Literature and Censorship in Restoration Germany

Studies in German Literature, Linguistics, and Culture

Literature and Censorship in Restoration Germany

Repression and Rhetoric

Katy Heady

Copyright © 2009 by Katy Heady

All Rights Reserved. Except as permitted under current legislation,
no part of this work may be photocopied, stored in a retrieval system,
published, performed in public, adapted, broadcast, transmitted,
recorded, or reproduced in any form or by any means,
without the prior permission of the copyright owner.

First published 2009
by Camden House

Camden House is an imprint of Boydell & Brewer Inc.
668 Mt. Hope Avenue, Rochester, NY 14620, USA
www.camden-house.com
and of Boydell & Brewer Limited
PO Box 9, Woodbridge, Suffolk IP12 3DF, UK
www.boydellandbrewer.com

ISBN-13: 978-1-57113-417-2
ISBN-10: 1-57113-417-4

Library of Congress Cataloging-in-Publication Data

Heady, Katy.
 Literature and censorship in Restoration Germany: repression and rhetoric / Katy Heady.
  p. cm. — (Studies in German literature, linguistics, and culture)
 Includes bibliographical references and index.
 ISBN-13: 978-1-57113-417-2 (hardcover: alk. paper)
 ISBN-10: 1-57113-417-4 (hardcover: alk. paper)
  1. German literature—19th century—History and criticism.
 2. German literature—Censorship. 3. Censorship—Germany—History
 —9th century. 4. Grabbe, Christian Dietrich, 1801–1836—Criticism,
 Textual. 5. Heine, Heinrich, 1797-1856—Criticism, Textual.
 6. Grillparzer, Franz, 1791-1872—Criticism, Textual. I. Title.

PT345.H39 2009
830.9'007—dc22

2009021013

A catalogue record for this title is available from the British Library.

This publication is printed on acid-free paper.
Printed in the United States of America.

Contents

Acknowledgments	vii
List of Abbreviations	viii
Introduction	1
1: Sex, Religion, and Violence: Christian Dietrich Grabbe's *Herzog Theodor von Gothland*	29
2: The Denomination of the Devil: Christian Dietrich Grabbe's *Scherz, Satire, Ironie und tiefere Bedeutung*	51
3: "Was soll ich nicht sagen?": Heinrich Heine's *Briefe aus Berlin*	69
4: Smuggling or Stalemate?: Heinrich Heine's *Reise von München nach Genua*	95
5: Too Nice a King for the People?: Franz Grillparzer's *König Ottokars Glück und Ende*	118
6: The Artist Fights Back: Franz Grillparzer's *Des Meeres und der Liebe Wellen*	170
Conclusion	197
Bibliography	203
Index	217

Acknowledgments

I AM EXTREMELY GRATEFUL to Michael Perraudin, who supervised the PhD thesis on which this book is based, for his guidance, insights, and feedback. I would also like to thank Henk de Berg, Gert Vonhoff, and the two anonymous Camden House reviewers for their invaluable comments and suggestions. Further thanks are due to Felix Eigenbrod for moral and practical support, to Alice Knight for proofreading several chapters of the book, and to the staff of the interlibrary loan department at Carleton University, Ottawa, for their unfailing cooperation. Last but not least, many thanks to Jim Walker at Camden House for his expertise, patience, and encouragement during the preparation of the book.

Abbreviations

DHA Heine, Heinrich. *Historisch-kritische Gesamtausgabe der Werke.* Düsseldorfer Ausgabe. Ed. Manfred Windfuhr et al. 16 vols. Hamburg: Hoffmann and Campe, 1973–97.

HSA Heine, Heinrich. *Werke, Briefwechsel, Lebenszeugnisse: Säkularausgabe.* Ed. Nationale Forschungs- und Gedenkstätten der klassischen deutschen Literatur in Weimar und Centre National de la Recherche Scientifique in Paris. 27 vols. to date. Berlin and Paris: Akademie Verlag and Editions du CNRS, 1970–.

HKG Grabbe, Christian Dietrich. *Werke und Briefe: Historisch-kritische Gesamtausgabe in sechs Bänden.* 6 vols. Ed. Akademie der Wissenschaften in Göttingen. Emsdetten: Lechte, 1960–73.

SW Grillparzer, Franz. *Sämtliche Werke: Historisch-kritische Gesamtausgabe.* 42 vols. Ed. August Sauer and Reinhold Backmann. Vienna: Schroll, 1909–48.

Introduction

Discourse Control and Censorship

THE SUPPRESSION OF UTTERANCE is a factor common to all forms of discourse. Not only is it impossible to express every idea that enters one's mind; in order to articulate a thought, it is also necessary to select the appropriate words from a wide range of possibilities, the rest of which are thereby rejected. Choices about what to say and how to say it inevitably involve choices about what not to say; and under most circumstances such decisions are shaped by an awareness of the rules of discourse applicable to a particular situation. Conversational etiquette may influence how much we choose to say, our adherence — or otherwise — to the rules of grammar, our choice of register and volume, as well as our responses to the actions, words, and silences of those around us. Social pressure may also cause us to avoid certain words or themes, either because they seem generally unacceptable or because we fear the response that they will provoke from particular listeners.

For many forms of discourse, a further level of restriction is imposed by the exclusion of certain categories of individual. In the case of specialized professional and academic debates, qualifications, knowledge of technical language or background knowledge are common prerequisites for participation. While the barring of those who do not meet these requirements may be necessary for pragmatic reasons, it nonetheless involves a silencing of their voices. Participation in more general, public discussions may also be limited by similar mechanisms. In many cases, the chances of a particular opinion being carried by the mass media will depend on the knowledge, connections, education, speaking ability, and charisma of those who wish to express it. Deficiencies in these areas can therefore result in the exclusion or marginalization of certain perspectives within public discourse.

Indeed, within the public domain as a whole, both social and economic structures influence patterns of marginalization and exclusion. The costs of dissemination through the media, as well as the limited time and attention span of media consumers, mean that not all viewpoints can be included in public debates and discussions. In general, the degree of publicity achieved by an utterance is determined to some extent by its compatibility with the interests of those with influence upon the media. Such interests are usually linked — at least in part — to the expected responses of media consumers, upon whose business media organs ultimately depend. Market forces can also determine patterns of exclusion from other forms of public discourse, such as literary writing. The choice to publish a certain book involves rejecting countless others; and once again, the tastes of the public — thematic, aesthetic, and ideological — can have a decisive impact on the choices made by both publishers and writers.

It is clear that a wide variety of mechanisms have the potential to hinder the communication of threatening or uncomfortable ideas, and, as such, can exercise a similar kind of control to formalized censorship institutions. One early acknowledgment of this continuity can be found in the writings of Sigmund Freud, who uses the term "Zensur" as a metaphor for the barrier function that prevents undesirable unconscious wishes from reaching the pre-conscious-conscious system.[1] On the level of cultural communities, the work of Aleida and Jan Assmann on canon formation has demonstrated close structural affinities between formal censorship and the processes involved in the maintenance of literary canons: both act as impediments to innovation and both preserve a hierarchy of more or less privileged (and, conversely, more or less marginalized) texts.[2] Within the French political arena, an awareness of the potential of the free market to produce censorship-like restrictions informed a 1986 verdict of the French council, which authorized the government to prevent excessive concentration of media ownership in order to safeguard the plurality of opinion represented by the media.[3]

An even broader conception of censorship emerged from the works of the Marxist sociologist Pierre Bourdieu in the 1970s and 1980s. According Bourdieu, all discourse is constrained by two factors: the rules of access to the arena (or "field") within which the discourse is produced and the modes of expression that are valued within that field. Bourdieu classifies these restraints (which frequently operate on a subconscious level) as structural censorship; and his theory of censorship — which expands the definition of censorship to include all forms of discourse control — has come to be known as "New Censorship."[4] According to proponents of "New Censorship" theory, phenomena such as the ordering of language into conformity with the rules of grammar, a parent stopping a child from talking, and the social pressure not to interrupt another speaker are all forms of censorship. Understood in this way, censorship is a precondition of intelligible discourse.

The implications of "New Censorship" theory are both far-reaching and problematic. On the one hand, recognition of the ubiquity of structural censorship has generated an important awareness of flaws in the traditional opposition between "censored" and "free" expression.[5] On the other hand, however, many researchers have been troubled by the way in which "New Censorship" gathers so many diverse phenomena under a single term. Beate Müller, for example, protests at the loss of analytical nuance that follows from such an expansive definition of censorship,[6] while Friedrich Schauer goes one step further and argues that "New Censorship" theory has rendered the very notion of "censorship" ontologically useless: "[. . .] if the use of the word *censorship* presupposes that censorship is a relatively identifiable subset of the set of human activity, then it makes no sense to identify as such a subset something that is part and parcel of all human activity."[7] Despite these misgivings, however, it is important to stress that even those who reject notions of "New Censorship" acknowledge the role that structural factors can play in excluding certain themes and ideologies from public discourse. Although censorship remains a disputed term, it is clear that public discourse is subject to a range of suppressive mechanisms, many of which produce censorship-like effects.

While recognizing the importance of informal censorship, this book will deal with the effects of state censorship: that is, censorship exercised by public institutions with the intention of regulating public discourse. Such formal control can take a variety of forms. Pre-publication censorship, for instance, involves a work being submitted to official scrutiny prior to publication and can result in its suffering deletions, additions or other alterations. Postpublication censorship, on the other hand, leads to either the deletion of passages of text already set in print, the prohibition of a completed piece, efforts to influence its reception, or the imposition of restrictions on its dissemination, for example by limiting the size of an edition or the number of performances. Censorship procedures can also include sanctions against the producers of proscribed utterance. Possible measures range from the exertion of psychological pressure, through professional restriction, fines and prison terms, to forced exile and even execution.

In contemporary society, formal censorship tends to be regarded with suspicion and is associated most closely with totalitarian regimes. Widespread modern distrust of censorship reflects the status of free expression as an essential democratic value, and is most evident in cases where the word "censorship" is used as a term of abuse in protests against unwanted attempts to limit or control public utterance. Typically, censorship is viewed as an exclusively repressive instrument that serves the sole purpose of protecting the interests and authority of those in power.[8] Yet, although state censorship is frequently linked to these aims, it is important not to ignore the function of censorship in protecting certain values and norms. While these values in some cases only reflect the interests of various elites, they may also represent — to a greater or lesser extent — social and ethical norms acknowledged by wider sections of the population. Censorship measures that would fall into the latter category include contemporary laws prohibiting the incitement of racial hatred or limiting the distribution of pornography. Clearly, state censorship can take a wide range of forms and produce a multitude of different effects.

In the German lands, as in other European countries, official censorship has been a continual, but constantly evolving factor for public utterance since before the invention of the printing press. Yet, while the development of state censorship in Germany in some respects mirrors that of official press controls in its neighboring countries, it is in other ways distinctive. Throughout history, religious, social, and political changes experienced by the German territories have been reflected in the evolution of censorship mechanisms and preoccupations. The variety and mutability of state censorship therefore demands a historically differentiated understanding of censorship and its relationship with public discourse.

Censorship before 1819

The first forms of censorship in the German lands were in place prior to the advent of printing, and involved ecclesiastical authorities overseeing the production of manuscripts and acting to prevent the dissemination of heretical writings. This kind of control, however, became ineffective after the invention of the printing press had made the reproduction of writings affordable for those outside church institutions. In 1486, the activities of Mainz's progressive, humanist printing firms prompted the establishment of the first German censorship commission by the Archbishop of Mainz, Berthold von Henneberg. During the following decades, both the pope and the kaiser initiated a series of censorship measures designed to repulse humanist challenges to the church's educational and political authority.[9]

During the sixteenth and seventeenth centuries, individual territories throughout the Reich developed censorship systems at different rates. This process became more pronounced from the late sixteenth century onwards as the ideal of a centralized state began to take root.[10] Censorship authorities during this period acted against threats to their international relations, breaches of decency, personal insults, and challenges to state authority; but in an age when religion was the main basis for ideological dispute, theology remained the central focus of censorship activity. As rulers came to recognize the advantages of a unified state religion, the censorship activities of ecclesiastical authorities in both Catholic and Protestant territories prevented alternatives to official theology from reaching the public. With few exceptions, works of Catholic theology could only be published in Catholic states, Lutheran theology only in Lutheran states, and Calvinist theology only in Calvinist states.[11]

During the eighteenth century, as politics began to grow more secular in character, the emphasis of state censorship shifted toward the repression of political expression. One reason for this was the dramatically increased presence of political writings within the German lands: a flood of French enlightened writings by authors such as Montesquieu, Voltaire, and Montaigne began to enter Germany from the mid-century onwards, and increased public interest in political questions led to the foundation of many new magazines and newspapers during the last decades of the eighteenth century.[12] Also decisive, however, were the periods of Enlightenment rule experienced by most German territories at some stage of the century. As the enforcement of confessional orthodoxy became less of a priority, enlightened states frequently took direct control of censorship functions previously exercised by ecclesiastical institutions. In the hands of progressive state officials, censorship practices became more tolerant of enlightened writings, although this rarely resulted in a blanket relaxation of press controls. Prevailing opinion held that, because most people were not yet enlightened, they still required guidance and tutelage from the state. During the reign of Maria Theresia (1740–80) in Austria, for instance, the likely effects of writing on the successful implementation of the empress's reform policies simply replaced religious conformity as the primary censorship criterion.[13] Similarly, the liberal attitude of Frederick II of Prussia (1712–86) toward religious works was also accompanied by stricter policies toward newspapers and political writings.[14]

In the long run, however, the most decisive effects of Enlightenment rule on censorship practices were structural. The bureaucratic reorganization and rationalization required to implement enlightened reforms resulted in more efficient systems of state censorship. Toward the end of the eighteenth century, these refined mechanisms were transformed into effective tools of repression, as reactionary monarchs ascended the thrones of Austria and Prussia, and the French Revolution produced an anxious backlash. Following the death of the enlightened Joseph II in Austria in 1790, for example, the state censorship apparatus fell under the influence of the conservative Archbishop Migazzi, and by 1810, all written works — regardless of length or subject matter — were subject to pre-publication censorship. A similar process took place during the reign of the reactionary Frederick William II in Prussia, who in 1788 also appointed a conservative, J. Christian v. Wöllner, to oversee censorship, with the result that enlightenment writings about religion became a target of state repression.[15]

This reactionary trend was briefly interrupted during the Napoleonic period, in which literary and scientific texts became exempt from censorship controls in many German states. As with the years of German Enlightenment, however, this phase did not result in a uniform relaxation of censorship controls, and draconian sanctions were imposed on those involved in the publication of subversive writings. Following the discovery of the anonymous anti-French pamphlet *Deutschland in seiner tiefsten Erniedrigung* in 1806, for example, Napoleon ordered the immediate execution of Johann Philip Palm, the Nuremberg bookseller charged with its publication.[16] Yet, despite these measures, such pamphlets continued to appear; and the loyalty of the German book trade toward their monarchs — also shown by the prominent participation of many leading publishers in the wars of liberation — gave rise to hopes that this valor would be rewarded with more liberal press laws following the final defeat of Napoleon.[17]

In fact, article 18d of the 1815 Bundesakte did indicate that the subjects of the newly-formed German Confederation would be granted the right to a free press.[18] Yet, as we will see, the reactionary climate that prevailed during the following years enabled and promoted the establishment of a comprehensive pan-German system of censorship. From 1819 onwards, all Confederation members were legally obliged to conform to a code of compulsory practices, which in most states resulted in a significant tightening of press controls. These controls were intended to defend the interests of the re-established absolutist order against threats to its legitimacy. However, in an age that saw many changes which promoted the free dissemination of information (such as rising literacy levels, urbanization, technological advances, improved communications, and the emergence of a liberal public sphere),[19] state censorship became not only severely compromised in its effectiveness, but also the source of considerable resentment. By the 1840s, press freedom had become a popular liberal cause, and the abolition of censorship was one of the chief aims of the 1848 revolutions.

Censorship after 1848

The March revolutions of 1848 quickly achieved the abolition of state censorship and ushered in a period of writing without any formal control. This freedom was short-lived, however, and the return of the old powers was briskly followed by the re-establishment of censorship. In 1854, a new set of federal laws instituted a revised system of press controls, which, instead of returning to the hugely unpopular pre-publication censorship of the Vormärz, enabled publications to be prohibited through the mechanisms of the criminal laws against blasphemy, obscenity and sedition. Authors, publishers, and printers became legally responsible for the publication of any offensive writings for which they were responsible, and a system of permits aimed to ensure the political conformity of those employed within the book trade.[20]

Whereas the system for printed works was thus designed to encourage self-censorship on the part of writers and publishers, theatrical performances remained subject to systematic control. In Austria, for instance, the old regime of universal pre-performance censorship was reinstated in 1849. The illegality of pre-publication censorship initially deterred other states from following suit, but Prussia soon found a way around the problem by declaring theatrical performances to be "öffentliche Lustbarkeiten," for which official permission was required. Prior to performance, dramatic works had to be vetted by the police, who would then attend performances to check that the actors followed the approved text. This procedure had to be repeated every time a production moved to a new location, a system which was soon adopted by most other states.[21] Only private theatrical performances — those that were closed to members of the general public — were exempt from the regulations.

Toward the end of the nineteenth century, these restrictions (which remained in place until the First World War) led to several high-profile clashes involving the morally, politically, and aesthetically radical plays of naturalism and expressionism. Although performance within a private club offered one means of avoiding pre-performance censorship, writers such as Gerhart Hauptmann (1862–1946) and, later, Frank Wedekind (1864–1918), wanted their plays to reach a wider audience and their determination to achieve this end resulted in a series of court cases. These conflicts — for example, that which preceded the first public performance of Hauptmann's socially critical drama *Die Weber* at the "Deutsches Theater" in Berlin in September 1894[22] — generated considerable public interest and intensified the antagonism between Wilhelmine traditionalists and the supporters of artistic modernism.[23]

Following the abdication of the kaiser in 1918, the constitution of the Weimar Republic forbade state censorship and even declared the arts to be free. In practice, however, this freedom soon became somewhat restricted: private citizens of the new republic were entitled to press charges against writers if they saw in their works a breach of criminal law. As in the old Reich, therefore, charges of indecency, immorality, and blasphemy could still be raised against literary works, with the old crime of lèse-majesté replaced by that of false accusation and personal insult. Within the polarized ideological climate of the Weimar Republic, conservative-minded citizens — in many cases encouraged by campaigns in the right-wing press — frequently made use of these rights and often succeeded in suppressing avant-garde writings and theater productions on the grounds of blasphemy or indecency.[24] Political writings could also provoke repressive measures, for despite the constitutional abolition of censorship, from 1922 onwards a "Gesetz zum Schutz der Republik" made possible the prohibition of critical writings. During the final, crisis-ridden years of the republic, a series of emergency decrees granted the police increasing powers to act against writing judged by them to represent a threat to state security.[25]

As is well-known, such measures were only a prelude to the unprecedented total control of public utterance that would be achieved by the National Socialists within a year of gaining power. In the first few months after coming into office, the new government expelled a dozen or so nonconformist artists and writers from the Preußische Kunstakademie, arrested several dissident writers during investigations into the burning down of parliament, and organized the public burning of Jewish and "subversive" writings in university towns throughout the land.[26] The result of these measures was a mass exodus of writers and other artists from Germany during the early months of National Socialist rule.[27] Those writers who remained were subject to the most effective regime of state censorship ever established in the German territories. The Reichskammergesetz of September 1933 required that all artists and writers belong to the relevant Reichskammer for his or her profession: expulsion from a Reichskammer, from which Jewish artists were automatically excluded, effectively meant the end of one's artistic career. Each year, the Reichskulturkammer issued a list of proscribed writings, and book traders who were found selling such publications were prohibited from practicing their profession.[28]

Censorship remained a feature of German public life even after the defeat of National Socialism. The allied forces that occupied Germany after 1945 established their own strict regimes of press control. Indeed, Soviet cultural policy remained decisive for East Germany even after the withdrawal of the Russian troops and the establishment of the GDR. For although official legislation and discourse avoided the word *Zensur*, and the existence of censorship was denied by many of the state's leading representatives,[29] in reality a rigorous regime of press control aimed at ensuring that the production of literature and art remained in the political service of the country's leaders. In addition to an intolerance of criticism, state cultural policy also demanded literary works that fostered "Freude, Erbauung, Kraft, Optimismus und Zuversicht" and — particularly in the first decades of the GDR — that fulfilled the aesthetic criteria of socialist realism. Avant-garde art was prohibited due to its alleged decadence, and even more conventional attention to the claims of subjectivity, as in Christa Wolf's novel *Der geteilte Himmel* (1963), gave rise to publication difficulties. All works destined for publication had to be presented to the Amt für Literatur und Verlagswesen, a central agency that was also charged with issuing licences to publishers and controlling the distribution of paper to state-approved printing firms. In addition, the establishment of a Schriftstellerverband, membership of which was a prerequisite for publication, aimed to control the activities of writers in the same way as had the system of Reichskammer under National Socialism. A final layer of control was provided by the Ministerium für Staatssicherheit, which actively searched for dissident literature and initiated steps to ensure its suppression. These measures ranged from the demanding of changes to a manuscript prior to publication and limiting the size of a particular edition, to the exclusion of the author from the Schriftstellerverband, the refusal of visa applications, house arrest, even imprisonment, and, as in the case of the hugely popular dissident songwriter Wolf Biermann, the withdrawal of citizenship. Pernicious psychological techniques, such as the organization of professional failures and the ruining of reputations, were also employed.[30]

The withdrawal of allied forces from western Germany, by contrast, brought about a swift end to systematic official control of the media and press. The 1949 Grundgesetz of the new Federal Republic of Germany explicitly outlawed state censorship and granted its citizens the right to freedom of expression. As in the Weimar Republic, however, the official abolition of censorship did not translate into complete freedom of the press and other utterance. Article 5 of the new constitution included a clause limiting this liberty of expression to utterance that complied with other demands of the Grundgesetz, such as the protection of young people, morality, personal *Ehre,* and the liberal, democratic character of the young state. And while the law suggests that art should be exempt from these restrictions,[31] the Federal Republic has borne witness to a number of attempts to prohibit literary works through the courts, usually through accusations of offenses against decency, personal honor, and the criminal law. The constitutional freedom of art has consistently been used as a defense in such cases, although not always successfully. Perhaps the most celebrated example is Klaus Mann's novel *Mephisto,* which was banned by a court in Hamburg in 1966 on the grounds that it attacked the personal honor of the author's former brother-in-law, Gustaf Gründgens, on whom the morally corrupt central character was ostensibly based. Although the court eventually recognized the artistic character of *Mephisto* and confirmed the freedom of art, it also issued the contradictory verdict that, in order to protect the personal honor of the recently deceased Gründgens, the novel should be prohibited.[32] While respect for the constitutional freedom of art has grown since the sixties,[33] several forms of state censorship — for instance, the restricted distribution of publications judged potentially harmful to young people and the prohibition of Nazi materials such as *Mein Kampf* — still operate within the contemporary Federal Republic.

Censorship from 1819 to 1848

Introduction

When compared to the various systems of press control in place during the history of the German lands, it is clear that state censorship between 1819 and 1848 was not the strictest (censorship in both the Third Reich and the GDR was certainly more severe), yet these years nevertheless occupy a distinctive place in the history of German press controls. For, despite the persistence of censorship throughout German history, it was during this period that the issue of press controls occupied the most prominent place on the political agenda and aroused the most widespread and intense public opposition. Part of this unpopularity can be related to the system itself, which was both one of the most far-reaching in Europe at the time,[34] and the most comprehensive hitherto seen in the German territories. Even more crucial, however, was the fact that this demonstration of state autocracy was pitted against the aspirations of a rapidly emerging public sphere, in an age characterized by sharp increases in literacy, book production, and political mobilization.[35]

In the years between 1818 and 1848, state censorship was not only employed with increasing desperation by the restoration powers to defend their values against the claims of an ever-growing, predominantly liberal, middle class; it also collided with the preoccupation of contemporary liberals with both constitutionalism and the codification of rights. The assurances of press freedom — albeit qualified — contained in the constitutions of Bavaria (1818),[36] Baden (1819)[37] and Württemberg (1819),[38] as well as in the constitution of the newly formed German Confederation, the 1815 Bundesakte,[39] initially seemed to represent progress toward liberal goals. The fact that state censorship was introduced despite these constitutional promises provided an additional reason for liberals to dislike it. By the 1840s, censorship had become so symbolic of repressive government that complaints relating to it were an important rallying call for the liberal opposition.[40] Indeed, the public antipathy toward censorship that took root during the period meant that Nachmärz governments avoided using the word *Zensur* to describe state control of utterance.

Historical Background

The system of censorship that provoked this hostility was made possible by the foundation of the German Confederation, or Deutscher Bund, in 1815. This organization — part of the wider European restoration system — was formed of predominantly absolutist German rulers who were anxious to consolidate their power following their recent humiliation at the hands of Napoleon. Although the Deutscher Bund guaranteed each member state a large degree of independence, it was inevitably dominated by the major powers of Prussia and Austria, and soon embarked on a reactionary course.

As already indicated, this conservative turn was not uncontested. Following the comparatively enlightened reforms of the Napoleonic era, liberals had hoped for further codification of rights and moves toward representative government. Their aspirations were encouraged by the promise made by the Prussian king, Frederick William III, in 1815 of a constitution for his people, and by the granting of new constitutions in eleven German states between 1818 and 1820; and they were reluctant to give up their demands as reactionary forces grew in strength. Another source of discontent was the decentralized structure of the German Confederation, as the patriotic sentiment generated by the wars of liberation had led to the birth of political movements demanding a free and united Germany. A national network of *Turnvereine* combined the goal of physical improvement with that of a rejuvenated Germany based on egalitarian principles. In universities, student societies known as *Burschenschaften* pursued similar aims, often with the help of professors. In October 1817, the *Burschenschaften* held a great rally at the Wartburg to mark the fourth anniversary of the Battle of Leipzig. During this event, a group of radical students burned a number of symbols of state power, including a copy of the Prussian police laws and a corporal's baton.[41]

The Carlsbad Press Laws and Their Implementation

Given the threats they faced, most German rulers were anxious to protect both their own power and the institution of monarchy as a whole. From the very beginning of the period, Prince Metternich, the foreign minister and later chancellor of Austria, was particularly keen to repress the activities and communication of the political opposition. In 1819, he used the murder of the reactionary poet August von Kotzebue by the radical student Karl Ludwig Sand to muster support for the Carlsbad Decrees,[42] which were legally binding for all Confederation members and, among other things,[43] laid the foundations for a pan-German censorship system. According to these decrees, each German state was responsible for censorship arrangements within its own territories. However, the laws were clearly designed to ensure that certain minimum censorship standards were applied throughout the Confederation, and to guarantee that — for the first time in German history — no state was able to provide a haven for heretical writers.

The decrees required that all works of less than twenty Bogen (usually 320 pages, depending on page size) be submitted for pre-publication censorship.[44] Ultimately, however, each German state had an obligation toward both its fellow states and the Confederation as a whole to act against any publications which, in the words of the decrees, "die Würde und Sicherheit anderer Bundesstaaten verletzt, die Verfassung oder Verwaltung derselben angegriffen [haben]." In addition, the Confederation reserved the right to take independent action against any offensive publications, and, if necessary, to use military action to enforce the decrees.[45] These press laws were initially valid for five years. However, they were renewed indefinitely in 1824 and remained in force until 1848.[46]

Although censorship controls were well established in many German states before 1819, the measures required by the Carlsbad Decrees represented a clear intensification of repression. The main elements of the decrees were agreed upon by the Prussian chancellor, Carl August von Hardenberg, and the Austrian foreign minister, Clemens von Metternich, prior to negotiation with the other states, who reacted to their proposals with a mixture of enthusiasm and skepticism. Pressure from Prussia and Austria led to the decrees being passed unanimously by the Bundestag in September 1819, but they provoked considerable resentment due to the violations of sovereignty they entailed.[47] Varying levels of support for the press laws among Confederation members translated into differing styles of implementation. While Austria, Prussia, and Hanover required that all written works, regardless of length, be submitted for pre-publication censorship, other governments were content to satisfy the minimum standards set out by the Bund.[48] Some member states were even less compliant. In Luxembourg, for instance, a stable political climate, combined with the opposition of the ruling monarch, King William I of the Netherlands, to the Grand Duchy's membership of the German Confederation, meant that the decrees were ignored until 1832.[49] In Bavaria, a strong sense of sovereignty combined with a tradition of press freedom established during the Napoleonic era weakened commitment to the Carlsbad Decrees. Consequently, all books were exempt from Bavarian pre-publication censorship until the decrees were renewed in 1824.[50]

Strictness with regard to the content of censored works also varied considerably between the different lands. Following the French Revolution of 1789, the anxieties of political elites in Austria had led to the establishment of a censorship system widely regarded as the strictest among all Confederation members.[51] In Baden, Württemberg, and the Bavarian Palatinate, on the other hand, liberal traditions developed during the Napoleonic period persisted, bringing a pronounced antipathy toward press controls.[52] For the first few years after 1818, for instance, censorship controls in Württemberg only applied to foreign affairs.[53] Other states maintained lenient censorship policies for economic reasons. The most important example is Saxony, which earned considerable revenue through its taxation of the book trade, the German center of which was situated in Leipzig.[54] Similar considerations led to the establishment of an even more liberal censorship regime in Saxony-Altenburg. This small state faced few threats to its internal order and was home to the thriving Piersche Hofbuchdruckerei, which largely owed its success to a liberal censor. During the 1820s, censorship in Altenburg was aimed primarily at escaping the attentions of the Confederation; and although a stricter censor was eventually appointed in 1833, conditions in the state still left considerable room for freedom of expression. The new censors' instructions of 1 February 1833, for example, explicitly allowed critical discussion of German politics, as long as this was carried out in an "anständige Form."[55]

Yet, despite these variations, a number of factors limited the sovereignty of individual states over their respective censorship controls. The most obvious of these were the press laws established in Carlsbad, which were later supplemented by further federal censorship legislation[56] in response to the political agitation that followed the 1830 July Revolution in Paris. Although some states initially fell short of the standards required by federal law, it became clear in the 1830s that the Confederation — dominated as it was by Austria and Prussia — was prepared to act against governments that did not fulfil its demands. In 1831, the liberal Archduke Leopold of Baden agreed to calls from the Baden Landtag to introduce a more permissive press law, which limited censorship to works relating to the German Confederation and its member states. These reforms were regarded with great displeasure by the Confederation's press commission, which was horrified by the growing number of left-wing publications appearing in the Grand Duchy. Using the threat of intervention, "mit allen ihm zu Gebote stehenden Mitteln," the Confederation presidency eventually forced Baden to capitulate and repeal its new press laws.[57]

Another form of centralizing pressure was exerted by the Confederation's authority to prohibit publications throughout the territories of its member states. The most famous example of this is the unprecedented campaign launched by the Confederation against the young, critical authors Heine, Gutzkow, Laube, Wienbarg, and Mundt, whom it collectively termed "Junges Deutschland." A federal decree of December 1835 called upon member states to prevent the circulation of all works by the Junges Deutschland authors. Initially, it seemed that even the writers' future works would be automatically prohibited, but they were in the end merely subjected to extra scrutiny by a specially appointed censor, Dr. John.[58] Less extreme measures could also have a profound impact on censorship procedures, however. The 1823 federal ban of the Württemberg-published newspaper *Teutscher Beobachter,* for example, was experienced as a painful violation of sovereignty in its home state and ultimately led to a tightening of press legislation in both Württemberg and neighboring Bavaria, which were anxious to avoid external interference in their censorship affairs.[59] At various times, fear of federal intervention had similar effects on censorship policy in Hamburg and Baden.[60]

Such formal measures were not the only factors limiting the variation in censorship practice. The federal assembly provided an informal meeting place in which representatives from the various states could discuss their press policies and notify each other of subversive publications. In addition, the publication of an offensive piece of work in one state frequently provoked complaints from other governments, and Prussia and Austria were particularly energetic in this regard. In a memorandum of 1845, for example, the Hamburg censor Merck complained, "[...] daß die kühnste

Phantasie nicht zu ergründen vermag, was Alles z.B. das königl. Preuß. Ministerium des Innern verletzen könnte."[61] Although the Hamburg authorities did not always accede to Prussia's wishes, it was generally true that the political and economic influence of the two major powers favored a compliant response to their protests.[62]

These centralizing forces were at their strongest during the 1830s, after the Paris July Revolution inspired a series of German uprisings and the emergence of a new climate of more rebellious utterance. Initially, a fear of further revolts led to a phase of more liberal censorship, but the authorities quickly regained their confidence and became determined to counter the bolder tone of many publications. The Confederation introduced measures aimed at repressing the activities of the political opposition, Prussia increased its efforts to influence the censorship policy of neighboring states,[63] and unsettled monarchs throughout the Confederation became more receptive to pressure for stricter press controls.[64] The Bund's campaign against the Junges Deutschland writers was part of this repressive wave, which also resulted in the establishment of a central *Untersuchungsbehörde* charged with investigating the production of oppositional literature, and in the tightening of federal censorship standards.[65] Following the "Zehn Artikel" of 1832, for example, German-language publications from outside the Confederation could no longer enter without first passing German censorship controls. Perhaps even more significant was the order given as part of the secret Wiener Beschlüsse of 1834, which forbade the use of "Zensurlücken" to indicate where the censor had removed parts of the text.[66] Although the Wiener Beschlüsse were never made public, they were nevertheless legally binding for all member states.[67]

Despite these severe measures, however, the political opposition continued to gather momentum. Shortly after his accession to the Prussian throne in 1840, Frederick William IV ordered a relaxation of censorship restrictions. The result of this liberal gesture was a flood of critical writings, which shocked him into introducing a more conservative policy.[68] But, by the end of the Vormärz, censorship systems in most German states were close to breaking point, as steady increases in public readership and a rising tide of political mobilization led to an enormous market for political literature.[69] As the censorship authorities within the German lands struggled to cope with an overwhelming workload, the expansion of the railways made it easier for the reading public to access works published in more liberal neighboring countries such as Switzerland or Denmark.[70] During the last few years before the 1848 revolutions, as calls for press freedom grew ever louder, both the German Confederation and the governments of many of its member states began to discuss the possibility of ending the pre-publication censorship and replacing it with a system of postpublication judicial liability.[71]

Censorship Organization

The bureaucratic organization of press controls between 1819 and 1848 varied from state to state, although the coordination of censorship was typically assigned to a censorship commission of some kind.[72] Other state agencies frequently had a role to play in the process, too: police forces all over the Confederation, for instance, regularly inspected bookshops to enforce the censors' decisions. The division of censorship tasks was particularly complex in the two major powers. In Prussia, the appointment and supervision of censors in each region was the responsibility of the provincial Oberpräsidenten. Until 1843, central control was assigned to an Oberzensurkollegium, the duties of which included prohibiting unsuitable works and dealing with complaints of both undue leniency and excessive strictness. This agency was supposed to coordinate censorship with the help of ministries charged with directing the censorship of certain themes: the foreign affairs ministry for newspapers and political works, the ministry of intellectual affairs and public education for academic theological writings, and the police department in the interior ministry for everything else.[73] In practice, however, the Oberzensurkollegium was too poorly resourced to provide comprehensive controls, and the ministries frequently pronounced bans independently.[74]

In Austria, censorship was more centralized, but also considerably slower. Uncensored writings were handed in at either the Wiener Zentralrevisionsamt or a provincial Revisionsamt. The provincial *Ämter* carried out the censorship of uncontroversial works independently, but passed everything else on to the Polizei- und Zensurhofstelle in Vienna. The Wiener Zentralrevisionsamt assigned two censors to each piece of writing; and each of these officials produced a separate report, which was likewise forwarded to the Hofstelle. Officials there examined the censors' verdicts and, in cases of uncertainty, consulted other state departments. The most important of these was the Staatskanzlei, which also issued guidelines for censorship practice. Once a decision had been reached, it was conveyed to the relevant Revisionsamt, which informed the parties concerned. This process could often take over a year.[75]

Existing research provides much evidence that the task of censorship was both strenuous and thankless. By no means all censors were reactionaries, and many took on the task out of necessity of one kind or another. Writers and unemployed academics frequently worked as censors in order to earn extra money, for instance;[76] and especially in smaller states, censoring duties were often assigned to civil servants, lawyers and police officers, who had no choice but to carry them out alongside their normal tasks and rarely received any compensation for their efforts.[77] Censors from all over the Confederation complained that they did not receive sufficiently detailed guidelines,[78] and intense time pressure often made the task even more difficult. Toward the end of the Vormärz, in particular, the sheer volume of material to be censored meant that it was rarely possible to submit publications to a thorough investigation. In Mannheim, for example, the censor responsible for newspapers had only one hour each day in which to examine the contents of all the newspapers appearing the next day. The higher authorities had little understanding for such difficulties, and if censors allowed through material that subsequently aroused complaints, they were often subject to official reprimands and in many cases had to pay fines.[79] For several years in Bavaria, censors had to pay twenty-five Gulden to a local poor fund for their first official reprimand, and fifty Gulden for their second.[80] Such sanctions doubtlessly caused many censors to err on the side of caution.

These were not the only hardships suffered by censors. As we have seen, the intense unpopularity of the state censorship system during the 1830s and 1840s led to a social stigma being attached to censorship as an occupation. In Baden, the 1840s saw cases of censors being confronted by liberal Landtag members in their own homes, and threatened with public admonishment in the Landtag if they went ahead with planned cuts. It is perhaps not surprising that the newspaper censor of Mannheim mentioned earlier, Stadtdirektor Riegel, begged several times to be released from his censorship duties. When the authorities in Baden finally granted his request in the early 1840s, the difficulty of finding a new censor led them to consider combing the list of state pensioners for a replacement.[81]

Censorship Criteria

Like most press control before and after the period, censorship legislation in place between 1819 and 1848 aimed to uphold the established political, religious, and social order. Contemporary censorship laws generally forbade attacks on the state, religion, and "die guten Sitten,"[82] and several prohibited the publication of personal insults.[83] A Prussian censorship order of 1824 also called for the protection of religious groups,[84] and several others demanded an "anständige[n] Ton."[85] A concern with tone is also expressed by a clause in the Austrian censorship law of 1810 — which remained in force until 1848 — that permitted discussion of mistakes made by the state bureaucracy, as long as these were expressed "mit Würde und Bescheidenheit, und mit Vermeidung aller eigentlichen und anzüglichen Persönlichkeiten."[86] Yet this concession should not be taken for leniency. Both Austrian and Prussian[87] censorship legislation also included lengthy lists of what would not be tolerated: attacks on the monarchy, ruling dynasty, and foreign administrations; attempts to spread dissatisfaction or undermine the bond between ruler and subject; and the positive depiction of movements opposed to the existing social and political order. Such publications, warned the Austrian law of 1810, "können so wenig auf Nachsicht, als Meuchelmörder auf Duldung Anspruch machen."[88] On the other hand, several contemporary censorship laws also expressly permitted a wider range of discussion for works aimed at an educated readership.[89] Censorship legislation in Austria, for instance, regulated the accessibility of a particular work through a system of categories clearly designed at granting social elites the right to read certain publications that were considered unsuitable for the rest of the population.

While undeniably interesting, such stipulations are too general to provide a complete picture of contemporary censorship practices. Not only were censorship laws in most states complemented at various times by instructions specifically prohibiting the discussion of sensitive topical issues,[90] but also studies of censorship in the different German lands contain many indications that — particularly, but not only, in Austria and Prussia — laws protecting the state, religion, and decency could have unexpected implications. It was presumably a fear of arousing discontent, for instance, that led the Austrian censorship authorities to prohibit reports of a deadly flooding of the Danube that occurred in the night from 28 February to 1 March 1830,[91] just as the discussion of typhoid and cholera epidemics was removed from newspapers in both Prussia and Austria.[92] Similarly, a deep-seated concern with social cohesion is demonstrated by the removal of demeaning depictions of both ethnic and professional groups by Austrian censors.[93]

The same could apply to the authorities' determination to protect religion. Austrian theater censors, for example, would not permit the depiction of any religious personages on stage.[94] And in Austria and Hesse-Kassel, censorship is known to have been charged with the task of combating superstition, so that "Ritter-, Geister-, Räuber- und Kriminalgeschichten" were routinely restricted in the former state,[95] and a treatise on animal magnetism, a collection of outlandish remedies and cures, and a recounting of "extraordinary occurrences" were among the publications banned during the 1820s in Hesse.[96] Finally, there is much evidence that censors could be extremely sensitive to any hint of sexual innuendo.[97] Clearly, censorship laws alone provide no more than an indistinct outline of contemporary censorship practices.

Resistance to Censorship

The extensive controls in place between 1819 and 1848 provoked a variety of responses from oppositional writers and publishers. One option was evasion of the strictest controls, for example by publishing works in states with less repressive censorship practices. At book fairs in Leipzig, writers and publishers could pass on information about liberal censors and states,[98] and Heinrich Heine's publisher, Julius Campe, for instance, was able to get books past the censors in Hamburg, Altenberg, or Holstein that were later banned in Prussia, Austria, and Hanover. Another approach was to leave considerable space between the lines in a book, use very large typefaces and margins, or add extra material in order to lengthen a volume beyond the twenty-Bogen limit.[99] Toward the end of the Vormärz, oppositional writers exploited the twenty-Bogen exception maintained by many states to publish previously censored articles with the deleted passages reinstated and accompanied by a critique of the censor's work.[100]

The late Vormärz also witnessed a massive growth in the illicit import of works published outside the Confederation. In Switzerland, for example, publishers such as the Schläpfersche Verlagsbuchhandlung in Herisau and Julius Fröbel's Literarisches Comptoir in Zürich became focal points for the German democratic opposition and developed a range of techniques for smuggling dangerous works into Germany. The pages of these were often transported unbound to look like spoiled sheets, covered by innocent prayer- or schoolbooks, and declared as returned wares so that they would not be opened by customs officials. Copies of the work *Die teutsche Revolution* by the socialist Karl Heinzen, for example, were reportedly smuggled into Germany under the name "Archiv für Tierheilkunde" during the late 1840s.[101]

In the long run, however, such tactics had their limits. Although they enabled offensive books to reach the market, the danger did not end there. Even if censored in one German state, a book could still be banned after publication by another member of the Confederation, with the result of large financial losses for the publisher. The consequences of exclusion from Prussia's very large book market — the state had 13 million inhabitants — were particularly severe.[102] And while licensed booksellers were not the only means used to distribute literature, they were certainly the most lucrative. Moreover, in addition to such financial risks, the publication of subversive literature also brought the danger of police action. In the 1830s, for instance, Karl Gutzkow, Heinrich Laube, and Georg Wirth were all imprisoned as part of the Confederation's campaign against Junges Deutschland writers, Karl Gutzkow and Ludolf Wienbarg were both expelled from their city of residence, Frankfurt, and, in 1841, August Heinrich Hoffmann von Fallersleben was stripped of his professorship at Breslau university following the publication of his second volume of *Unpolitische Lieder*.[103] Although Heinrich Heine was already in French exile when he wrote the radical foreword to his *Französische Zustände* in 1832, his publisher underwent a police interrogation lasting several hours in the course of an investigation into the work. After this experience, Campe was extremely reluctant to publish any of the author's later works unless they had been passed by the censors.[104]

Under such circumstances it was inevitable that literary writing during the Restoration would be affected by the pressures of state control. For, although political newspapers and leaflets were the primary focus of official anxiety, belletristic works were also subject to censorship. Indeed, the censors' primary preoccupations — morality, religion, and politics — are also popular literary topics. Censorship affected literature both through the deletion of prohibited content during pre-publication censorship and through writers' own efforts to preempt external controls. In its most simple and devastating form, such self-censorship involved authors suppressing illicit material entirely; but it is also generally acknowledged that writers employed a range of techniques with the aim of hiding their subversive ideas from the censors.[105] One dimension of this was a preference for certain forms: travel literature and historical works offered a means of addressing current issues while appearing to be concerned with geographically or temporally remote settings; and the adoption of verse forms enabled a similar distancing from contemporary society. It is also recognized that censorship pressure led to the emergence of a distinctive style of writing — now termed *Zensurstil* —, characterized by evasive modes of expression such as allegory, allusion, association, and irony.[106]

Censorship and Literary Writing

Despite widespread acceptance of the influence of censorship on literature during the Restoration, little systematic attention has been paid to the specific effects of censorship pressure on literary texts. Recent decades have seen the emergence of a number of fascinating studies into Restoration censorship in the different German lands based on correspondence, legal documents, and censorship files. Yet such research has focused predominantly on the organization and administration of censorship systems, rather than its impact on texts. During the early twentieth century, Heinrich Hubert Houben composed extensive and entertaining accounts of passages removed and altered by the censors,[107] but a lack of referencing and an unmistakable delight in the more absurd examples of censorship practice may lead us to question the reliability of his work. Moreover, like much contemporary secondary literature on the topic, Houben concentrates only on the passages that were removed by the censors and makes no attempt to establish the logic behind such deletions by comparing such excisions with similar passages the publication of which was permitted.

The need for detailed analysis of state censorship's impact on literary texts has been suggested by several researchers,[108] and such analysis is desirable for a number of reasons. For one thing, the vagueness of censorship laws and the imprecision of contemporary censorship guidelines have left us with little information about the boundaries between permitted and forbidden utterance. More detailed knowledge of these borders would generate a greater understanding of how the composition of literary texts was constrained by state censorship. In addition, our knowledge of *Zensurstil* techniques stems primarily from statements made by authors themselves and is therefore unlikely to be exhaustive. Finally, little is known about the frequency or success with which evasive strategies were pursued; or about other ways in which censorship pressure shaped the structures, styles, and linguistic forms of literary writing during the Restoration.

As several scholars have observed, investigations into the effects of censorship on a given literary text face two crucial limitations. The first of these is the futility of speculation about the form a particular literary text would have taken within an alternative censorship context. Systems of censorship are an intrinsic part of the world from which literary texts emerge and, as Nicholas Harrison has pointed out, their very existence influences both authorial intentions and reader reception.[109] Secondly, and on a more concrete level, attempts to discern instances of self-censorship are necessarily restricted by methodological difficulties. For not only is material frequently suppressed by authors before being recorded,[110] but it is also often impossible to distinguish between alterations made for censorship reasons and those motivated by considerations such as aesthetics or audience response.[111]

Yet although the complete influence of censorship on any text must remain obscure, many of the restrictions which press controls placed on contemporary writings are nevertheless accessible to empirical examination. One important source of information are the manuscripts which were submitted to the censors and on which the required cuts were marked: such manuscripts provide direct evidence of impact of censorship on texts. In addition, a careful examination of textual alterations made by authors can frequently permit the detection of self-censorship. By considering such factors as the circumstances under which changes were made, the aesthetic effect of a given alteration and the question of whether or not the amendment in question forms part of a wider pattern of changes relating to a known censorship concern, it is often possible to reach relatively secure conclusions about the role of censorship in motivating authorial changes. Such an approach involves detailed attention to both the circumstances and the nature of pre-censorship changes, and inevitably involves an element of speculation. Yet as I hope to show, such consideration can yield persuasive results.

This book aims to provide more precise insights into the way in which censorship impinged on Restoration literature through detailed studies of six literary texts by three authors. The case studies in question enable us to see how censorship affected literary texts both directly, through censorship cuts, and indirectly — through the efforts of authors and editors —

to avoid externally-imposed alterations and/or prohibition. Of course, it is inevitable that such judgments (by writers, editors, and censors) varied from one individual to another, and that they were influenced by such factors as tiredness, time pressure, and market forces. Indeed, recent theoretical works on censorship have tended to insist upon the arbitrariness of censorial decisions.[112] However, such claims are not backed up by substantial empirical evidence, and it is important to remember that a degree of inconsistency in censorship implementation does not preclude the existence of more general trends. For despite variations between the practices of those preparing texts for dissemination within a given state, all such individuals were confronted with the same set of political and administrative circumstances, which included the possibility of measures initiated by the Bund. As the following case studies of works prepared for publication within Austria and Prussia — the two largest German states — will reveal, there were significant parallels in the effects of censorship on the individual texts; and such parallels are highly suggestive of wider trends.

Texts and Authors

The works under examination in this book are Christian Dietrich Grabbe's *Herzog Theodor von Gothland* and *Scherz, Satire, Ironie und tiefere Bedeutung*, Heinrich Heine's *Briefe aus Berlin* and *Reise von München nach Genua*, and Franz Grillparzer's *König Ottokars Glück und Ende* and *Des Meeres und der Liebe Wellen*. These texts provide a productive basis for studying the effects of state censorship on literary writing for a number of reasons. First, they were all composed during the 1820s, a time when state repression succeeded in preventing serious challenges to the status quo and when the isolation and vulnerability of oppositional thinkers rendered the censorship system particularly effective. Secondly, each of the three authors held ideological views that conflicted with those of the Restoration authorities and, as we will see, attempted to express these views in their writings. Also significant is the fact that all of the texts received considerable contemporary public attention, and therefore provide an indication of the modes of literary expression that were allowed to reach a wide audience.

In addition to their comparability in these respects, however, the texts under discussion also provide an interesting cross section of literary writing under censorship. One dimension of this is the different forms represented by the works: while *Briefe aus Berlin* and *Reise von München nach Genua* are quasi-Romantic prose texts, Grillparzer's verse dramas were prepared (by the playwright, the theater management, and the censors) for immediate stage performance, and the structurally innovative plays of Grabbe under examination in this work were published as texts during the period, but, for various reasons, were not performed until much later.[113] The censorship controls faced by the texts also emerged from contrasting political climates. As a playwright of the Viennese Burgtheater, Grillparzer had to produce texts acceptable to the Austrian censorship authorities, generally held to be the strictest of the entire Confederation. Grabbe and Heine, on the other hand, were able to publish their texts in states or regions with relatively liberal censorship controls, but ultimately had to avoid prohibition in Prussia in order to reach a wide readership. One further area of divergence is the attitudes of the three writers toward the status quo. For although all of the men were opposed to elements of the social and political establishment, the nature and intensity of their dissent was different in each case. While Heine desired a complete overhaul of the established order, Grillparzer was basically loyal to the Habsburg monarchy, but deplored the excessive authoritarianism of the Metternich system and wished for a return to Josephinist principles of enlightened government. Grabbe, meanwhile, left few written records of his political views, but diverged from Restoration state ideology in both his anti-religious nihilism and his frustration with what he considered to be the mediocrity of contemporary society. Between them, the writers therefore had a range of objections to the political, religious, and social order that contemporary censorship aimed to protect. The effects on literary texts of the tension between the authors' dissident imaginations on the one hand, and the pressure exerted by state censorship on the other, are the subject of the following chapters.

Notes

[1] See, for example, Sigmund Freud, *Die Traumdeutung*, 11th ed. (Frankfurt am Main: Fischer, 2001).

[2] See Aleida Assmann and Jan Assmann, "Kanon und Zensur als kultursoziologische Kategorien," in *Kanon und Zensur: Archäologie der literarischen Kommunikation II*, ed. Aleida Assmann and Jan Assmann (Munich: Fink, 1987), 7–27 (especially 11 and 21).

[3] For a detailed account of the debates which preceded this verdict, see Nicholas Harrison, *Circles of Censorship: Censorship and its Metaphors in French History, Literature and Theory* (Oxford: Clarendon Press, 1995), 42–43.

[4] See, for example, Pierre Bourdieu, "Censorship and the Imposition of Form," in *Language and Symbolic Power*, ed. John B. Thompson, trans. Gino Raymond and Matthew Adamson (Oxford: Polity, 1992), 137–76; esp. 137–38.

[5] For more on the political effects of the breakdown of this opposition, see Robert C. Post, "Censorship and Silencing," in *Censorship and Silencing: Practices of Cultural Regulation*, ed. Robert C. Post (Los Angeles: Getty Research Institute, 1998), 1–12; here 2.

[6] Beate Müller, "Über Zensur: Wort, Öffentlichkeit und Macht. Eine Einführung," in *Zensur im modernen deutschen Zeitraum,* ed. Beate Müller, Studien und Texte zur Sozialgeschichte der Literatur 94 (Tübingen: Niemeyer, 2003), 1–30; here 4–5.

[7] Friedrich Schauer, "The Ontology of Censorship," in *Censorship and Silencing,* 147–68; here 149.

[8] This view of censorship is articulated in Ulla Otto, *Die literarische Zensur als Problem der Soziologie der Politik,* Bonner Beiträge zur Soziologie 3 (Stuttgart: Enke, 1968), 137.

[9] See Bodo Plachta, *Zensur* (Stuttgart: Reclam, 2006), 50–54.

[10] See Plachta, *Zensur,* 39.

[11] See Plachta, *Zensur,* 69.

[12] See Ulrich Eisenhardt, "Wandlungen von Zweck und Methoden der Zensur im 18. und 19. Jahrhundert," in *"Unmoralisch an sich . . ." Zensur im 18. und 19. Jahrhundert,* ed. Herbert G. Göpfert and Erdmann Weyrauch, Wolfenbütteler Schriften zur Geschichte des Buchwesens 13 (Wiesbaden: Harrassowitz, 1988), 1–35; here 18.

[13] See Bodo Plachta, *Damnatur — Toleratur — Admittitur: Studien und Dokumente zur literarischen Zensur im 18. Jahrhundert* (Tübingen: Niemeyer, 1994), 33–40.

[14] See Plachta, *Damnatur,* 95–101.

[15] See Plachta, *Damnatur,* 106–7.

[16] See Karlheinz Fuchs, *Bürgerliches Räsonnement und Staatsräson. Zensur als Instrument des Despotismus dargestellt am Beispiel des rheinbündischen Württemberg (1806–1813)* (Göppingen: Kümmerle, 1975), 59–63.

[17] See Dieter Breuer, *Geschichte der literarischen Zensur in Deutschland* (Heidelberg: Quelle und Meyer, 1982), 151–52.

[18] See Ulrich Eisenhardt, "Die Garantie der Pressefreiheit in der Bundesakte von 1815," *Der Staat* 10 (1971): 339–56; here 339.

[19] The significance of the emergence of a public sphere (which began in the German lands in the eighteenth century) is discussed in Jürgen Habermas, *Strukturwandel der Öffentlichkeit: Untersuchung zu einer Kategorie der bürgerlichen Gesellschaft,* 17th ed. (Frankfurt am Main: Suhrkamp, 1990), 69–133.

[20] For a detailed account of this system, see Wolfram Siemann, "Von der offenen zur mittelbaren Kontrolle. Der Wandel in der deutschen Preßgesetzgebung und Zensurpraxis des 19. Jahrhunderts," in Göpfert and Weyrauch, *"Unmoralisch an sich . . .,"* 293–308; esp. 298–305.

[21] See Martin Pagenkopf, *Das preußische OVG und Hauptmanns "Weber": Ein Nachtrag zum 125. Geburtstag von Gerhart Hauptmann* (Cologne: Bundesanzeiger, 1988), 84–85.

[22] The first, closed performance of *Die Weber* had taken place at a private club, the "Neues Theater" in Berlin, in February 1893. For a detailed account of the legal battle that preceded the first public staging of the play, see Pagenkopf, *Das preußische OVG und Hauptmanns "Weber,"* 56–70.

[23] See Gerhard Schulz, "Naturalismus und Zensur," in *Naturalismus: Bürgerliche Dichtung und soziales Engagement,* ed. Helmut Scheuer (Stuttgart: Kohlhammer, 1974), 93–121.

[24] For examples, see John Willett, *Art and Politics in the Weimar Period: The New Sobriety 1917–1933* (New York: Pantheon, 1978), 175 and 185–86.

[25] See Breuer, *Geschichte der literarischen Zensur,* 231–33.

[26] See Joseph Wulf, *Literatur und Dichtung im Dritten Reich: Eine Dokumentation* (Gütersloh: Sigbert Mohn, 1963), 28–42.

[27] See Hans-Helmuth Knütter, "Zur Vorgeschichte der Exilsituation," in *Die deutsche Exilliteratur 1933–1945,* ed. Manfred Durzak (Stuttgart: Reclam, 1973), 27–39; here 35–36.

[28] See Dietrich Aigner, "Die Indizierung 'schädlichen und unerwünschten Schrifttums' im Dritten Reich," *Archiv für Geschichte des Buchwesens* 11 (1971): 933–1034; here 943–44.

[29] See Manfred Jäger, "Das Wechselspiel von Selbstzensur und Literaturlenkung in der DDR," in *"Literaturentwicklungsprozesse": Die Zensur der Literatur in der DDR,* ed. Ernest Wichner and Herbert Wiesner (Frankfurt am Main: Suhrkamp, 1993), 18–49; here 18.

[30] See Joachim Walther, "Der fünfte Zensor — das MfS als letzte Instanz," in Müller, *Zensur im modernen deutschen Kulturraum,* 131–47; here 136–37.

[31] See Silke Buschmann, *Literarische Zensur in der BRD nach 1945,* Gießener Arbeiten zur Neueren Deutschen Literatur und Literaturwissenschaft 17 (Frankfurt am Main: Lang, 1997), 47.

[32] See Wilfried F. Schoeller, "Unerwünschte Zeugenschaft: Klaus Mann," in *Schriftsteller vor Gericht: Verfolgte Literatur in vier Jahrhunderten,* ed. Jörg-Dieter Kogel (Frankfurt am Main: Suhrkamp, 1996), 266–80; here 277–78.

[33] See Breuer, *Geschichte der literarischen Zensur,* 252.

[34] See, for example, Robin Lenman, "Germany," in *The War for the Public Mind: Political Censorship in Nineteeth-Century Germany,* ed. Robert Justin Goldstein (Westport, CT: Praeger, 2000), 35–80; here 35.

[35] See David Blackbourn, *History of Germany 1780–1918: The Long Nineteenth Century,* 2nd ed. (Malden, MA: Blackwell, 2003), 96–98.

[36] See "Verfassungsurkunde für das Königreich Bayern vom 26. Mai 1818," in Ernst Rudolf Huber, *Dokumente zur deutschen Verfassungsgeschichte,* 2nd ed., 3 vols. (Stuttgart: Kohlhammer, 1961–66), 1:141–56; here 148.

[37] See "Verfassungsurkunde für das Großherzogtum Baden vom 22. August 1818," in Huber, *Dokumente zur deutschen Verfassungsgeschichte,* 1:156–70; here 158.

[38] See "Verfassungsurkunde für das Königreich Württemberg vom 25. September 1819," in Huber, *Dokumente zur deutschen Verfassungsgeschichte,* 1:171–200; here 174.

[39] See "Deutsche Bundesakte vom 8. Juni 1815," in Huber, *Dokumente zur deutschen Verfassungsgeschichte,* 1:75–81; here 80.

⁴⁰ See, for example, Elke Blumenauer, *Journalismus zwischen Pressefreiheit und Zensur: Die Augsburger "Allgemeine Zeitung" im Karlsbader System (1818–48)*, Medien in Geschichte und Gegenwart 14 (Cologne: Böhlau, 2000), 33–37.

⁴¹ See Thomas Nipperdey, *Deutsche Geschichte 1800–1866: Bürgerwelt und starker Staat*, 2nd ed. (Munich: Beck, 1984), 278–80.

⁴² See Nipperdey, *Deutsche Geschichte*, 246.

⁴³ The decrees also included a set of laws that established procedures for the surveillance of universities and the exclusion of political dissidents from institutions of higher learning. A third set of laws dealt with the foundation of a central authority to investigate "revolutionäre[. . .] Umtriebe." For the full text of the decrees, see Huber, *Dokumente zur deutschen Verfassungsgeschichte*, 1:90–95.

⁴⁴ It is generally thought that the Carlsbad Decrees did not require longer works to be submitted for pre-publication censorship because their length and higher cost made them unsuitable for demagogic purposes.

⁴⁵ See "Die Karlsbader Beschlüsse," in Huber, *Dokumente zur deutschen Verfassungsgeschichte*, 1:90–95.

⁴⁶ See Edda Ziegler, *Literarische Zensur in Deutschland, 1819–1848: Materialien, Kommentare* (Munich: Hanser, 1983), 118.

⁴⁷ See Matthias Meyn, "Staatliche Repressionsmaßnahmen und "Karlsbader Beschlüsse" (1819–1832)," in *Deutsche Kommunikationskontrolle des 15. bis 20. Jahrhunderts*, ed. Heinz-Dietrich Fischer (Munich: Saur, 1982), 75–96; here 82–83.

⁴⁸ See Wolfram Siemann, "Ideenschmuggel und das Los deutscher Zensoren im 19. Jahrhundert," *Historische Zeitschrift* 245 (1987): 71–106; here 86.

⁴⁹ See Gast Mannes und Josiane Weber, *Zensur im Vormärz (1815–1848): Literatur und Presse in Luxemburg unter der Vormundschaft des Deutschen Bundes* (Luxembourg: Bibliothèque Nationale, 1998), 17–19.

⁵⁰ See Meyn, "Staatliche Repressionsmaßnahmen," 85.

⁵¹ See James J. Sheehan, *German History 1770–1866* (Oxford: Oxford UP, 1989), 445.

⁵² See Edda Ziegler, "Zensurgesetzgebung und Zensurpraxis in Deutschland 1819 bis 1848," in *Buchhandel und Literatur: Festschrift für Herbert G. Göpfert zum 75. Geburtstag am 22. September 1982*, eds. Reinhard Wittmann und Bertold Hack (Wiesbaden: Harrassowitz, 1982), 185–220; here 109–10.

⁵³ See, Ziegler, "Zensurgesetzgebung," 215.

⁵⁴ See, for example, Lenman, "Germany," 43.

⁵⁵ See Edda Ziegler, *Julius Campe: Der Verleger Heinrich Heines* (Hamburg: Hoffmann und Campe, 1976), 34–36.

⁵⁶ The new legislation was promulgated within the framework of "Die Zehn Artikel vom 5. Juli 1832" and "Die Sechzig Artikel vom 12. Juni 1834" (Huber, *Dokumente zur deutschen Verfassungsgeschichte*, 1:120–22 und 123–35).

⁵⁷ See Ziegler, "Zensurgesetzgebung," 216.

⁵⁸ See Breuer, *Geschichte der literarischen Zensur*, 155–57.

[59] See Michaela Breil, *Die Augsburger "Allgemeine Zeitung" und die Pressepolitik Bayerns: Ein Verlagsunternehmen zwischen 1815 und 1848* (Tübingen: Niemeyer, 1996), 72.

[60] For Hamburg, see Margarete Kramer, *Die Zensur in Hamburg 1819–1848: Ein Beitrag zur Frage staatlicher Lenkung der Öffentlichkeit während des deutschen Vormärz* (Hamburg: Buske, 1975), 177; for Baden, see Breil, *Die Augsburger "Allgemeine Zeitung,"* 78.

[61] See Kramer, *Die Zensur in Hamburg*, 247.

[62] See Frederik Ohles, *Germany's Rude Awakening: Censorship in the Land of the Brothers Grimm* (Kent, OH: Kent State UP, 1992), 101–7.

[63] See Ziegler, "Zensurgesetzgebung," 206–7.

[64] See, for example, Breil, *Die Augsburger "Allgemeine Zeitung,"* 170–76, and Mannes and Weber, *Zensur im Vormärz*, 17–19.

[65] See Ziegler, "Zensurgesetzgebung," 196.

[66] Huber, *Dokumente zur deutschen Verfassungsgeschichte*, 1:123–35.

[67] See Ziegler, "Zensurgesetzgebung," 195.

[68] See Hans-Ulrich Wehler, *Deutsche Gesellschaftsgeschichte*, 4 vols. (Munich: Beck, 1987–2003), 2:543.

[69] See Blumenauer, *Journalismus zwischen Pressefreiheit und Zensur*, 33–37.

[70] For details of this phenomenon in Hamburg, see Kramer, *Die Zensur in Hamburg*, 241.

[71] See Blumenauer, *Journalismus zwischen Pressefreiheit und Zensur*, 33–37.

[72] For example in Saxony (see Ziegler, "Zensurgesetzgebung," 209), Hamburg (see Kramer, *Die Zensur in Hamburg*, 257) and Hesse-Kassel (see Ohles, *Germany's Rude Awakening*, 32).

[73] See the "Preußische Zensur-Verordnung vom 18. Oktober 1819," in Huber, *Dokumente zur deutschen Verfassungsgeschichte*, 1:95–98; here 96.

[74] See Meyn, *Staatliche Repressionsmaßnahmen*, 86–87.

[75] See Julius Marx, *Die österreichische Zensur im Vormärz* (Vienna: Verlag für Geschichte und Politik, 1959), 17–24.

[76] See Siemann, "Ideenschmuggel," 100.

[77] See, for example, Ziegler, "Zensurgesetzgebung," 199, Mannes and Weber, *Zensur im Vormärz*, 139, and Breil, *Die Augsburger "Allgemeine Zeitung,"* 100.

[78] See, for example, Ziegler, "Zensurgesetzgebung," 201–2., and Breil, *Die Augsburger "Allgemeine Zeitung,"* 122.

[79] See Norbert Deuchert, *Vom Hambacher Fest zur badischen Revolution: Politische Presse und Anfänge der Demokratie 1832–1848/9* (Stuttgart: Thiess, 1983), 82–85.

[80] Breil, *Die Augsburger "Allgemeine Zeitung,"* 120.

[81] Deuchert, *Vom Hambacher Fest*, 82–84.

[82] See, for example, Mannes and Weber, *Zensur im Vormärz*, 147–48, Kramer, *Die Zensur in Hamburg*, 74–75, and Breil, *Die Augsburger "Allgemeine Zeitung,"* 122.

[83] See, for example, Mannes and Weber, *Zensur im Vormärz*, 148, Breil, *Die Augsburger "Allgemeine Zeitung,"* 133, and the Prussian censorship law of 1819 in Huber, *Dokumente zur deutschen Verfassungsgeschichte*, 1:95–98.

[84] For the original order, see *Preussische Gesetz-Sammlung 1824* (Berlin: Staatsministerium, 1810–1933), 2–3.

[85] See, for example, Mannes and Weber, *Die Zensur im Vormärz*, 147–48, and Breil, *Die Augsburger "Allgemeine Zeitung,"* 134.

[86] The full text of this law can be found in Marx, *Die österreichische Zensur*, 73–76.

[87] See "Preußische Zensur-Verordnung vom 18. Oktober 1819," in Huber, *Dokumente zur deutschen Verfassungsgeschichte*, 1:95–98; here 96.

[88] See Marx, *Die österreichische Zensur*, 75.

[89] See, for example, Mannes and Weber, *Die Zensur im Vormärz*, 148, and Kramer, *Die Zensur in Hamburg*, 233.

[90] See, for example, Kramer, *Die Zensur in Hamburg*, 75, Breil, *Die Augsburger "Allgemeine Zeitung,"* 122, Donald E. Emerson, *Metternich and the Political Police: Security and Subversion in the Habsburg Monarchy* (The Hague: Martinus Nijhoff, 1969), 144.

[91] This flood plays an important role in Franz Grillparzer's novelle *Der arme Spielmann* (1848).

[92] Austrian examples from Julius Marx, "Die amtlichen Verbotslisten. Neue Beiträge zur Geschichte der österreichischen Zensur im Vormärz," *Mitteilungen des österreichischen Staatsarchivs* 9 (1956): 150–85; here 159; Prussian example from Wehler, *Deutsche Gesellschaftsgeschichte*, 2:653.

[93] See W. E. Yates, *Theatre in Vienna: A Critical History, 1776–1995* (Cambridge: Cambridge UP, 1996), 28.

[94] See Yates, *Theatre in Vienna*, 28.

[95] See Marx, "Die amtlichen Verbotslisten," 167–68.

[96] See Ohles, *Germany's Rude Awakening*, 94.

[97] See Yates, *Theatre in Vienna*, 38.

[98] See Siemann, "Ideenschmuggel," 87.

[99] At one stage, Heinrich Heine's publisher, Julius Campe, planned to use this strategy for Heine's fourth *Reisebilder* volume. See Heinrich Heine, *Historisch-kritische Gesamtausgabe der Werke*, Düsseldorfer Ausgabe, ed. Manfred Windfuhr and others, 16 vols. (Hamburg: Hoffmann und Campe, 1973–97), vol 7, ed. by Alfred Opitz, 1986, 1439–40.

[100] See Breil, *Die Augsburger "Allgemeine Zeitung,"* 79.

[101] See Siemann, "Ideenschmuggel," 90–91.

[102] See Siemann, "Ideenschmuggel," 91.

[103] See, for example, Robert Justin Goldstein, ed., *The War for the Public Mind: Political Censorship in Nineteenth-Century Europe* (Westport, CT: Praeger, 2000), 48.

[104] See Heinrich Heine, *Historisch-kritische Gesamtausgabe,* vol. 12, ed. J. Derrë and C. Giesen, 662–70.

[105] See, for example, Ziegler, *Literarische Zensur in Deutschland,* 172–74.

[106] Studies that demonstrate the use of evasive strategies within contemporary literary writing include Elvira Grözinger, "Die 'doppelte Buchhaltung.' Einige Bemerkungen zu Heines Verstellungsstrategien in den *Florentinischen Nächten,*" *Heine-Jahrbuch* 18 (1979), 65–83, and René Anglade, "Die Engländer in der Hofkirche. Zugleich ein kleiner Beitrag zur Poetik Heines," *Euphorion* 78 (1984): 415–34.

[107] In particular, Heinrich Hubert Houben, *Der gefesselte Biedermeier: Literatur, Kultur, Zensur in der guten, alten Zeit* (Leipzig: Haessel, 1924; reprinted, Hildesheim: Gerstenberg, 1973).

[108] See, for example, Klaus Kanzog, "Textkritische Probleme der literarischen Zensur. Zukünftige Aufgaben einer literaturwissenschaftlichen Zensurforschung," in Göpfert and Weyrauch, "*Unmoralisch an sich . . .,*" 309–25, and Ziegler, *Literarische Zensur in Deutschland,* 176.

[109] Harrison, *Circles of Censorship,* 86 and 178.

[110] Cf. Ziegler, *Literarische Zensur in Deutschland,* 172.

[111] For an examination of a case in which either aesthetic or censorship considerations could have motivated a series of amendments, see the discussion by Klaus Kanzog of a manuscript of Gerhard Hauptmann's *Die Ratten* in Kanzog, "Textkritische Probleme," 318–320.

[112] See, for example, Armin Bierman, "Gefährliche Literatur: Skizze einer Theorie der literarischen Zensur," *Wolfenbütteler Schriften zur Geschichte des Buchwesens* 13.1 (1988): 1–28; here 10–11.

[113] *Herzog Theodor von Gothland* was first performed in Vienna in 1892, and *Scherz, Satire, Ironie und tiefere Bedeutung* was first staged in Munich in 1907.

1: Sex, Religion, and Violence: Christian Dietrich Grabbe's *Herzog Theodor von Gothland*

IN 1822, THE YOUNG and rather unenthusiastic law student Christian Dietrich Grabbe sent a copy of his recently completed drama, *Herzog Theodor von Gothland*,[1] to the celebrated poet Ludwig Tieck. In his letter of reply, Tieck acknowledged the young writer's talent and the *Gothland* play's "große Gedanken, die auch mehr wie einmal kräftig ausgedrückt sind,"[2] but also expressed disappointment at the play's cruelty and cynicism, a reaction that was echoed in later responses to the drama following its publication in 1827.[3] Such elements of disapproval in the contemporary reception of *Gothland* can be related both to the brutal language of the play and to the disturbing events contained within its elaborate plot.

Set in Sweden at an unspecified time during the Middle Ages, *Gothland* follows the descent into nihilism and amorality of its title character, Duke Theodor von Gothland. This descent is largely set in motion by the scheming of Gothland's archenemy, Berdoa, the African leader of the Finns. The play opens during the course of a Finnish raid on Sweden and, shortly after reaching Swedish territory, Berdoa discovers that one of Gothland's brothers has died unexpectedly. Aware of the Duke's devotion to both his brothers, Berdoa sets out to convince him that Manfred was in fact murdered by his other brother, the chancellor, Friedrich. With the forced help of the chancellor's servant, Rolf, the Finnish leader defaces Manfred's corpse to make it look as though he had been murdered and then leads Gothland to the tomb to view his brother's body.

Unable to dispute the sight that meets his eyes, Gothland immediately becomes convinced of the chancellor's guilt. He seeks justice from the Swedish king, but when this fails, he kills the chancellor himself and is forced to flee when the king issues his death warrant. Shortly afterwards, Rolf informs Gothland of Berdoa's deception, and this revelation plunges the Duke into such a rage that he throws the servant off a cliff. Devastated by the knowledge that he unjustly killed his own brother, Gothland is overwhelmed by despair, and soon comes to reject the existence of both God and human goodness.

Gothland's new amoral philosophy frees him from the shackles of conscience and religion, and this initially brings him a certain amount of success. He uses deception, for example, to persuade the Finns to take Berdoa prisoner and to select him as their new leader. Yet even after leading his new army to victory against the Swedes, Gothland does not find peace. His son comes increasingly under the corrupting influence of Berdoa, and Gothland himself becomes tormented by nightmares about the brother he murdered. As the Duke conducts anxious dialogues with Berdoa about the existence of God and the afterlife, it is made clear that the consequences of his murderous actions prey on his mind. This unease does not induce Gothland to return to a belief in morality, however. When his wife, Cäcilie, turns up at the Finnish camp to seek reconciliation, he rejects her, declaring that he is no longer the man she married and turning her out into the wilderness on a cold night. We observe her death two scenes later.

In the closing scenes of the drama, the Finns realize Gothland's deception and reinstate Berdoa as their leader, just as a renewed Swedish army appears to reclaim their conquered land. Berdoa takes Gothland prisoner, but before he gets round to killing him, the Swede escapes and eventually manages to murder his enemy. With this task accomplished, Gothland realizes that his life no longer holds any meaning and that all he can look forward to is death. He is killed shortly afterwards and the drama ends with Gothland's aged father lamenting the demise of his family.

Although the composition of *Gothland* was clearly influenced by contemporary fate tragedies,[4] the play was in many respects highly unusual. By the standards of the time, for example, its language was frequently blasphemous and its cruelty and nihilistic atheism shocking.[5] In addition, the convoluted plot, with its chaotic battle scenes and relatively formless structure[6] did not make the drama an inviting prospect for theater producers.[7] It is likely that these factors played a role in its author's failure to find either a publisher or a director for *Gothland* during the early 1820s.

Grabbe had begun work on the tragedy while attending the Gymnasium in his home town of Detmold, continued it during the two years he spent studying in Leipzig, and completed the play in June 1822, shortly after his arrival in Berlin.[8] Hoping for recognition from the literary establishment, Grabbe showed *Gothland* to many people in the Prussian capital, where it met with divided reactions: while some readers were appalled by the play's violent language and cynicism, others were fascinated by its energy and originality.[9] In 1823, however, Grabbe's parents were no longer able to support him financially; and after an unsuccessful attempt to establish himself as an actor, the aspiring writer was forced to return to Detmold, where he took his final exams and started work as a lawyer.

In April 1827, Grabbe received a letter from his old friend Georg Ferdinand Kettembeil, a fellow student whom he had first met in Leipzig. The two men had continued to meet in Berlin, where Kettembeil learned the book trade and socialized with the same group of literary bohemians as Grabbe. By 1827, Kettembeil had become the owner of the J. C. Hermannsche Buchhandlung in Frankfurt am Main and was interested in publishing his friend's work. It was soon agreed that Grabbe's four completed dramas, including *Gothland,* would be collected into one book alongside his essay on German admiration for Shakespeare. The two volumes of *Dramatische Dichtungen von Grabbe. Nebst einer Abhandlung über die Shakspearo-Manie* went on sale in September 1827.

In the intervening months, a certain amount of work was necessary in order to prepare the works for publication.[10] Grabbe was well aware that two of his plays in particular, *Gothland* and *Scherz, Satire, Ironie und tiefere Bedeutung,* would be likely to offend the censors in their current form. Each volume of *Dramatische Dichtungen* was longer than twenty Bogen, which meant that the comedy would not have to undergo prepublication censorship in the relatively liberal city-state of Frankfurt am Main, where it was printed. Yet the danger of a postpublication ban remained and Grabbe's correspondence twice mentions the likely response of Prussian censors to his plays. A ban in this largest North German state would have had a severe impact on the book's sales.

At first, the young author seemed remarkably relaxed about changes to his works and, in a letter of the 25 June 1827, gave his editor permission to "Streich oder laß streichen, so viel Du willst" (*HKG* 5:162). At the same time, however, Grabbe also made it clear which places in the dramas he was most anxious to conserve and, over the course of five lengthy letters, conducted a detailed dialogue with his editor regarding ways of rendering those works less offensive to the censors. Unfortunately, Kettembeil's letters have not survived and our picture of this dialogue remains incomplete. Nevertheless, we do have access to the original 1822 version of *Gothland* as well as the setting copy for the 1827 first edition and the first edition itself. Alongside Grabbe's comments in his letters regarding censorship concerns, the differences between these versions give us a clear idea of how the editing of *Gothland* was shaped by censorship pressure.

Of course, not all the differences between successive versions of the drama can be attributed to censorship considerations. Aesthetic concerns played a role too. In particular, a considerable amount of excess material was removed from the later versions of *Gothland,* presumably in order to heighten the play's dramatic energy. However, it is in most cases relatively easy to distinguish such aesthetic cuts from those resulting from censorship pressures.

For one thing, the censors were known to be sensitive to certain topic areas such as religion and politics;[11] where the removed sections touched upon these themes, it is probable that they were excised due to censorship considerations. Secondly, where changes to the setting copy have been explicitly attributed to Kettembeil, it seems safe to assume that they did not arise out of aesthetic considerations alone. As mentioned above, although Grabbe initially told Kettembeil to make whatever changes he wanted, he later gave his editor very precise instructions about which parts of the dramas he was most anxious to see retained. It is therefore highly unlikely that Kettembeil would have felt free to change the plays according to his own tastes. Indeed, whereas changes arising from censorship concerns are discussed in great detail throughout Grabbe's letters to Kettembeil during the months running up to the publication of *Dramatische Dichtungen,* there is no mention of any alterations on artistic grounds. Finally, in cases where the excised words are replaced by dashes, it also seems safe to rule out the possibility that the cuts were motivated by aesthetic considerations.

Despite such clues, it may be judged controversial to attribute all non-aesthetic changes to censorship pressure. As we will see later, many of these amendments can be related to the area of "gute Sitten" or decency. And in the "Anzeige des Verlegers" that precedes the first edition of *Gothland,* specific mention is made of modifications that had to be made "des großen Publici wegen" (*HKG* 1:8). As a result, it could be argued that some of the changes may have been more a response to the sensibilities of the drama's potential audience than a means of escaping the censor's pen.

On the other hand, however, the area of "Sittlichkeit" was itself within the remit of Restoration censors;[12] and one imagines that their concerns overlapped considerably with the ideas of polite society on what it was acceptable to say. Moreover, Grabbe's letters to Kettembeil do not mention any concern on the part of his editor to tone down the more shocking parts of *Gothland.* On the contrary, in a letter to Kettembeil of 4 May 1827, Grabbe writes, "den sittlichen Eindruck, welchen bei albernen, kurzsichtigen Personen jene Producte machen könnten, trage ich unbedingt, und geht er den Verleger nichts an" (*HKG* 5:152). Although it is impossible to be certain in every case, I would therefore argue that the need to appease the censorship authorities was overwhelmingly the main motive for Kettembeil's changes to the setting copy, which are discussed in the following sections.

Religion

Judging from the plot of *Gothland,* we might expect the treatment of religion in the play to have suffered under the threat of censorship. After all, the fall of Duke Gothland away from morality and religion is one of its central themes. Although religion is not mentioned explicitly in the Carlsbad Decrees,[13] it nevertheless represented a cornerstone of Restoration society. Accordingly, the Prussian censorship law of 1819 declared that one of the principal aims of state censorship was "demjenigen zu steuern, was den allgemeinen Grundsätzen der Religion, ohne Rücksicht auf die Meinungen und Lehren einziger Religionsparteien und im Staate geduldeter Sekten, zuwider ist,"[14] an intention which is reiterated in a cabinet order of 1824.[15] It is therefore interesting that only one passage relating to religion was removed from the text prior to publication (*HKG* 1:544). This concerned a statement of Berdoa's that linked pious devotion with human sensuality in a manner that would clearly be offensive to Christians:

> Ich kenne unter
> Den Christen gar nicht wen'ge Laffen, die
> Im selben Sinn, in welchem sie
> Von ihrem Mädchen sprechen, Gott
> Die Liebe nennen! (*HKG* 1:116)

To be sure, even the 1822 version of *Gothland* contains no attacks on the Christian churches or their members, and Jesus is not mentioned at all. Perhaps as a result of self-censorship by the young Grabbe, the God from whom Gothland becomes alienated remains a vague creator figure whose relationship with Christianity is never made explicit. Nevertheless, it is still significant that the first edition of *Gothland* contains many statements that question the central tenets of Christianity.

During the act 4 scene 1, for example, Gothland summons Berdoa to his tent for a metaphysical discussion. Gothland's first question for his prisoner is "Was ist Unsterblichkeit?" — to which Berdoa supplies the impious answer, "Ein Wort" (*HKG* 1:124–25). And when questioned further on the origins of this commonly held belief, Berdoa responds that it is a result of our psychological needs:

> Bloß
> Um unsrer ungeheuren Eitelkeit
> Zu schmeicheln und die Furcht vor der
> Vernichtung unsres Daseins zu besänftgen,
> Erfanden wir uns die Unsterblichkeit [. . .]. (*HKG* 1:125)

Admittedly, Berdoa does change his tune somewhat later on in the conversation and begins to suggest the existence of both an afterlife and an omnipotent God. However, the value of such assertions is undermined by the circumstances under which they are made. For, freed from the fear of divine retribution by Berdoa's assurances in the first part of their conversation, Gothland orders the killing of 5,000 prisoners. And as the Swede eventually realizes, it is only in order to arouse his enemy's fears of the consequences of this murderous command that Berdoa seems to change his theological views (*HKG* 1:125–31). Not only are convincing psychological explanations for religious beliefs put forward in this scene, but these convictions are also casually employed in a game of psychological manipulation.

It may be suggested that the anti-religious comments in this scene were able to appear in the first edition because they originated from Berdoa. As a savage villain from the "heathen" continent of Africa, he could not be expected to behave any better. Be that as it may, we must also consider the fact that Berdoa is not the only character in *Gothland* to make blasphemous statements. Indeed, probably the most profound expression of distrust in God comes from Gothland himself, a representative of Christian Sweden.[16] In act 3 scene 1, for example, Rolf tells Gothland of Berdoa's scheming and reveals to him that he has killed the chancellor unjustly. In the face of Gothland's horrified reaction to this news, the servant suggests that he prays to God for forgiveness, but Gothland refuses, insisting that "Beten / Ist Betteln" (*HKG* 1:78). His subsequent monologues advance the idea that human beings are incapable of distinguishing right from wrong (*HKG* 1:79) or controlling their own actions (*HKG* 1:82). This scene also contains the blasphemous declaration that "Es ist kein Gott" (*HKG* 1:81), as well as the pronouncement that "Allmächtge Bosheit also ist es, die / Den Weltkreis lenkt und ihn zerstört" (*HKG* 1:82). The ultimate conclusion of this train of thought is reached when Gothland finally cries out:

> Ja, Gott
> Ist boshaft, und Verzweiflung ist
> Der wahre Gottesdienst! (*HKG* 1:82–83)

Two scenes later, Gothland's alienation from God appears to have led him to a philosophy of atheist materialism. During his metaphysical discussion with Berdoa, the Swedish Duke repeatedly declares that God does not exist (*HKG* 1:128–29) and his evocative description of the end of the universe clearly implies that reality consists only of physical matter:

> Dann rollen jene feurgen Welten
> Mit ihren Erden und
> Mit ihren Monden, andre Welten mit
> Sich niederreißend, in die Schlünde der
> Vernichtung, und die Himmelswölb'
> Fällt ihnen nach, wie'n müdes Augenlid! —
> Ewig ist nur der Staub. (*HKG* 1:128)

Although none of these statements were removed from the setting copy, both Kettembeil and Grabbe were clearly worried about how the censors might react to them. Within the context of a specifically Christian society, both atheistic proclamations and insults hurled against even an unspecified "Gott" represented a potential attack on Christianity. On the other hand, however, Gothland's blasphemous speeches supplied several dramatic highpoints within the play, and Grabbe was anxious for them to be included in the published version. In his letter to Kettembeil on 25 June 1827, the writer at first responded to his editor's worries with the request that "die Stelle im Gothland im 3t Acte dürfte wohl nur in den schlimmsten *directe* contra Gott gerichteten Stellen verändert werden" (*HKG* 5:162). Later on in the same letter, he suggests a strategy to protect Gothland's blasphemous outbursts:

> Schlimmstens könntest Du beim Beginn derselben die Note setzen: "Die 3te Scene des 5ten Actes und in gegenwärtigem Auftritt die Zwischenreden Berdoas zeigen daß der Dichter, nachdem er zwar die Flamme des Abgrundes auflodern ließ, er sie auch durch eigene Kraft [...] zu schwächen, ja zu vernichten versteht. (*HKG* 5:162-63)

Berdoa's "Zwischenreden" in the third act consist of a series of statements that reassert the existence and power of God in the face of Gothland's denials. Together with the menacing rolls of thunder that punctuate this scene, such comments bring a strong sense that the Swede's abandonment of God will bring him no good. At one point, for example, Gothland's words cause Berdoa to exclaim gleefully, "Wie er sich gegen Gott zu bäumen meint" (*HKG* 1:81). And perhaps even more significantly, in act 5 scene 3, Berdoa condemns his enemy's treatment of his brother, and suggests that the torments of hell await him, before trying to persuade Gothland to pray for repentance (*HKG* 1:186).

Of course, it may be hard to accept Berdoa as a defender of Christian values. Indeed, his uncharacteristic acknowledgment of these values stems from a very unchristian sense of triumph at his adversary's downfall. Nevertheless, his pronouncements are confirmed by the unenviable fate of Gothland, whose nightmares and tormenting visions only give way to a sense of meaninglessness. The Swede certainly makes a poor advertisement for atheism. Within this context, it seems, expressions of defiance toward and disbelief in a vaguely defined creator could be tolerated.

Sexual Morality

> Die Zoten sind in den Gesprächen zwischen Berdoa und Gustav (der ein Hauptcharakter ist) am nöthigsten; da schone soviel es Dir möglich ist. (*HKG* 1:165)

This request, made by Grabbe in a letter to Kettembeil on 12 July 1827, was one that his editor was unable to grant. Like other contemporary censorship legislation, the Prussian law of 1819 insists that censors should not pass anything "was die Moral und gute Sitten beleidigt."[17] Indeed, it seems that Kettembeil's experience led him to judge that, unlike the play's blasphemous statements, Berdoa's "Zoten" could not be rendered less offensive, either by footnotes or by other means. Several other passages in *Gothland* were also affected by the censors' duty to uphold standards of morality and decency; and, in fact, the majority of alterations — almost twenty in total — made to the setting copy for the first edition of Grabbe's plays involve the removal of sexual references from the original text.

Most of these arise from Berdoa's efforts to use the prospect of sexual adventure with a certain woman named Milchen to tempt Gothland's son, Gustav, away from his faraway beloved, Selma. Examples of passages that had to be excised range from Berdoa's matter-of-fact report that Gustav "liegt / In Milchens Arm" (*HKG* 1:141), through his crude reference to a girlfriend of one of the Finnish officers as "deinem hübschen Nachtgeschirre" (*HKG* 1:117), to his graphic wish that, upon making the acquaintance of Selma, Gustav's reaction will be "ihr vor Wollust in die Brüste beißen" (*HKG* 1:118).[18]

Yet, despite the quantity of erotic reference removed from the setting copy of *Gothland*, even the completed first edition did not allow its readers to forget about the sensual side of human nature. Certain types of sexual reference, it seems, were more acceptable than others. One such example is Berdoa's description of how he expects Gustav to behave toward Milchen:

>   Hier
> Wird sich der Bube nicht mehr halten können,
> Entzückt, begeistert, weinend wird
> Er in die Arm' ihr fallen, ihr beistimmen,
> Mit "himmlisch" und mit "göttlich" um
> Sich werfen, wie Straßendreck,
> Venus Urania sie heißen. (*HKG* 1:118)

The emotional agitation ("Entzückt, begeistert, weinend") and vigorous movement ("um sich werfend") described here indicate that Gustav's envisaged powerlessness is not of a completely spiritual nature, and this impression is reinforced by the series of dashes that follow the passage. However, Berdoa's words do describe this erotic activity in exclusively poetic terms, and one suspects that they were acceptable to both Kettembeil and the censorship authorities for that reason.

Such oblique references to sexuality were not the only ones to survive the editing process. More direct comments were also left in. In particular, Gustav's defiant declarations of love for Selma arouse some cynical responses from Berdoa, who refuses to see this emotional attachment as an obstacle to his scheming. His thinking on the matter is perhaps most neatly summed up in his pronouncement that "Ein Schritt nur ists, der von der Liebe zu / Der Unzucht führt" (*HKG* 1:116) and the even more explicit, "wer verliebt ist, der ist geil" (*HKG* 1:112). Although it is possible that these brief statements were overlooked by inattentive censors and editors, the same cannot be suggested of Berdoa's response to Gustav's assurance that love is "das Höchste auf der Erde":

> [. . .] das Höchste?
> Aufs Kindermachen läuft's hinaus! — Was liebt
> Ihr denn am Weib? Etwa den Geist? [. . .]
> Ihr liebt das Fleisch! (*HKG* 1:115)[19]

In the end, Gustav does surrender to the temptations offered to him by Berdoa in the form of "das blonde Milchen." However, the intense sexual experiences he enjoys with her do nothing to diminish his love for Selma; and this outcome could be seen to undermine Berdoa's cynical equation of love with sex. Nevertheless, the fact that he is allowed to make such pronouncements in the first place indicates that the theme of human sexuality was not a complete taboo.

This raises the question of why the above-mentioned comments were included in the first edition of *Gothland* when so many others were removed. It is possible that, as an essentially evil character, as well as an "uncivilized" non-Christian African, Berdoa was allowed to be more sexually explicit than other figures in the drama. However, as we have already seen, many of Berdoa's other sexual comments were removed from the text, so that his status as a black representative of evil does not provide the complete explanation.

Although it is difficult to come to firm conclusions on the basis of such a limited number of examples, there is one noticeable difference between the sexual references that were left in the first published edition, and those that were removed from the setting copy. Unlike most of the excised passages, none of the explicit sexual comments in the first edition are at all graphic. While the latter acknowledge sex as a factor in human behavior, they do not even hint at the details that could be used to compose erotic images. Berdoa's conviction that love is only a step away from "Unzucht" may be crude, but it does not supply the same inviting food for fantasy as even the casual report that Gustav "liegt in Milchens Arm." Although Kettembeil did not feel obliged to turn *Gothland* into a play that denied human sexuality, he clearly saw the need to remove any concrete examples of the types of behavior to which it led.

The idea that sexuality could be acknowledged, as long as the audience were not presented with graphic examples of its manifestations, is supported by one further aspect of the treatment of sexual reference in *Gothland*. For, many of the erotic references that were removed from the setting copy of the play did not disappear completely, but were replaced by dashes. Although up to two or three such dashes were also employed throughout the play to denote a pause, longer series of dashes were only ever used to replace forbidden material.[20] As a result, these dashes served as a signal that the author had originally intended to include illicit material at a particular point. And in many cases, the nature of the excised material was frequently clear from the words surrounding the dashes.

In act 4 scene 2, for instance, during one of Berdoa's banquets, Gustav exclaims, "Das Lied ist aus — wir wollen tanzen!" In the 1822 version of the text, Irnak replies to him with the following words:

> Ne, tanzt nicht! reitet lieber! *Zu einer Dirne*
> Nicht wahr, mein Kind?[21]

In the first edition, however, Irnak's words from "reitet" to "Kind" are replaced by four dashes (*HKG* 1:551). Although the exact nature of the original content remains obscure, the clear indication of an illicit alternative to dancing gives us a fair idea of the nature of Irnak's speech. Similarly, in the 1822 version of act 4 scene 1, Berdoa asks Gustav whether his sexual experiences with Milchen have made him forget Selma. The young man indignantly replies that they have not and explains why he spends so much time with Milchen:

> Bloß weil ich Selma liebe, bloß
> Daß meine Qual um sie in etwas doch
> Sich lindre, gehe ich zu deinem Milchen;
> O selig, überselig wär ich, hörte ich
> Nur rauschen ihres Kleides Saum! (*HKG* 1:143)

Berdoa's response to this question is to evoke for Gustav an image that was taken out of the setting copy and replaced by seven dashes (*HKG* 1:549):

> Du!
> Mit Selma unter einer Decke —
> Im bloßen Hemde du und sie —
> Und dann der süß Errötenden
> Mit wollustvollem Zögern leise, leise
> Das Hemde aufzuheben! (*HKG* 1:143)

As we have seen, these dashes are introduced by Gustav's revelations of sexual tension in the previous speech and are immediately followed by his response of "Ah, der Wonne!" Although such hints do not reveal precisely the scenario described by Berdoa's words, they do strongly indicate some kind of sexual encounter between Gustav and Selma, leaving only the details to the reader's imagination.

A further borderline between acceptable and unacceptable sexual reference is suggested by a comment of Berdoa's in act 4 scene 1. This example is the only exception to Kettembeil's practice of removing potentially erotic images from the setting copy. It comes when Gustav asks Berdoa if he has ever loved, a question that prompts a feigned rhapsody on the merits of "Ella [. . .] Holdeste der Afrikanerinnen":

> Wie edel war ihr Herz! wie wollig war
> Ihr Haar! zwei Schuhe lang ihr Busen! (*HKG* 1:144)

The presence of the phrase "zwei Schuhe lang ihr Busen!" in the published first edition is particularly significant because it is highly unlikely that Kettembeil could have overlooked it during the course of the editing process. For the editor actually changed the wording of the next passage from the puzzling "Und ach! sie war Euch schwarz," to the more comprehensible, "Und ach! sie war so schwarz" (*HKG* 1:550). Although Kettembeil actually had to copy out the phrase "zwei Schuhe lang ihr Busen" during the course of his corrections, he did not see any need to remove it.

One suspects that two factors were decisive in allowing this phrase to remain in the first published edition of *Gothland*. First, a reference to "Busen" may have been considered less offensive than comments about the "Arsch" or "Steiß" of other women, both of which were removed from the setting copy (*HKG* 1:549). In addition, it is also possible that, because she was an African, Ella was not protected from explicit personal remarks in the same way that European women were. Kettembeil's toleration of this passage may therefore reflect the same attitudes that allowed images of bare-breasted African women in various contexts long before the equivalent images of white women.

The Family

In many ways, *Gothland* does not seem to be marked by much consideration for the family, containing as it does several instances in which family bonds appear to be negated. Gothland's distrust of the chancellor, for example, leads him to become rapidly convinced that his brother has killed Manfred and to exact an unjust revenge. Later on, Gothland rejects his wife's offer of reconciliation and shows a complete disregard for her welfare by throwing her out into the cold night. Shortly before his death, Gothland states that family ties no longer mean anything to him; and the drama closes with old Gothland lamenting the end of the family line.

Yet despite these brutal events, the editing process for the first edition of *Gothland* does suggest that the family was offered some protection by the censorship authorities. One indication comes following the Finns' victory over the Swedish army. Here, Gothland's wife, Cäcilia, turns up at the Finnish camp to seek reconciliation with her husband. As already mentioned, this request is refused and she and her aged father are turned out of the camp. In the setting copy, Gothland's relief at her departure is expressed initially by the following rather harsh words:

> Endlich hat das Geschrei ein Ende!
> Was tuts denn auch, ob so ein Weib krepiert? (*HKG* 1:140)

Later on, however, Kettembeil replaced "krepiert" with "verdirbt" (*HKG* 1:549). Although *Gothland* abounds with examples of murderous intent, it was apparently inadvisable for a man to express such energetic indifference toward the death of his wife.

More evidence for a concern to protect the sanctity of the family is provided by the occasions in which comments linking sex and childbearing are removed from the setting copy. The first example of this comes following Gothland's murder of his brother, when his father approaches the Finnish camp with the intention of fighting a duel with his only surviving son. A disguised Gothland asks his father whether he regrets having given life to such a son; and when old Gothland replies in the affirmative, cursing his offspring, the son answers angrily:

> Den Fluch auf dich! Wer hatte dir das Recht
> Verliehn, das Leben ihm zu geben?! Fluch der Geilheit
> Die Dich antrieb. (*HKG* 1:92)

In the first edition of *Gothland*, the final sentence, "Fluch der Geilheit, Die Dich antrieb" is missing, having been crossed out of the setting copy by Kettembeil (*HKG* 1:540). There are several possible reasons for its removal. First, it might be argued that either the word or the concept of "Geilheit" was in itself unacceptable. However, we have seen from Berdoa's theories on love and sensuality that this was not the case. A more plausible suggestion is that it was considered unacceptable for a specific person's sexual drives to be discussed in such a way, especially by his own son. In addition, however, Gothland's excised comments also make very explicit the link between sex and childbearing.

Further evidence of official sensitivity toward this issue is supplied by another example of Kettembeil's editing. For, although we have seen that Berdoa is allowed to proclaim confidently, "Wer verliebt ist, der ist geil," the editor's forbearance did not extend to a similarly generalized and impersonal reminder of the link between sex and children: Gothland's angry cursing of a world in which "jeder Bauerlümmel / Mit Hülfe einer Viehmagd / Etwas Unsterbliches verfertgen kann" (*HKG* 1:93) was crossed out of the setting copy and is absent in the 1827 first edition (*HKG* 1:540). It may be suggested that the passage was removed because the word "verfertigen" was considered an inappropriate verb with which to describe the conception of a human being. However, this is unlikely within the context of a play of which the hero is allowed to pronounce all human life worthless. Moreover, if the word "verfertigen" had been the only problematic element of the passage, it could have been replaced by another, less offensive verb. Although the explicit mention of a general link between love and sex was tolerable, the connection between sex and childbearing, just like a man's emphatic indifference to his wife's death, was evidently considered unacceptable.

The Human Body

Another subject area that was significantly affected by the editing process of *Gothland* was that of bodily functions. Admittedly, it may seem unremarkable that, during Gothland's diatribe about childhood, the second line of the following quotation was removed and replaced by dashes (*HKG* 1:548):

> Kindheit, fahr hin
> Samt deinen Kindern, welche sich bekacken! (*HKG* 1:134)

However, on other occasions, changes made to the setting copy of *Gothland* indicate that contemporary sensibilities regarding the organic dimension of human existence went much further. During one of the many instances in which Gustav impresses upon Berdoa the strength of his love for Selma, the African's response in the 1822 version is to remind the young man that "Deine Göttin ist ein Mensch wie du!":

> Hat sie auf ihrem Kopf viel Haare,
> Was du rühmst, so hat sie sicher auch
> Viel Ungeziefer drauf, und ihre Nas
> Ist schleimig, wie die Nasen andrer Leute!
> Sie trinkt und ißt so gut als du
> Und so wie du gibt sie's auch wieder von sich! (*HKG* 1:115)

In the setting copy, the whole of the above quotation was crossed out and replaced by ten dashes (*HKG* 1:544). It could be suggested that the final two lines were the only reason for the excision. This is improbable, however, since they could easily have been removed on their own. As we have seen, Kettembeil was prepared to allow speeches to end abruptly elsewhere; and on this occasion, taking out the final two lines would not have disrupted the flow of the passage. Instead, it seems that comments regarding insects in hair and nasal mucus were themselves too provocative be included in the first edition of *Dramatische Dichtungen*.

This concern to protect the dignity of the human body was not restricted to female characters. At the end of the play, Berdoa decides to torment Gothland by describing to him how his brother Manfred really died. In the 1822 version of the play we can read how:

> Manfred war
> Jählings am Schlagflusse verreckt —
> Wahrscheinlich hatte er beim Abendschmaus
> Zu viel gefressen und es nicht
> Verdauen können [...]. (*HKG* 1:184)

On the setting copy for the 1827 first edition, on the other hand, Kettembeil removed all references to the role of eating and digestion in Manfred's death, and we are simply told that "Manfred war / Jählings am Schlagflusse gestorben" (*HKG* 1:556). Similarly, in the following inoffensive pronouncements on a cow's purpose in life, Kettembeil changed "gefressen" to "gegessen" in the setting copy (*HKG* 1:556):

> Sein Dasein hat 'nen Zweck — es wird
> Gefressen — [...]. (*HKG* 1:85)

Once again, Kettembeil's editing reveals a concern to protect the dignity of the physical processes of life.

Perhaps the most obvious interpretation of this embarrassment about bodily functions would be to see it arising out of a desire to protect the dignity of the characters concerned. Yet it is interesting that not all aspects of the material basis of life were considered equally degrading. A death from indigestion may have been considered too undignified a fate for Manfred, yet, following a serious injury in the first scene of the play, it seems perfectly acceptable for Berdoa to tell us of how his "Eingeweide löst / Sich los" (*HKG* 1:14). Other inclusions in the first edition reinforce the idea that the routine physical processes of life may have been considered more sensitive than gore within the context of violence and death. Manfred's corpse, for example, is not granted the same protection as the dying man. Berdoa's gruesome description of seeing Manfred in his tomb, "Von dem Gewürme der Verwesung wimmelnd" (*HKG* 1:41), is unchanged in the first edition, as is Rolf's later account of how, while trapped in the tomb, "Schaudernd naht / Ich mich den würmdurchnagten Leichen, sie / Zu speisen" (*HKG* 1:75). Most horrific of all is Rolf's fictional tale of Manfred's alleged murder at the hands of his brother. Egged on by Berdoa, the servant concocts a story in which the chancellor strikes his sleeping brother on the head with an axe, waking him:

> Manfred
> Erwacht, kreischt auf und fährt
> Schlaftrunken mit der Rechten
> Nach dem gespaltnen Haupt, — und greift krampfhaft in
> Die eigne, offenstehnde Hirnschal

> Und reißt die Faust geballt, befleckt mit Blut,
> Voll von Gehirn daraus zurück! (*HKG* 1:45)

Kettembeil was evidently less worried about the censors' response to corpses and internal organs than he was about their reactions to undignified descriptions of eating, digestion, and other physical processes involved in human life.

Stylistic Variation: "Reizwörter"

Several studies of censorship during the German Restoration period have asserted the importance of "Reizwörter" that had to be avoided, no matter how innocuous their meaning in a particular context.[22] At first glance, the pre-publication alterations made to *Gothland* appear to support such accounts and include one extreme example of hypersensitivity to an individual word. In the first draft of the play, shortly after discovering that he has unjustly murdered his brother and coming to the conclusion that human existence is meaningless, Gothland declares:

> Bei einem Mastschwein
> Bedenke ich mich eh ich das Messer zücke,
> (Sein Dasein hat 'nen Zweck — es wird
> Gefressen —) doch bei einem Menschen
> Bedenke ich mich nicht; sein Leben
> Nützt weder anderen, noch ihm [. . .]. (*HKG* 1:85)

Although the second half of this quotation may at first appear more controversial, containing as it does an irreligious denial of the value of human life, it was left intact. Instead, the word "Mastschwein" was crossed out of the setting copy by Kettembeil, and replaced initially by "Tier" and then by "Vieh" (*HKG* 1:539). The fact that this alteration was made by Kettembeil (and not Grabbe) suggests that it was motivated by censorship concerns; and the only possible reason for the amendment is the circumstance that the word "Schwein" can be used as a serious insult in German. Although it did not convey that meaning in this instance, and its replacement did nothing to alter the sense of the passage, Kettembeil apparently considered it safer to remove the word "Schwein" from Grabbe's text.

The pre-publication editing of *Gothland* contains other examples of sensitive words being removed from the text without altering the meaning it conveys. As he rages at his father in the 1822 draft of *Gothland,* for instance, the title character proclaims:

> Verdammte Schuldigkeit ists, daß
> Ihr die Geschöpfe, welche ihr zu eurer Last
> In diese Welt der Qual setzt, auch ernährt! (*HKG* 1:92)

In the setting copy, however, Kettembeil removed the word "Verdammte" from Gothland's "Schuldigkeit," and that is how it remained in the first edition (*HKG* 1:541). The word "verdammt," it seems, was expected to arouse the authorities' disapproval.

A similar instance occurs during act 3 scene 1, where Berdoa describes his scheme to corrupt Gothland's son, saying in the 1822 version:

> [. . .] erst verführe ich
> Ihn mit Hilfe seiner Liebe zur Hurerei [. . .]. (*HKG* 1:116)

Here again, the word "Hurerei" is crossed out on the copy set and replaced by two dashes, which is how it appears in the first edition (*HKG* 1:544). Since we have already witnessed Berdoa's plan in action, it may well be easy for us to guess at what is indicated by those two dashes, and our understanding of Berdoa's words is not significantly altered. The important thing, it appears, is that we are spared exposure to the word "Hurerei."

On closer examination of the first edition of *Gothland*, however, it becomes apparent that neither "verdammt" nor "Hurerei" are completely taboo words. During a battle against the Swedes, for example, Berdoa uses the first word to curse the positioning of the Finnish army:

> ROSSAN: [. . .] Hier auf der offnen Heide können wir
> Nicht widerstehn!
> BERDOA: Das ist verdammt! (*HKG* 1:91)

And during the act 2 scene 1, when interrogating his surviving brother about the death of Manfred, Gothland asks the Chancellor whether he ever recollects the three brothers swearing an oath of eternal friendship. When his brother replies "Es war 'ne schöne Stunde," Gothland is angered by his lack of feeling and cries out:

> 'Ne schöne Stunde!
> 'Ne schöne Hure! Mehr war es
> Dir nicht? (*HKG* 1:50)

Although the word "Hurerei" was removed from Berdoa's quotation later in the text, Kettembeil did not feel compelled to excise Gothland's utterance of the word "Hure" here.

With the cases in which the words "verdammt," "Hure/Hurerei," and "Mastschwein" were excised or tolerated by Kettembeil, it is striking that the terms were allowed to remain in the manuscript when employed in innocent passages and removed from discussions that address sensitive topic areas. Berdoa's "zur Hurerei" was deleted from a statement about sex, and Gothland's "verdammt" from an accusation against his own father that also denounced the basis of family ties. Similarly, the "Mastschwein" reference was excised from a speech that denounces human life as worthless. Although these deletions did not alter their controversial subject matter, they removed a source of emphasis, and, as a result, diminished the impact of the sections in question. The fact that such words were included in the first edition of *Gothland* at all, however, suggests that the attitude of the censorship authorities toward "Reizwörter" was not entirely rigid, and that Grabbe's editor knew this to be so.

"Vorwort" and "Kopie eines Briefes von L. Tieck"

One of the most intriguing passages in Grabbe's letters to Kettembeil about the editing of *Dramatische Dichtungen* refers to the importance of the collection's prefaces: "Die Vorworte! [...] Glaub' mir, sie schützen, sie helfen. Tiecks Briefe gleichfalls. Manches kann stehen bleiben, weil die Vorreden davor stehen" (*HKG* 5:159). Given Grabbe's indifference to the possibility that his plays might offend some readers, it is most probable that this reference to the preface "protecting" certain elements of the plays' contents refers to the likelihood of *Dramatische Dichtungen* being prohibited by censorship authorities. Certainly, the strategic function of the prefaces is confirmed by an examination of their contents.

The most pressing concern of the author in the *Vorwort* appears to be that of distancing himself from his works. Grabbe begins the first preface by telling us how much time has elapsed since he composed the dramas, which "ihrem Verfasser längst fremd geworden [sind]" (*HKG* 1:1). He also claims to have been anxious at first about publishing these early works, fearing that they might cause him to be misunderstood; and he expresses both astonishment and displeasure at the "Extreme" that are contained within them. This point is reinforced by both the sober tone of the preface — which forms a sharp contrast with the energetic language of Grabbe's correspondence — and by other aspects of the writer's self-portrayal. An impression of conscientious respectability is strengthened, for example, by the report that, in the years since he composed his plays, he has had hardly any time to occupy himself with art due to the demands of "ein fünfjähriges Geschäftsleben und eine währenddem wieder aufgegriffene bloß wissenschaftliche Richtung seiner Studien" (*HKG* 1:1). Similarly, the author assures us that he has no interest in achieving literary fame; and that owing to his "bürgerliche Stellung," he cannot consider continuing with a literary career until his early works have been accepted by the public (*HKG* 1:2).

Several aspects of Grabbe's self-portrait as a respectable and serious member of the establishment are unconvincing. We have already seen, for example, that, even in 1827, the author was eager to conserve *Gothland*'s most shocking expressions of atheism and obscene sexual references. And indeed, the tactical considerations behind his somber writing style are revealed by the following comment from a letter to Kettembeil: "Meine

Vorworte sind so trocken, daß sie vielleicht manche Stelle der Stücke retten" (*HKG* 5:159). While perhaps initially obscure, the strategy behind the forewords can be related to the attitude of the authorities toward readers of different social origins. The prevalent contemporary belief that the lower orders were more corruptible than members of the aristocracy and bourgeoisie is reflected by censorship policies designed to enforce stricter standards for works likely to be read by the masses.[23] One can therefore imagine that by emphasizing his bourgeois lifestyle and serious intentions, Grabbe sought to suggest that *Dramatische Dichtungen* was aimed at other prosperous and educated traditionalists, who would be morally unimpaired by the provocative material it contained.

This intention also accounts for another striking tendency of the forewords, namely the repeated emphasis that they place on the high-brow character of *Dramatische Dichtungen*.[24] The letter from Tieck that is reprinted after the first preface, for instance, constitutes a signal of acceptance by a celebrated member of Germany's literary establishment. Alongside much criticism of *Gothland*, Tieck's letter also expresses considerable appreciation for the play's poetic merits. Indeed, the respected poet also hints that he considers his younger colleague to be an equal, explaining at the end of the letter, "Ich habe mich so in das Urteil hineingeschrieben, als wenn ich mit einem Freunde etwa über ein längst gedrucktes Buch mich unterhielte" (*HKG* 1:6). In a footnote to the letter, Grabbe emphasizes the honor implied by Tieck's response:

> Der freimütige und herzliche Tadel, den L. Tieck ausspricht, müßte dem Dichter des Gothland schon insofern höchst angenehm sein, als er die Unparteilichkeit des vielleicht übergroßen Lobes am besten verbürgt. (*HKG* 1:6–7)

These efforts to stress the artistic quality of his works correspond to assertions made by Grabbe that the more controversial elements of his writings are justified by a deeper level of significance. In the first foreword, for instance, Grabbe suggests that, upon closer examination of the play's excesses, the reader should also discover "eine[n] consequent befolgt[en] Plan [. . .], der jene Extreme nicht nur bedingt, sondern hier und da auch rechtfertigt [. . .]" (*HKG* 1:1). And in a footnote to Tieck's letter, Grabbe defends *Gothland* against the poet's attack on the alleged "Zynismus" of the drama. The author's detailed response to this charge begins with the explanation that "[d]er Zynismus wollte nach der Tendenz des Verfassers sich in diesem Trauerspiel in keiner Art als das Höchste und Letzte geben" (*HKG* 1:4), and includes the discussion of examples from the play to support his argument.

Grabbe's belief — expressed in the quotation that opens this section — that his preface and the letter from Tieck would protect certain elements of his plays was evidently based on a confidence that the contents of these writings would influence the authorities' reaction to *Dramatische Dichtungen*. It seems that, by presenting these volumes as the artistically sophisticated works of a serious and conscientious member of the establishment, the author hoped to determine the censors' perception of their likely reception. Instead of appearing as cynical, shocking, and sensationalist writings capable of threatening the fragile morality of uneducated, lower-class readers, his dramas were to be understood — so Grabbe clearly wished — as the complex, profound, and artistically valuable works of a talented and morally upstanding individual.

Conclusion

All indications suggest that the editing process for *Gothland* was relatively successful, at least for producing a marketable reading text. *Dramatische Dichtungen* was widely reviewed in the years following its publication;[25] and although the work caused quite a stir, there is no mention of it being banned in any state in northern Germany. Once edited, it seems, *Gothland* was judged harmless enough to escape banning and confiscation.

Given the shocking content of even the published version of *Gothland*, it is improbable that Kettembeil was an unusually cautious editor. And in view of the financial losses associated with prohibition — especially in Prussia — it is unlikely that he would have published a book that risked being banned. Instead, one imagines that Kettembeil's experiences in the book trade had given him a confident understanding of censorship practices; and that he consequently felt able to anticipate the reactions of the censorship authorities — particularly those in Prussia — to different parts of Grabbe's play.

As a result, it seems likely that, for some thematic areas at least, censorship practices were stable enough to be predicted with a degree of certainty, and that many of the concerns suggested by Kettembeil's changes to the text were fairly typical, at least within northern Germany during the period before 1830. Admittedly, the evidence presented here may not be conclusive. Yet the editing of *Gothland* does give us an idea of the criteria that were important to North-German censorship authorities. In addition to the well-known themes of politics, religion, and sexual morality, for instance, there are clear suggestions that concern for "Sittlichkeit" also involved a degree of protection for the sanctity of the family and the dignity of bodily functions (if not that of corpses and murder victims).

At the same time, however, the editing process for the first edition of *Gothland* suggests that the attitudes of North-German censorship authorities toward literature were more tolerant, or at least more flexible, than might have been thought. As we have seen, the first edition includes many challenging and modern statements on such controversial issues as the psychological background to religious belief and the relationship between sex and love. The publication of Gothland's powerful expression of atheist materialism ("Ewig ist nur der Staub") is also significant. Despite the existence of censorship controls, it is clear that certain significant deviations from moral and religious orthodoxy could be articulated within published literary works.

To be sure, part of the reason for this unexpected leniency may well lie in the play's historically remote setting and its use of verse, which distanced it further from the discourse of contemporary Germany. In many cases, however, editing decisions seem to have been influenced by either the presentation or the context of dangerous content. While potentially arousing images were removed from the setting copy of *Gothland,* for example, other parts of the play are able to communicate the sexual thoughts and activities of its characters through the use of exclusively poetic language or the strategic placing of dashes. Similarly, the author's footnote suggestions indicate that Gothland's blasphemous attacks on his creator would be regarded as less of a threat when accompanied by ominous rolls of thunder and Berdoa's gleeful (and accurate) predictions of doom. Finally, the importance attached by Grabbe to the edition's prefaces indicates that works of literary seriousness — associated, one imagines, with a bourgeois and aristocratic readership — were censored less strictly than popular fiction.

These flexible editing — and, by implication, censorship — practices have significant consequences for our understanding of the production of literature during the Restoration period. Most obviously, they reveal that certain types of presentation could allow authors to express subversive ideas with a remarkable degree of clarity. And similarly, an awareness of the relevance of literary context to censorship decisions may have prompted authors to construct unproblematic sections of their works in a manner designed to elicit a more lenient approach to other, more controversial, passages. In addition to leading to the concealment and exclusion of certain types of content, censorship pressure could therefore mold the composition of both permitted and openly nonconformist literary expression.

Notes

[1] Christian Dietrich Grabbe, *Werke und Briefe: Historisch-kritische Gesamtausgabe in sechs Bänden*, ed. Akademie der Wissenschaften in Göttingen, 6 vols. (Emsdetten: Lechte, 1960–73), 1:9–208 (edition subsequently as *HKG*).

[2] Letter of 6 December 1822, *HKG* 5:48–52; here 49.

[3] See Michael Vogt, *Literaturrezeption und historische Krisenerfahrung: Die Rezeption der Dramen Christian Dietrich Grabbes 1827–1945* (Frankfurt am Main: Lang, 1983), 35–37.

[4] As, for example, Ladislaus Löb suggests. See Löb, *Christian Dietrich Grabbe* (Stuttgart: Metzler, 1996), 23.

[5] Several critics have interpreted such elements as a deliberate attempt to shock contemporaries. See, for example, Roy C. Cowan, *Christian Dietrich Grabbe* (New York: Twayne, 1972), 52.

[6] For a detailed discussion of *Gothland's* formal peculiarities, see Wolfgang Hegele, *Grabbes Dramenformen* (Munich: Fink, 1970), 9–24.

[7] *Gothland* was not performed on stage until 1892.

[8] See Jörg Aufenanger, *Das Lachen der Verzweiflung: Grabbe. Ein Leben* (Frankfurt am Main: Fischer, 2001), 44–46.

[9] See Aufenanger, *Das Lachen der Verzweiflung*, 60–64.

[10] Being passed for publication did not enable a work to be performed on stage. An extra round of censorship was required for theatrical productions.

[11] See, for example, the "Preußische Zensur-Verordnung vom 18. Oktober 1819," in *Dokumente zur deutschen Verfassungsgeschichte*, ed. Ernst Rudolf Huber, 1:95–98; here 95.

[12] See "Preußische Zensur-Verordnung vom 18. Oktober 1819," in Huber, *Dokumente zur deutschen Verfassungsgeschichte*, 1:95–98; here 95.

[13] For the full text of the Carlsbad press laws, see Huber, *Dokumente zur deutschen Verfassungsgeschichte*, 1:91–93.

[14] Article 2 of the "Preußische Zensur-Verordnung vom 18. Oktober 1819," in Huber, *Dokumente zur deutschen Verfassungsgeschichte*, 1:95.

[15] This order declares that no writings should be allowed to attack "den Grund aller Religion überhaupt" or the Christian church and its teachings. See *Preussische Gesetz-Sammlung 1824* (Berlin: Staatsministerium, 1810–1933), 2–3.

[16] A number of textual references establish the religion of *Gothland's* Sweden as Christianity. See *HKG* 1:14, 28, 36, and 76.

[17] Article 2 of the "Preußische Zensur-Verordnung vom 18. Oktober 1819," in Huber, *Dokumente zur deutschen Verfassungsgeschichte*, 1:95.

[18] See *HKG* 1:544–45 and 549 ("Lesarten" for all the cited examples).

[19] Kettembeil replaced "Kindermachen" with "Gemeines" in the setting copy, but otherwise left the speech as it was (*HKG* 1:544).

[20] Such series of dashes resemble those used by censors engaged in pre-publication censorship to indicate excised material until 1834. In that year, the practice was banned throughout the German Confederation by article 28 of the "Schluß-protokoll der Wiener Konferenz vom 12. Juni 1834." See Huber, *Dokumente zur deutschen Verfassungsgeschichte*, 1:128.

[21] The phrasing and punctuation of the 1822 version of these lines quoted here is slightly different from that found in the *Gothland* text printed in the *HKG*. For the latter version, see *HKG* 1:151; for details of the relevant deviations, see *HKG* 1:551 (part of the "Lesarten" section for the play).

[22] See, for example, Klaus Kanzog, "Zensur: literarische," in *Reallexikon der deutschen Literaturgeschichte*, eds. Klaus Kanzog, Dorothea Kanzog, and Achim Masser, 2nd ed., 5 vols. (Berlin: de Gruyter, 1958–88), 4:998–1049; here 1038–39.

[23] See, for example, the account of Luxembourgish censorship instructions in Mannes and Weber, *Zensur im Vormärz (1815–1848)*, 147.

[24] A policy of more lenient censorship for works of artistic seriousness is indicated by paragraph 7 of the Austrian censorship law of 1810, which reveals that the standards applied to "die klaßischen Werke" are not as strict as those for "Broschüren, Jugend-und Volksschriften" and "Unterhaltungsbücher." For the full text of this law, see Marx, *Die österreichische Zensur*, 73–76.

[25] See Vogt, *Literaturrezeption*, 35–38.

2: The Denomination of the Devil: Christian Dietrich Grabbe's *Scherz, Satire, Ironie und tiefere Bedeutung*

AS MENTIONED IN the previous chapter, Grabbe's first comedy, *Scherz, Satire, Ironie und tiefere Bedeutung*,[1] also had to be adapted to the demands of state censorship before its publication within *Dramatische Dichtungen von Grabbe. Nebst einer Abhandlung über die Shakspearo-Manie* in 1827. The *Lustspiel* was originally composed within a few weeks during the summer of 1822, shortly after the completion of *Gothland*. Following Ludwig Tieck's disapproving reaction to the tragedy's nihilistic pessimism, Grabbe sent him a copy of *Scherz, Satire, Ironie und tiefere Bedeutung* in December 1822, with an assurance that "ich will mich von jetzt an bemühen, bloß heitere Sachen zu dichten" (*HKG* 5:53).

The mood of *Scherz, Satire* is certainly less oppressive than that of *Gothland*, but in other respects the two plays have much in common. A hint that the comedy's author had not moved beyond the pessimism of *Gothland* is contained within a letter from Grabbe to Kettembeil written in December 1827, in which the playwright refers to the "Lachen der Verzweiflung"[2] that he expects his comedy to provoke. Though less brutal than Grabbe's early tragedy, *Scherz, Satire* contains episodes that involve callous violence and the undermining of family ties. Finally, like *Gothland*, the Lustspiel has an anti-classical form[3] as well as an assertively complex plot intended to perplex the reader or spectator.

Grabbe's comedy tells the story of a visit by the devil to an unnamed German village. He is discovered shivering on a hilltop by a passing scientist and, more accustomed to the fiery climate in hell, freezes solid during their first encounter. The scientist drags him off to be analyzed indoors with the help of some colleagues, who prove unable to identify the newly found specimen. Eventually the devil wakes up and assures the scientists that he is, in fact, a high-ranking churchman. The scientists believe him, and then proceed to introduce him to the local nobility: the baron, his niece Liddy, and her fiancé, Wernthal.

With his false identity thus established, the devil embarks upon his main project, that of buying Liddy from her fiancé and selling her to the Freiherr von Mordax. The price that Mordax has to pay for Liddy is to make his eldest son study philosophy and to kill a large group of tailors.

After some negotiation, these terms are accepted; persuading Wernthal to sell his fiancée proves even less problematic, and all that remains is for Liddy to be lured to a remote place so that she can be transferred into the Freiherr's hands.

Unfortunately for the devil, however, his plan is thwarted. A visit to a blacksmith to have a loose horseshoe refastened leads to his identity being revealed to the local schoolmaster. The latter decides to capture the devil and show him at fairs as a money-making venture. With the devil imprisoned in a cage, Mordax tries to seize Liddy. Yet, fortunately for the Baroness, she is rescued by yet another admirer, the ugly, yet noble Mollfels — to whom she becomes engaged on the spot. A rescuer also comes to the aid of devil: his grandmother, a beautiful young woman in a stylish Russian coat, who negotiates his release with the schoolmaster. The play ends with the disgraced noblemen, Mordax and Wernthal, breaking the dramatic illusion by fleeing into the audience to escape punishment, and its author, Grabbe, trying to enter the stage, only to be insulted by the schoolmaster, his own dramatic creation.

As several critics have noted, however, this central plot does not form the main source of interest for most of the play;[4] instead, it provides the framework for a series of unrelated comic episodes that include much literary and other satire. Not only is contemporary writing attacked by a variety of figures, but jibes are also made at canonical writers such as Klopstock, Schiller, and Shakespeare. Although *Scherz, Satire* does exploit various Romantic techniques, the comedy also mocks several key tenets of Romanticism, and several episodes represent parodies of stock elements within the "Trivialliteratur" of the time.[5] Another source of humor is the moral and social inadequacies of its characters, which in many cases can be seen to exemplify the failings of various social and professional groups,[6] and make a substantial contribution to the vision of a mediocre reality advanced by the play.[7] On the other hand, however, while the contemporary setting of *Scherz, Satire* is established by references to politics and literature, such realist elements are offset by the many absurdist features contained within the play, as well as the lack of concrete indicators of time and place.

There can be little doubt that the composition of the first manuscript of *Scherz, Satire, Ironie und tiefere Bedeutung* in 1822 (identified as H1 in the *HKG*)[8] was shaped by an awareness of state censorship. Although Grabbe was at that time enrolled at the University of Berlin, he devoted little time to his studies and immersed himself in the artistic life of the Prussian capital. Censorship restrictions were at that time a widespread preoccupation and the writer had ample opportunity to become acquainted with the effects of state censorship. He frequently attended theatrical performances, for example, and was acquainted both with Heinrich

Heine and Friedrich Wilhelm Gubitz, who had edited the journal *Der Gesellschafter* since 1817 and was extremely experienced at dealing with censorship. In addition, the bohemians with whom Grabbe socialized were all intensely interested in literature. Two of these friends had already published books by 1822, and one of them, Karl Köchy, was an expert on theatrical history.[9] Grabbe's consciousness of censorship concerns during the composition of *Scherz, Satire* is confirmed by one scene of the comedy, in which the devil complains that one of his own dramatic creations, the *Französische Revolution*, cannot be performed in Prussia or Austria because of the strict censorship there (*HKG* 1:241).

Despite this early awareness, however, censorship considerations also played a role in revisions of the 1822 manuscript prior to publication. These commenced with Grabbe's preparation of a new manuscript of *Scherz, Satire*, which he promised to a friend, Moritz Leopold Petri, in November 1826 (*HKG* 1:569). The effort that the writer put into writing out his play suggests that he was hoping that Petri might help him to get it published. Although many of the changes made at this stage seem to have been motivated by stylistic or other aesthetic concerns, we will see that there are reasons to suspect that others were a response to censorship pressure.

In 1827, Grabbe sent this manuscript, referred to as H2 in the *HKG*,[10] to Kettembeil, who eventually used it as the setting copy for *Dramatische Dichtungen*. As was the case for *Gothland*, however, the two men discussed in their correspondence changes that were needed in order to appease the Prussian censorship authorities.[11] These final alterations, many of which are discussed by Grabbe and Kettembeil in their correspondence, are clearly identified in H2. As a result, they provide us with the most reliable indications of how different thematic areas of *Scherz, Satire, Ironie und tiefere Bedeutung* were affected by the threat of censorship.

Religion

Despite the evident concern of Grabbe and his publisher to avoid a ban in Prussia, the first edition of *Scherz, Satire, Ironie und tiefere Bedeutung* contains several violations of sections in the Prussian censorship law requiring the protection of religion. The "Allerhöchste Kabinetsorder"[12] of 28 December 1824 insisted that no writings could be permitted to attack "den Grund aller Religion überhaupt" or the Christian religion and its teachings. In addition, the article expressly forbade all "unanständige, lieblose, zur Vertheidigung der eigenen oder ruhigen Widerlegung entgegen gesetzter Meinungen nicht unmittelbar gehörenden, verletzenden Angriffe auf andere Glaubens-parteien."[13]

Yet despite this apparent determination by the censoring authorities to protect both Christian churches and all religious groups, the final editing process for Grabbe's comedy suggests that such stipulations were not applied scrupulously. Contemporary anti-Semitism,[14] for instance, is reflected in several comments included in the first edition of *Scherz, Satire, Ironie und tiefere Bedeutung*. In act 2 scene 1, for example, the devil indignantly asks, "Meinen Sie, ich ließe mit mir handeln wie ein Jude?";[15] and in act 1 scene 3, the baron refers to the contemporary literary establishment disdainfully as "Judenjungen, deren Bildung im Schweinefleischessen besteht" (*HKG* 1:227).

More remarkable, however, is the deliberate inclusion of anti-Catholic content in the first edition. Some anti-Catholic elements had already been present in the 1822 version of *Scherz, Satire Ironie und tiefere Bedeutung*. In act 1 scene 3 of the 1822 manuscript, for example, the devil, in his "role" as a priest, claims to have been awarded by the Pope the status of "Ritter des päpstlichen Zivilverdienstordens" (*HKG* 1:222). This creates a potentially offensive association between the devil and the Catholic Church that is re-emphasized later on in the scene when the former has left his hosts to sit in their fireplace in the next room. As the devil sings with joy at his hell-like situation, the baron cries out in astonishment, "Alle Wetter, das ist die Stimme des Ritters vom päpstlichen Zivilverdienstorden!" (*HKG* 1:229).

Despite their illegitimacy in principle, Grabbe seems to have considered these lines a potential asset to his play. In a letter to his editor of 12 August 1827, he wrote, "Hör mal, laß doch (wenn möglich) den Teufel ja Ritter des päpstlichen Civilverdienstordens bleiben; die Katholiken anpacken, heißt Manchen gewinnen" (*HKG* 1:179). Far from fearing the censorship consequences of these attacks, Kettembeil apparently agreed with Grabbe's assessment and allowed the devil to retain his papal award.

The impression that the Catholic religion was not granted the protection promised to it by Prussian censorship law is confirmed by an important change made by Kettembeil to the setting copy of *Scherz, Satire, Ironie und tiefere Bedeutung*. Having thawed out and woken up during his examination by the scientists, in act 1 scene 3 of the 1822 version of the comedy, the devil had introduced himself as a high-ranking Protestant clergyman,[16] namely "Theophil Christian Teufel, Generalsuperintendenten in herzoglich — schen Diensten" (*HKG* 1:222). The link that this created between Satan and the Protestant churches was strengthened by the response of the other characters, who, despite their bewilderment at the new visitor's behavior, never challenged his identity. Even as the devil pulled out his own arm, stuck his finger into the flame of a lamp, and set one of his host's chairs on fire, he was continually both referred to and addressed as "Herr General Superintendent."

When preparing the play for publication in 1827, however, Grabbe and Kettembeil seemed to feel nervous about this association between the devil and Protestantism. In a letter of 12 July 1827, Grabbe wrote to his editor: "Der Teufel als Generalsuperintendent? Meinetwegen! Doch wäre "Eremit," "Canonicus," "Bonze" (in China) oder "Derwisch" oder "Druide" nicht zulässiger?" (*HKG* 5:165). Although four of these suggestions would have been compatible with Prussian censorship law, Kettembeil apparently shared Grabbe's views on the benefits of insulting Catholics, for it is as a *Canonikus*, a high-ranking Catholic churchman, that the devil makes his appearance in the first edition of *Dramatische Dichtungen* (*HKG* 1:572). While the two men considered insulting the domininant Protestant churches to be dangerous, equivalent attacks on the Catholic Church did not seem to worry them at all.

In addition to abusing Catholicism, Grabbe's Lustspiel also contains a less obvious violation of a clause in the Prussian censorship law of 1824 designed to protect "den Grund aller Religion überhaupt."[17] In act 2 scene 3, the devil implicitly denies the existence of both God and meaning, when he tells the poet Rattengift that the world is nothing more than a mediocre comedy:

> So will ich Ihnen denn sagen, daß dieser Inbegriff des Alls, den Sie mit dem Namen Welt beehren, weiter nichts ist, als ein mittelmäßiges Lustpiel, welches ein unbärtiger, gelbschnabeliger Engel, der in der ordentlichen, dem Menschen unbegreiflichen Welt lebt, und wenn ich nicht irre, noch in Prima sitzt, während seiner Schulferien zusammengeschmiert hat. Das Exemplar, in dem wir uns befinden, steht, glaube ich, in der Leihbibliothek zu X, und eben jetzt wird es von einer hübschen Dame gelesen, welche den Verfasser kennt und ihm heute abend, d.h. über sechs Trillionen Jahre, beim Teetische ihr Urteil darüber mitteilen will. (*HKG* 1:241–42)

The nihilism of the devil's vision is underlined later on in the conversation by his account of hell. When questioned by a nervous Rattengift about how criminals are punished, Satan replies that a murderer would be laughed at, "bis er selber mitlacht, daß er sich die Mühe nahm, einen Menschen umzubringen" (*HKG* 1:242). As murder is presented as an absurdly trivial offense, it is fitting that hell loses its traditional theological status as a place of terrifying retribution and becomes a vehicle for satire. The devil assures Rattengift, for example, that the worst possible punishment is being forced to read two well-known publications of the time, the *Abendzeitung* and *Der Freimütige,* without spitting at them. And when Rattengift inquires about the fate of various literary figures, he is told how, for example, Marquis Posa has become a pimp, Wallenstein the headmaster of the "höllische" grammar school, and Ariosto has just bought himself a new umbrella (*HKG* 1:242–45).

These breaches of traditional moral and theological teachings did not seem to worry Grabbe and Kettembeil. Neither this section, nor the "Welt als Lustspiel" passage that directly precedes it, is mentioned in the writer's correspondence with his editor, suggesting that both men were unconcerned about their impact on the censoring authorities. This attitude cannot be attributed to a belief that the censors were indifferent to the literary treatment of theology. On the contrary, the devil's claim that he had studied theology at the university is removed from the setting copy,[18] no doubt in order to protect the dignity of the discipline. And as we saw in the previous chapter, Grabbe was apprehensive about the authorities' reaction to Duke Gothland's nihilistic diatribes.

Consequently, it is clear that the presentation of the devil's heretical metaphysics made them appear less of a threat to religious orthodoxy. For one thing, they originate from Satan, who is both a self-confessed liar[19] and the archenemy of Christ, so that attacks on religion are to be expected from him. In addition, the implausibility and comic nature of the scenario described by the devil mean that it can hardly be considered a serious alternative to traditional religious teachings. Instead, it seems to belong in the same category as other fantastical lies told by both the devil and the schoolmaster at intervals throughout the play.[20] Finally, it is also striking that, like Duke Gothland's atheistic rants, the metaphysical accounts provided in these sections avoid key religious vocabulary that could signal an intention to compete with Christianity. When outlining his model of a meaningless universe, for example, the Devil does not mention God at all, let alone his absence; and he refers to his charges not as "Seelen" but as "Geister" (*HKG* 1:242).

It is impossible to determine the extent to which these presentational aspects were motivated by censorship pressure. However, they clearly did offer a safe way of advancing the vision of a world without a God or meaning. The importance of this idea to *Scherz, Satire, Ironie und tiefere Bedeutung* is indicated by several of Grabbe's statements that declare its affinity with *Herzog Theodor von Gothland,* in which, as we have seen, the central character loses his belief in God and descends into amorality. In a letter to Kettembeil of 1 June 1827, for example, Grabbe writes that his comedy is "aus den nämlichen Grundansichten entsprungen" as *Gothland* (*HKG* 5:158). Moreover, as many critics have noted, several aspects of the play's structure and content serve to support the devil's description of a meaningless world.[21] The comedy discredits or ridicules many common belief systems, for example, yet seems to propose no alternative values of its own.[22] In addition, incidental side episodes take up far more text space than those that develop the central plot, so that the play has little sense of direction or purpose.[23] The wealth of absurd happenings and inconsistent character portrayal[24] further increase the impression of a world devoid of purpose. Comical though it may be, Satan's description of a Godless and senseless universe can therefore be seen as an articulation of the play's nihilistic spirit. The absence of professions of nihilism that are either more serious or expressed by more trustworthy characters points toward the restrictions censorship placed on the delivery of such attacks on the "Grundsätze aller Religion."

Insults

The 1827 edition of Grabbe's comedy also retained breaches of a law designed to prevent the publication of personal insults. Paragraph 2 of the Prussian "Allerhöchste Kabinetsorder vom 28sten Dezember 1824" contained a reminder that a 1788 law to this effect was still in force, and insisted that no works be permitted "welche zur Kränkung der persönlichen Ehre und des guten Namens anderer abzielen."[25] To insult writers may not have been the main aim of the Grabbe's play, but it did represent an important element of the text. Lengthy passages denouncing the contemporary literary scene as a whole are complemented by vicious jibes at the works of named writers. Although it may be argued that criticism of someone's literary works does not, in itself, constitute an assault on their personal honor, at several points in the play the tone of this criticism becomes distinctly abusive. For example, in act 1 scene 3, after the schoolmaster announces that he has been sold herrings wrapped in fresh copies of recent literary works, the baron exclaims, "Bedenke! Houwald, der sinnige, zarte Houwald! Um einen Hering gewickelt! welche Beleidigung!," to which the schoolmaster responds, "Keine Beleidigung, Herr Baron, sondern eine Verbesserung!" (*HKG* 1:226).

A similar assault on the dignity of particular contemporary authors takes place in an exchange between Mollfels and the poet Rattengift in act 3 scene 1. Here, Liddy's ugly admirer condemns the cruelty of the government, who "immer noch zaudern endlich einmal ein Schock Poeten wegen ihrer elenden Gedichte hinzurichten" (*HKG* 1:258). Although Mollfels himself does not mention which writers he would like to see executed, the poet's outrage at this suggestion betrays who would apparently have been the obvious choices:

> (*in unbegreiflicher Unruhe*) Nein! nein! das wäre doch zu stark! Zu stark! Hinzurichten! Gütiger Himmel, welche schauderhafte Idee! Heinrich Döring, Friedrich Gleich, Wilhelm Blumenhagen, Methusalem Müller, Karl Stein — O mir klappern die Zähne, mir klappern die Zähne! (*HKG* 1:258)

Although he had not removed them himself, Grabbe was evidently worried that censorship considerations might compel his editor to delete these attacks. In a letter to Kettembeil on 1 June 1827, he insisted that they should be allowed to stay (*HKG* 5:160). His first argument was that, because many of the writers concerned were not important, his assaults on them would not cause him any problems. This reasoning suggests that, as with the Prussian laws designed to protect religion, enforcement of the "Persönliche Ehre" clause was at least partly dependent on the status and power of the injured party. In addition, however, Grabbe referred to the play's preface, which includes a sentence aimed at excusing his literary attacks: "Im übrigen verspottet [das Lustspiel] sich selbst und werden daher die literarischen Angriffe von den beteiligten Personen leicht verziehen werden" (*HKG* 1:214).

Indeed, Grabbe's belief that self-mockery could offer a means of escaping censorship cuts may have encouraged the inclusion of a powerful attack on the author himself in the final scene. For, when the schoolmaster sees his author approaching at the close of the play, he gives full vent to his annoyance:

> O so schlage der Donner darein! Kommt mir der Kerl mit seiner Laterne noch spät in der Nacht durch den Wald, um uns den Punsch aussaufen zu helfen! Das ist der vermaladeite Grabbe, oder wie man ihn eigentlich nennen sollte, die zwergige Krabbe, der Verfasser dieses Stückes! Er ist so dumm wie'n Kuhfuß, schimpft auf alle Schriftsteller und taugt selber nichts, hat verrenkte Beine, schielende Augen und ein fades Affengesicht! Schließen Sie vor ihm die Tür zu, Herr Baron, schließen Sie vor ihm die Tür zu! (*HKG* 1:273)[26]

This energetic piece of self-denigration offered Grabbe an opportunity to condemn the play's other literary insults and to relativize them by launching an even more lengthy, direct, and vehement attack on himself. As such, it acts as a counterbalance to proscribed material in a similar way to the warning "Zwischenreden" of Berdoa, which, as we saw in the previous chapter, punctuate Gothland's speeches proclaiming the meaninglessness of existence. It has been argued that, although breaking the dramatic illusion was a well-established Romantic technique, the bitterness of the schoolmaster's diatribe undermines the sovereignty of art normally associated with this device and thereby enhances the nihilistic spirit of *Scherz, Satire*.[27] Paradoxically, therefore, censorship pressure may have stimulated a further contribution to the pessimistic mood of the play.

Sexual Morality

As we have seen, the 1827 first edition of *Scherz, Satire, Ironie und tiefere Bedeutung* contained several violations of sections of Prussian censorship law concerning religion and personal insults. The play's sexual content, by contrast, was edited far more strictly. The two most important modifications to sexual reference within the Lustspiel, for instance, can be related to the Prussian censorship law's proclaimed intention "zu unterdrücken, was die Moral und gute Sitten beleidigt."[28]

Perhaps the best-known effect of censorship on *Scherz, Satire* concerns the condoms that, in the 1822 version, Mollfels brings back from his travels and are eventually used by the schoolmaster to lure the devil into a cage. At first Grabbe suggested replacing the word "Kodons" with "K——" (*HKG* 5:163), but Kettembeil evidently judged this too obvious a hint. In the end, the condoms are replaced by the memoirs of Jakob Casanova de Steingalt (*HKG* 1:580–82), which were published in Germany in the 1820s. The memoirs were infamous due to their erotic content, which had also led to censorship difficulties.[29]

The other substantial change made to the setting copy of *Scherz, Satire* also involves a section of fairly explicit sexual reference. In act 3 scene 1, the schoolmaster is pressed by his drinking companions to tell them about his first love. Hannchen Honigsüß was the daughter of his headmaster, whose house he used to visit on winter evenings. The schoolmaster remembers how, sitting next to Hannchen on a bench in the darkness, "pflegte ich ihr verstohlen das Patschhändchen zu drücken, und wenn ich einen Gegendruck fühlte, so ging ich weiter." In the 1822 version of the Lustspiel, the schoolmaster describes how he "schlang allmählich den Arm um ihren zierlichen Nacken, zupfte ihr am Busenwärzchen, und krabbelte ihr zuletzt ohne Umstände im Schoße" (*HKG* 1:261). This account was evidently considered too obscene for the first edition, which contained a toned-down version of the schoolmaster's adventures. Here, the youth "schlang allmählich den Arm um ihren Hals, zupfte ihr am Busentuche und krabbelte sie im Nacken" (*HKG* 1:584).

Much less obvious sexual references had to be removed from the setting copy of *Scherz, Satire, Ironie und tiefere Bedeutung*, too. At the beginning of act 3 scene 1, for instance, the blacksmith suggests that his son, Jürgen, has not learned much at school. The schoolmaster attributes this to Jürgen's low intelligence, and, in the 1822 version, goes on to inquire, "Im Vertrauen, woran hat Eure Frau gedacht als sie mit dem Jungen schwanger war? Der Bengel trägt 'ne Art Pferdekopf!," to which the blacksmith replies, "Das tut der vermaladeite Hengst, welcher sich beim Beschlagen losriß und meiner Frau, die in der Stube stand und Essig auf den Salat goß, plötzlich durch das Fenster ins Gesicht kuckte!" (*HKG* 1:254).

On the surface, this exchange concerns itself with the fairly innocent idea of a shock to the expectant mother during pregnancy causing damage to her child. Although the use of the word "schwanger" could be considered coarse, and the description of Jürgen's "Pferdekopf" brutal, both of these terms could have been exchanged for milder alternatives. Instead, however, the entire exchange is deleted from the setting copy (*HKG*

1:581–52). The reason for this was probably the association it created between Jürgen's physiognomy and an encounter his mother had with a horse while pregnant. Although the passage contains no concrete hints of bestial desires or practices, the appearance of the word "Hengst," with its "stud" associations, would have strengthened the hint of sexual innuendo it contained. Although the section is not sexually explicit, it appears to have been considered too risky for the first edition.

It is likely that this cautious editing was a reflection of censorship practices. There is considerable evidence that many censorship authorities were aware of the efforts made by writers to disguise forbidden reference. The Prussian censorship law of 1819,[30] for example, specifically warns writers against trying to disguise forbidden content from the censors. That the censors were known to be particularly vigilant with regard to hidden sexual allusion is confirmed by other alterations to the setting copy of the Lustspiel. At the end of act 2 scene 2, for example, the devil tells Rattengift how to reach hell in order to visit him. In the 1827 first edition, he instructs the poet to go to Dresden or Leipzig and look for "[die] am Abend am besuchtesten Straßen." From there, he says, the entrance to hell is only five minutes' journey away, adding, in the 1822 version, "Sie werden noch dazu auf ausgezeichnet guten, vielfältig ausgebesserten Chausseen dahin reiten können" (*HKG* 1:246). In the setting copy, however, Kettembeil crossed out the word "reiten" and replaced it with "gelangen" (*HKG* 1:579). Given the reference to prostitution earlier on in the sentence, the connotations attached to "reiten" meant that, even when used as an verb of transportation, it could arouse suspicions of sexual allusion.

Similar worries may have caused Grabbe to omit exclamation marks from a couple of lines at the end of the play's final scene. Here, Emperor Nero has just arrived in livery to carry the books that the devil wants to take back to hell with him. Nero, the devil and the devil's grandmother then briskly depart from the villagers, leaving the baron and the schoolmaster to exchange expressions of astonishment. The baron asks his niece if she is not bewildered as well:

BARON: Verwunderst du dich denn nicht, Liddy?

MOLLFELS: Liddy und ich haben nicht gehörig darauf geachtet!
                                                    (*HKG* 1:273)

Although Mollfels's excitement at his recent engagement may seem to justify the exclamation mark present in the 1822 version, it is absent from the setting copy (*HKG* 1:588). The alteration appears all the more strange given the animated character of this page, in which two-thirds of the sentences that are not questions end with an exclamation mark in the 1827 first edition. Thus, it is likely that Grabbe was anxious that making Mollfels appear too excited about his and Liddy's distraction could lead to a sexual interpretation being placed on his words.

Stylistic Variation: Exclamation Marks

The above exchange is not the only example of an exclamation mark present in the 1822 version of *Scherz, Satire, Ironie und tiefere Bedeutung* being absent from the setting copy of the play. In total, the 1827 first edition of the Lustspiel contains thirty-six fewer exclamation marks than the 1822 version. Although it might seem obvious to ascribe this reduction to the distaste of the older and potentially wiser Grabbe of 1826 for this Sturm-und-Drang type of punctuation, such an explanation is not entirely convincing. For even after the author's modifications, the play's setting copy still contains a total of 673 exclamation marks: an average of just over 11.6 per page of the *HKG*, which is an especially high figure given the relatively low number of sentences per page.

It is therefore more likely that Grabbe had specific reasons for removing each of the exclamation marks that are absent from the setting copy. In some cases, these reasons were no doubt grammatical or stylistic: when revising his play, Grabbe no longer thought an exclamation mark appropriate at that particular point. There are other examples, however, where the content or mood of a sentence is suited to the exclamation mark that was present in the 1822 version of the play, but is missing from the setting copy. Such instances almost always concerned particularly provocative lines. Since exclamation marks often signal the importance or excitement of the words that precede them, the removal of an exclamation mark in such cases had the effect of reducing the prominence or altering the tone of a dangerous statement.

Grabbe appears to have exploited this in the scene in which the devil purchases Liddy from Wernthal. Although the depiction of a fiancé selling his future bride was doubtless somewhat scandalous, this episode is central to the play and could not readily have been removed. It is therefore interesting that, despite the momentous nature of this event, the H2 version of the page of the *HKG* on which this deal is secured contains only four exclamation marks, well below the average for the play. Indeed, of the thirty-six exclamation marks that disappear between the 1822 and 1826 manuscripts, four were taken from the page and a half in which Wernthal and the Devil negotiate a price for Liddy. Wernthal's initial reaction to hearing that the devil is a collector of brides, for example, changes from an exuberant "So so!!" in the first manuscript (*HKG* 1:237) to a less enthusiastic "So so!" in the setting copy. Just two lines later, in another apparent attempt to reduce the nobleman's excitement, his initial boast that Liddy is "ausgezeichnet schön!" (*HKG* 1:237) appears in the more subdued form of "ausgezeichnet schön" in the later versions. The devil's offer to pay "nicht mehr als 3 Gr. 1 Pf. in Kupfer!" (*HKG* 1:237) for Liddy's virginity also loses an exclamation mark in the 1826 manuscript, as does Wernthal's accusation to the devil that "Sie haben einen ziemlich ekeln Geschmack!"[31] Of course, there is a chance that Grabbe merely decided he did not want these exclamation marks any more, or that he simply overlooked them when writing out the 1826 manuscript. However, the high density of those changes (all four examples occur on the same page) within such a potentially controversial scene suggests that the writer wished to diminish both the scene's prominence and the excitement it conveys.

Further evidence for the use of this technique comes in the play's opening scene. Here, the schoolmaster is visited by a farmer, Tobies, whom he asks about his family. In the 1822 version of the play, their conversation continues as follows:

TOBIES: So lala! Meine Frau ist gesund, aber mein bestes Schwein liegt in den letzten Zügen. Es stöhnt und ächzt wie ein alter Mann!

SCHULMEISTER: Bedaure, bedaure, sowohl das Schwein als wie den alten Mann! (*HKG* 1:215)

Here, the exclamation mark at the end of Tobies's speech seems appropriate, given the startling comparison he draws between the sounds produced by his dying pig and those emitted by an old man. In the case of the schoolmaster's line, the joke he makes by expressing sympathy for a figurative old man also seems to call for an exclamation mark. In the setting copy, however, it is replaced by a full stop:

TOBIES: So Lala! Meine Frau ist gesund aber mein bestes Schwein liegt in den letzten Zügen. Es stöhnt und ächzt wie ein alter Mann.

SCHULMEISTER: Bedaure, bedaure, sowohl das Schwein als wie den alten Mann. (*HKG* 1:570–71)

Here, the fact that Tobies's jolly opening of "So Lala!" is retained makes the absence of an exclamation mark at the end of his speech appear the more incongruous. It is therefore probable that Grabbe removed the other two exclamation marks from the scene in order to avoid drawing attention to a vulgar comparison between an old man and a pig.

It is unlikely that Grabbe's desire to obscure distasteful elements of the original play was motivated by embarrassment at his youthful impropriety. As we saw in the last chapter, the writer seemed completely indifferent to the possibility that his works could shock people, and, when addressing the subject of how his play *Herzog Theodor von Gothland* should be prepared for publication, expressed the desire that, if possible, many of the obscenities it contained should be preserved (*HKG* 5:162). Given that several of these lines are considerably cruder than anything found in even the 1822 version of *Scherz, Satire, Ironie und tiefere Bedeutung*, it is hard to believe that the older Grabbe really had become more restrained.

Another possibility is that the author removed the exclamation marks to make a more favorable impression on potential editors. At the time when Grabbe prepared the manuscript that was later to become the setting copy for *Dramatische Dichtungen*, Kettembeil had not yet expressed interest in publishing his works. Grabbe may, therefore, have been concerned that potential publishers would be reluctant to invest money in works that their readers would find offensive. But, although there may be truth in this, it is unlikely to provide the whole explanation. First, we have seen that, prior to the alterations undertaken by Kettembeil and Grabbe in 1827, the 1826 manuscript contained material that was so obscene that it was expected to provoke a ban. Had publisher sensibilities been of serious concern to the writer in 1826, it would have made sense to remove a good deal more of the play's provocative content when producing the new manuscript.

The role of censorship considerations in Grabbe's removal of exclamation marks from dangerous statements, on the other hand, seems even more probable given his use of the technique to reduce the prominence of many lines that portrayed his aristocratic characters in an unflattering light. Although Prussian censorship laws did not mention the way members of the different social classes could be portrayed, the Prussian "Zensur-Verordnung" of 1819 expressly forbade "alles was dahin zielt im Preußischen Staate, oder den deutschen Bundesstaaten Mißvergnügen zu erregen und gegen bestehende Verordnungen aufzureitzen."[32] Given the position of the nobility within the social hierarchy, the negative portrayal of aristocracy could readily be perceived as a violation of that clause. In addition, the fact that the higher reaches of the Prussian bureaucracy, and hence the censorship authorities as well, were dominated by members of the nobility meant that an assertively negative portrayal of aristocratic characters was unwise.

Indeed, it is striking that, while we are repeatedly invited to laugh at the failings of almost all of the non-noble characters in *Scherz, Satire, Ironie und tiefere Bedeutung*, none of the aristocratic characters ever become objects of mockery in the same way. And although it is true that the play provides the potential for Wernthal and Mordax to develop into comic characters during performance, for readers of the text, their humorous moments are outweighed by far longer sections of straightforward presentation. Of course, it may be objected that these two aristocrats are also the villains of Grabbe's comedy. Yet, not only is the dramatic profile of the two characters relatively low, but they are also condemned as "die

Schande des Adels" at the end of the play (*HKG* 1:270), and are compensated for by the positive portrayal of Liddy and the baron, who are both higher-ranking aristocrats and more prominent characters.[33]

A deliberate effort to obscure Liddy's flaws from readers of the Lustspiel appears to have motivated the removal of an exclamation mark from a command given by her in act 1 scene 3. Here, the arrival of the schoolmaster and Gottliebchen at the castle has just been announced. Well aware that the schoolmaster will yet again be attempting to present one of his pupils to them as a genius, the baron initially instructs his servant to tell them to go away. Liddy, on the other hand, finds the schoolmaster's attempts to deceive them amusing, and, in the 1822 version, protests to her uncle: "Ei, lieber Onkel, verderben Sie uns den Spaß nicht!" (*HKG* 1:223) The exclamation mark at the end of this sentence appears legitimate since Liddy is giving her uncle a command. Nevertheless, is it absent from the setting copy, where her instruction ends in a full stop: "Ei, lieber Onkel, verderben Sie uns den Spaß nicht" (*HKG* 1:572).

Due to the missing exclamation mark, Liddy's instruction becomes less conspicuous in the 1827 version. Since fifty-two of the fifty-eight commands in the 1827 first edition end in an exclamation mark, this absence is unusual; and one suspects that it was motivated by nervousness about a statement in which an aristocrat announces her intention to laugh at a member of the lower orders. For, although we later observe Liddy making fun of Tobies (*HKG* 1:228), at no stage in the text is this mockery described explicitly. And the removal of the exclamation mark at the end of Liddy's instruction to her uncle also renders her intention to laugh at her visitors relatively discreet.

The baron also appears in a more virtuous light following the removal of exclamation marks in the 1826 and 1827 manuscripts. In act 1 scene 3 of the 1822 manuscript, for example, his rude reaction to the arrival of the schoolmaster at the castle is followed by the exclamation mark usually found at the end of an instruction: "Sag dem Saufaus vom Schulmeister, daß er sich mit seinem Genie zum Henker packen möge!" (*HKG* 1:223) The removal of this exclamation mark in the 1826 and 1827 manuscripts, however, diminishes the prominence and vigor of this aggressive command. Similarly, after the departure of Satan and his entourage in the final scene, the baron makes the following suggestion: "Wir wollen uns zur Restauration einige Terrinen Punsch machen!" (*HKG* 1:273). While relief at the happy outcome of Liddy's adventure may seem to justify the exclamation mark at the end of this suggestion in the 1822 manuscript, it was removed for the 1826 and 1827 versions (*HKG* 1:588). As a result, the baron appears much less enthusiastic about the prospective drinking session.

Of course, few, if any, of the statements from which exclamation marks were removed would have been offensive enough to provoke a ban on their own. Indeed, it is unlikely that the deletion of exclamation marks was sufficient to conceal the meaning of such utterances from censors. However, it is important to remember that, by the standards of the time, the language of *Scherz, Satire, Ironie und tiefere Bedeutung* was violent and most of its content shocking. One suspects that, by reducing the vigor and prominence of a portion of the play's provocative contents, Grabbe hoped to improve the general impression made by the drama on the authorities.

Conclusion

As we saw in the previous chapter, *Dramatische Dichtungen* seems to have been available in most states in northern Germany in the years following its publication. This means that the editing process for *Scherz, Satire, Ironie und tiefere Bedeutung* rendered the volume harmless enough to escape banning and confiscation. This success provides further evidence that, at the time when *Dramatische Dichtungen* appeared, censorship practices were stable enough to be predicted with a reasonable degree of certainty. In particular, those sections of the Lustspiel that contravened Prussian censorship law point toward widespread acceptance of such violations. Given the financial losses that would have been incurred by a ban, it seems unlikely that Kettembeil, who had been in the book trade since leaving the university, would have risked publishing illicit content without being fairly certain that it would be tolerated. His belief that it would be safe to include attacks on the Catholic Church, for example, is almost certainly a reflection of either his own experiences or those of his associates. It is likely that the decision to include insults against mediocre writers, as well as the devil's comical nihilistic vision of the universe, was also founded on a broader knowledge of the censorships authorities' priorities and concerns. Indeed, the fact that a play was allowed to insult the minority Catholic Church and "unimportant" literary writers suggests the indifference of the predominantly Protestant elite toward such issues.

Our understanding of the responses of Grabbe and Kettembeil to censorship pressure can also be broadened by a comparison of the editing processes for *Gothland* and *Scherz, Satire*. The two men's uninhibited approach to the gruesome description of murder in *Gothland*, for example, also applied to the treatment of violence in the 1827 published version of *Scherz, Satire*. Although the Lustspiel's storyline does not require readers to witness Freiherr von Mordax killing the thirteen tailors, stage directions for the Lustspiel clearly describe this murderous act. Similarly, in both early plays, a speech proclaiming a nihilistic atheism is allowed to remain in the published version, and it is striking that both heretical passages avoid religious vocabulary that could signal an intention to compete with established religious institutions. Indeed, the fact that the devil's atheist metaphysical vision caused Grabbe and Kettembeil far less worry than Gothland's expressions of despair suggests a belief in other ways that presentation could influence the censors' responses to subversive material. In this case, it is likely that using the devil as a mouthpiece for an unconvincing and comical blasphemous account of the universe was considered a safer means of advancing the idea of an existence without purpose.

Kettembeil's meticulous treatment of possible sexual allusion in *Scherz, Satire* sheds further light on editing decisions within *Gothland*. Both plays were prepared for publication during the same four-month period, and the correspondence between editor and author during this period does not contain any suggestion that the editing process was rushed. Given Kettembeil's fastidious editing of the Lustspiel, it is hard to imagine that he simply missed the clear, yet nongraphic references to sexuality that were allowed to appear within the 1827 published version of *Gothland*. Instead, it is more plausible that the retention of these elements was based on an understanding that Prussian censors would be unlikely to take exception to them.

Finally, parallels can be drawn between Berdoa's warning "Zwischenreden" during Gothland's atheistic diatribe and the schoolmaster's attack on Grabbe at the end of *Scherz, Satire*. Although there is no conclusive evidence that the latter speech was included due to censorship considerations, we have seen that the contents of Grabbe's "Vorwort" to the play suggest a belief that self-mockery could be expected to compensate for insults directed at others. State censorship clearly encouraged Grabbe to incorporate into his literary works material designed to counterbalance dangerous content. Such strategies can be seen as part of a wider pattern of attempts made during the preparation of both plays for publication to diminish the prominence of controversial material while preserving its essential meaning. This purpose was also served both by Kettembeil's deletion of provocative language from controversial passages within *Gothland* and by Grabbe's removal of exclamation marks from potentially disturbing statements in *Scherz, Satire*. Regardless of the extent to which such subtleties influenced the authorities' reaction to writings, they certainly demonstrate that censorship pressure could stimulate a wide range of literary responses.

Notes

[1] Christian Dietrich Grabbe, *Werke und Briefe: Historisch-kritische Gesamtausgabe in sechs Bänden,* ed. Akademie der Wissenschaften in Göttingen, 6 vols. (Emsdetten: Lechte, 1960–73), 1:213–74 (edition subsequently as *HKG*).

[2] Letter of 28 December 1827, *HKG* 5:195.

[3] For a detailed discussion of the structure of *Scherz, Satire, Ironie und tiefere Bedeutung,* see Hegele, *Grabbes Dramenformen,* 24–29.

[4] See, for example, Hegele, *Grabbes Dramenformen*, 28.

[5] See Löb, *Christian Dietrich Grabbe*, 26.

[6] For more details, see Lothar Ehrlich, *Christian Dietrich Grabbe: Leben, Werk, Wirkung* (Berlin: Akademie, 1983), 18.

[7] Cf Hans-Georg Werner, "Komik des Niedrigen. Zu Grabbes *Scherz, Satire, Ironie und tiefere Bedeutung*," in *Grabbe und die Dramatiker seiner Zeit: Beiträge zum II. Internationalen Grabbe-Symposium 1989*, eds. Detlev Kopp and Michael Vogt (Tübingen: Niemeyer, 1990), 135–48; here 143–45.

[8] See *HKG* 1:568–69.

[9] See, for example, Aufenanger, *Das Lachen der Verzweiflung: Grabbe. Ein Leben*; Ehrlich, *Christian Dietrich Grabbe*; and Löb, *Christian Dietrich Grabbe*.

[10] See *HKG* 1:569.

[11] As mentioned in the previous chapter, satisfying the Prussian censorship authorities was particularly important because prohibition in the largest North German state would have a disastrous impact on the book's sales.

[12] For full text of the order, see *Preussische Gesetz-Sammlung 1824* (Berlin: Staatsministerium, 1824), 2–3.

[13] *Preussische Gesetz-Sammlung 1824*, 2.

[14] After 1815, for example, earlier emancipatory legislation in many German states was reversed, and the "Hep-Hep" riots of 1819 were the worst anti-Jewish attacks in Germany since the early 1600s. See Eric Dorn Brose, *German History 1789–1871: From the Holy Roman Empire to the Bismarckian Reich* (Providence: Berghahn, 1997), 128–29.

[15] The phrasing and punctuation of the setting copy version of this line, quoted here, is slightly different from that of the *Scherz, Satire* text found in the *HKG*. The edition's version of this speech can be found on *HKG* 1:236; *HKG* 1:576 (part of the "Lesarten" section for the play) gives details of the differences between the setting copy version and the version printed in full in the *HKG*.

[16] The title "Generalsuperintendent" was employed within both the Lutheran and the Calvinist churches.

[17] See *Preussische Gesetz-Sammlung 1824*, 2.

[18] The devil's line "Ich habe auf der Universität zu — die Theologie studiert" has the words "die Theologie" crossed out on the setting copy, and appears in the first edition as "Ich habe auf der Universität zu — studiert." *HKG* 1:572.

[19] See *HKG* 1:221.

[20] In act 1 scene 1, for example, the schoolmaster tells Tobies that better roads mean it is possible to receive news of events before they happen (*HKG* 1:216). In act 1 scene 3, the devil informs one of the scientists that, although he was alive in the Middle Ages, he is in fact only eleven years old (*HKG* 1:222).

[21] For instance, Aufenanger, *Das Lachen der Verzweiflung*, 77–78.

[22] See Cowen, *Christian Dietrich Grabbe*, 58.

[23] See Herbert Kaiser, "Scherz, Satire, Ironie und tiefere Bedeutungslosigkeit. Zu Grabbe's Lustspiel," in *Grabbes Gegenentwürfe: Neue Deutungen seiner Dramen,* ed. Winfried Freund (Munich: Fink, 1986), 17–31; here 21.

[24] See Kaiser, "Scherz, Satire, Ironie und tiefere Bedeutung," 25.

[25] See *Preussische Gesetz-Sammlung 1824,* 2.

[26] The wording and punctuation of the 1822 version of the speech quoted here and reproduced in the *HKG* deviates slightly at a couple of points from the version that appears in the setting copy and published edition. For details, see *HKG* 1:599.

[27] See, for example, Cowen, *Christian Dietrich Grabbe,* 60.

[28] Article 2 of the "Preußische Zensur-Verordnung von 18. Oktober 1819," in Huber, *Dokumente zur deutschen Verfassungsgeschichte,* 1:95.

[29] See Heinrich Heine, *Briefe aus Berlin,* in Heine, *Historisch-kritische Gesamtausgabe der Werke,* 6:7–53; here 50.

[30] See Article 13 of the "Preußische Zensur-Verordnung von 18. Oktober 1819," in Huber, *Dokumente zur deutschen Verfassungsgeschichte,* 1:97–98.

[31] See *HKG* 1:576 ("Lesarten" for both cited examples).

[32] Article 2, "Preußische Zensur-Verordnung vom 18. Oktober 1819," in Huber, *Dokumente zur deutschen Verfassungsgeschichte,* 1:95–96.

[33] One suggestion that Grabbe was concerned about the portrayal of these characters is provided by a discrepancy between the 1822 manuscript for the play and the setting copy. In act 1 scene 3, following a vigorous denunciation of contemporary literature by the baron, a stage direction in the 1822 version reads "Liddy wendet sich bei den ersten unedlen Ausdrücken rasch weg und redet eifrig mit dem Herrn von Wernthal, indem sie tut, als ob sie von den Worten des Barons nichts hörte" (*HKG* 1:227). In the setting copy, however, this direction appears as "Liddy wendet sich weg und redet mit Wernthal" (*HKG* 1:573). In view of the fact that other interpretative stage directions remained in the first edition, it seems likely that Grabbe wanted to get rid of the references to the baron's "unedle Ausdrücke" as well as of the direct description of Liddy pretending not to hear him.

3: "Was soll ich nicht sagen?": Heinrich Heine's *Briefe aus Berlin*

LIKE THE ENDING OF GRABBE'S *Herzog Theodor von Gothland* and the whole of his *Scherz, Satire, Ironie und tiefere Bedeutung*, Heinrich Heine's *Briefe aus Berlin*[1] was composed in Berlin in the early 1820s. As mentioned in the previous chapter, the two young writers were reasonably well-acquainted, and there is even a story that Grabbe threatened to kill Heine if he ever discovered that the latter had attacked him in print.[2] Yet, if this incident took place, it did not prevent Heine from reading an early manuscript of *Gothland* and expressing confidence that it would be a success.[3] Both men published their works within northern Germany and, like Grabbe's early plays, *Briefe aus Berlin* also faced Prussian censorship controls. As its title suggests, however, Heine's early prose work pays more sustained and detailed attention to contemporary reality than either *Gothland* or *Scherz, Satire*, and thus provides a distinctive perspective on the interaction between censorship and literary writing in the 1820s.

When Heine arrived in Berlin in March 1821, the Prussian capital was undergoing a period of rapid expansion. In the years between 1815 and 1837, the city grew in population from 190, 000 to 283, 000;[4] and it counted many leading German writers and intellectuals among its inhabitants.[5] The theatrical scene of Berlin was thriving,[6] and its eleven-year-old university had already emerged as a center of German scholarly life.[7] This cultural importance was matched by Berlin's industrial development. The city was a commercial and manufacturing center[8] and it has been reported that, by 1821, one in every three Berliners worked in the city's 436 factories.[9]

Not all areas of Berlin life shared this vitality, however. In common with other German cities, the proportion of the Prussian capital's citizens living in poverty rose dramatically during the early decades of the nineteenth century.[10] In the Napoleonic era, the Prussian government had initiated reforms including economic liberalization, the abolition of serfdom,[11] the expansion of the education system,[12] and the improvement of the Jews' legal position.[13] By the 1820s, however, groups representing conservative and feudal interests had gained decisive influence in both court circles and the government. One consequence of this was a reining in, and in some cases reversal, of the reform process.[14] The reactionary climate was further intensified by an ongoing suppression of political movements ordered by the Carlsbad Decrees: university lectures were subject to surveillance, civil servants became subject to a strict disciplinary code, and all printed matter, no matter how long, had to be submitted for prepublication censorship.[15]

Heine came to Berlin after having been suspended from Göttingen University for challenging another student to a duel. He could have returned after only one semester away, but instead remained in the Prussian capital for over two years. During this time, he half-heartedly continued his study of the law and attended lectures on other subjects, including some by Georg Wilhelm Friedrich Hegel. In addition to these academic pursuits, Heine explored the artistic, social, and wider intellectual life of the capital. He regularly visited the Varnhagen and Hohenhausen salons, made many important connections, and became significantly involved in a society for the advancement of Jewish culture and education.[16] At this stage, Heine was a relatively unknown writer,[17] but interest in his work was growing. His poems regularly appeared in newspapers and journals, and his first volume of poetry was published in December 1821.[18] Two of his essays on literary aesthetics were also printed in 1820 and 1821,[19] but *Briefe aus Berlin* was Heine's first prose work to declare as its purpose the description of contemporary society.

Reports from distant cities were a standard feature of newspapers at the time; and the idea of writing a series of *Korrespondenzen* (as such articles were known) on the Prussian capital came to Heine shortly after his arrival in Berlin. Following a failed attempt to interest the renowned liberal publisher Brockhaus in the project, he reached an agreement with Dr. Heinrich Schulz, the editor of the *Rheinisch-westfälischer Anzeiger*, in early 1822.[20] Published in Hamm, the *Anzeiger* was one of the two most important newspapers in the provinces of Rhineland and Westphalia and was read with interest by many in Berlin.[21]

This curiosity was evidently reciprocated by sections of the *Anzeiger*'s provincial readership. The paper had a tradition of publishing reports on the goings-on in Berlin,[22] and Schulz seems to have been particularly impressed by Heine's *Briefe aus Berlin*. While most *Korrespondenzen* appeared in small print on the final pages of contemporary newspapers, each of Heine's reports on Berlin provided either the lead or the second article of the *Anzeiger*'s weekly *Kunst- und Wissenschaftsblatt*.[23] The first letter was dated 26 January 1822, and was published in two instalments on 8 and 15 February of the same year. The second letter, of 16 March, was split into four parts, which appeared on 12, 19, and 26 April, and 3 May 1822. The final letter, dated 7 June, was included in the 28 June and 5, 12, 19 July editions of the *Kunst- und Wissenschaftsblatt*.[24] Heine's *Briefe aus Ber-*

lin were therefore a major feature in the *Anzeiger* during the six months in which they appeared.

Most contemporary *Korrespondenzen* consisted of a list of news items;[25] and the appearance of similar lists in many parts of *Briefe aus Berlin* has provoked accusations of formlessness[26] and conventionality[27] from critics. While such charges are not entirely unjustified, it is also clear that the letters differed from most other contemporary *Korrespondenzen* in a number of ways. They were longer than other travel reports published in the *Anzeiger*,[28] for example, and caused a stir in Berlin by their author's unusual boldness in naming contemporary figures, which almost led to another of his duels.[29] More importantly, the letters include accounts of the narrator's inner life, fictional elements, poetry, and extended narrative episodes. These literary sections anticipate an important aspect of Heine's distinctive *Reisebilder* style, in which such features become very prominent.[30]

The political content of the *Briefe aus Berlin* provides another link with the later *Reisebilder* works:[31] behind their superficial emphasis on the city's cultural life, the *Briefe* also include many attacks on Restoration ideology. To Heine's great annoyance, one passage in the third letter was censored into incomprehensibility prior to publication[32] and the second letter also contains one series of the dashes that at the time indicated censorship.[33] Unfortunately a lack of manuscript evidence means that it is now impossible to know exactly what was cut.[34] Yet, on the whole, the letters remained unscathed; and they were able to express opposition to government policies, uncomplimentary descriptions of the nobility, contradictions of religious orthodoxy, and praise for liberal ideals.

The publication of such comments was due partly to the favorable censorship conditions that existed in the *Anzeiger*'s home province of Westphalia, part of the Rhineland territories acquired by Prussia at the Congress of Vienna. The Prussian censorship edict of 1819 had placed responsibility for censorship in the hands of provincial Oberpräsidenten. In the case of Westphalia, this was Ludwig Freiherr von Vincke, a firm believer in press freedom. The instructions he issued to censors in his province represented a very mild interpretation of the Prussian censorship edict of 1819,[35] and concentrated on the need to avoid offending allied governments without mentioning the protection of the Prussian state's "Würde und Sicherheit."[36] During his entire term in office, von Vincke did not initiate any official action against the newspapers in his province; and in 1820, he even persuaded the Prussian Oberzensurkollegium to reconsider a planned prohibition of the *Anzeiger*.[37]

External supervisory control of censorship in Westphalia could only provide a partial corrective to von Vincke's liberal principles. The Prussian Oberzensurkollegium had appointed only one member to oversee the implementation of censorship in each province; and the responsible official in Westphalia was *Geheimer Regierungsrath* von Körner.[38] According to the most detailed account of the Prussian Oberzensurkollegium,[39] none of its members were paid for their censoring duties, which were generally carried out alongside other careers. Von Körner also worked as a senior civil servant and, like his colleagues, was not even provided with funds to purchase the publications he was required to censor.[40] Under such circumstances, it is hard to imagine how he could have provided a comprehensive control.

Despite these limitations, state censorship remained an important factor for writers in Westphalia. As well as the limited controls imposed by von Vincke, the Prussian Foreign Ministry kept an eye on all newspapers[41] and the Prussian Oberzensurkollegium took action against several violations of censorship law in Westphalia. In 1820, for example, the *Anzeiger*'s brush with prohibition was prompted by its publication of an article reminding the Prussian king of his promise of a constitution.[42] This experience doubtlessly decreased Schulz's willingness to publish articles that criticized the Prussian government, thereby imposing another layer of censorship on the *Anzeiger*. Given the liberal local pre-publication censorship, the acceptance of material likely to provoke a ban by the Prussian central authorities would have been an extremely dangerous undertaking.[43]

One would therefore expect dissent in *Briefe aus Berlin* to be expressed with restraint, and this is by and large the case. Indeed, although no early drafts of the work have survived,[44] an analysis of the version published in the *Anzeiger* allows us to observe Heine's interaction with censorship. An examination of the letters' critical comments suggests a number of principles that consistently determined both the scope and the presentation of subversive expression in *Briefe aus Berlin,* and thus reveals the effects of self-censorship on the work. At the same time, however, we will also see that, as the letters progress, Heine develops a range of techniques for articulating dissent with increasing boldness. The young writer's willingness to test the boundaries of censorship toleration may have been increased by the context within which the letters were published: writing in a newspaper subject to pre-publication censorship meant that its editor and censor had to take responsibility for illegal material. In the end, however, most of the critical content in *Briefe aus Berlin* was approved by both Schulz and the local censor in Hamm, and does not appear to have provoked any action by the central Prussian authorities. This success reveals the power of the evasive strategies pursued by Heine, and, as we will see, illustrates the role of censorship in shaping the development of his prose style.

The First Letter

The importance of critical messages to Heine's *Briefe aus Berlin* series is made clear early on in the first letter. Before beginning his account of life in the Prussian capital, the writer reflects upon the difficulties of the task in hand, asking himself, "was darf [das Publikum] nicht wissen?" (DHA 6:9). This allusion to restrictions imposed by censorship on the letters is briskly followed by the revelation of a defensive strategy. For Heine also warns his readers that the reports will not proceed systematically and declares that "Assoziazion der Ideen soll immer vorwalten" (DHA 6:9). This principle is illustrated by a juxtaposition of the famous reactionary law professor Savigny with a group of clowns that both demonstrates the critical power of association[45] and encourages readers to read between the lines of Heine's text:

> Ich spreche heute von den Redouten und den Kirchen, morgen von Savigny und den Possenreißern, die in seltsamen Aufzügen durch die Stadt ziehen, übermorgen von der Giustinianischen Gallerie, und dann wieder von Savigny und den Possenreißern. (DHA 6:9)

Yet although association plays an important role in generating critical meanings in the first report from Berlin, at this stage Heine's subjectivity is granted far less freedom than in much of his later prose. This is because the narrator's imagination is subjugated to the purpose of describing a fictional walking tour of Berlin with a Westphalian reader. The role adopted by the narrator here is therefore similar to that of the modernist "flaneur" who goes on leisurely, goalless walks through urban settings and allows his mind to wander as he observes his surroundings. The narrator of Heine's *Briefe aus Berlin,* however, appears committed to the task of showing his visitor around the Prussian capital and pays constant attention to both the physical reality of Berlin and his companion's reactions to it. An impression of brisk movement is conveyed by the rapid succession of sights mentioned, and in addition to these, other external factors such as loud coach wheels, the indifference of the narrator's companion, and his own hunger also appear to determine the direction of his account.

This apparent absorption in the external reality of Berlin offered Heine's narrator a means of referring to political issues without revealing an ideological agenda. As we will see, most of the subversive comment in this first letter is far from explicit, and consists of suggestive juxtapositions, allusions, or reminders of uncomfortable facts. The majority of these are made to seem as if they are prompted by the narrator's surroundings, thereby diminishing his apparent responsibility for the content of the text. In many cases, indeed, the narrative framework serves to obscure the subversive nature of Heine's comments. After showing his visitor the new stock exchange and remarking upon the greed on the faces of the dealers there, for example, the narrator's subsequent reference to the poverty in Berlin does not reveal any signs of socially critical intent: "Wie viel glücklicher ist doch mancher arme Teufel, der nicht weiß, ob ein

Louisd'or rund oder eckig ist" (DHA 6:11). Later on in the letter, Heine's rejection of proposals to provide prostitutes with some kind of uniform is immediately followed by a remark about the large number of men on "Unter den Linden" wearing medals. This juxtaposition was doubtless intended as a comment on Frederick William III's habit of granting state honors as a reward for political conformism, as well as the general militarization of society in Prussia. Nevertheless, given the letter's attention to geographical location, the proximity of the sketches of prostitutes and soldiers appears to be a natural consequence of the presence of these two groups in the streets near the university buildings past which the narrator has apparently just walked.

In other cases, the narrative framework does not conceal the political relevance of various reports, but provides a seemingly innocent explanation for their presence. This is the case for the text's references to censorship and suppression of student associations, both of which were closely associated with the Carlsbad Decrees, the laws passed by the German Confederation to eliminate political opposition to the status quo. These measures generated much controversy, which the Prussian government attempted to quell in 1820 with a censorship instruction specifically prohibiting their criticism.[46]

Although Heine's first letter from Berlin contains several clear references to political repression, the narrative framework means that such allusions do not appear to be motivated by the author's interest in the subject. At the end of the first letter, for example, Heine and his companion stop at the Café Royal, where, among several prominent Berlin figures, they meet an unidentified *Kammermusikus*, who furnishes them with a long list of recent events. The bulletin provided by this apparently independent figure is dominated by innocuous news from the artistic world, but also includes two reports of government censorship measures.[47] Such issues were clearly important to Heine — as we will see, he refers to them repeatedly in the two later letters. At this stage however, the writer was evidently keen not to appear concerned with them.

In addition to such structural measures, Heine also uses a number of presentational techniques to signal that the accounts of government repression contained within the first letter from Berlin are not intended as cues for political protest. First, he consistently refrains from mentioning the government agencies responsible for carrying out these measures, reverting instead to the passive. He also shows restraint in his choice of vocabulary, avoiding political keywords such as "verboten" and "Zensur" in favor of vaguer, more neutral terms; and, in the following example, using the verb "soll" — which indicates the reporting of a rumor — to weaken the authority of the statement: "Die Landsmannschaften sind aufgehoben. Die Verbindung, die, unter dem Namen Armenia, aus alten

Anhängern der Burschenschaft bestand, soll ebenfalls aufgelöst seyn" (DHA 6:13).

It is also striking that none of these accounts hint at disapproval; on the contrary, the nature of their presentation reinforces an impression of authorial indifference.[48] The insignificance of the censorship reports, for instance, is signaled both by their positioning within a list consisting largely of cultural trivia, and by the *Kammermusikus*'s preceding warning that nothing much has happened in Berlin recently (DHA 6:17). The relegation of the decisive verbs to the end of each sentence reinforces this impression of authorial apathy; and in the following example, the use of the casual qualifier "dann und wann" implies a decidedly relaxed attitude toward government action taken against the Brockhaus publishing firm: "Vom Brockhausischen Conversazionsblatte werden hier noch dann und wann Blätter konfisziert" (DHA 6:18).

A similar approach to vocabulary and phrasing can also be found in the few cases where the logic of the text suggests the author's subversive intentions. Although the first letter's narrative framework furnished much of its dangerous content with an innocent purpose, other passages were more manifestly critical. While the first letter's references to such issues as poverty and political oppression were well integrated within the narrative structure, the writer evidently felt able to sail much closer to the wind when addressing other topics. In addition to conveying factual information, for example, Heine, in his treatment of the Prussian king's attempts to introduce a new liturgy, implicitly reveals his own opinion on the matter. Motivated by a desire to integrate the newly acquired Rhine province into the rest of Prussia, this reform aroused the resistance of orthodox Lutherans and led to a conflict that lasted throughout the 1820s.[49] As Heine leads his readers past the Domkirche, he remarks upon two of its newer towers that look like birds' nests, and then goes on to describe how Friedrich August Wolf, a renowned Berlin philologist, had explained their strange appearance to a visitor with the words, "Hier werden Dompfaffen abgerichtet" (DHA 6:11).

This implicit comparison of conformist pastors with trained song birds is presented in a distinctly cautious manner. Heine is careful to signal its distance from his own consciousness: the anecdote is introduced by the words "man erzählt" and the scholars involved are identified by name. Moreover, by not mentioning either the Prussian government or the central issue — the new liturgy itself — and by maintaining a good-humored tone, the writer avoids supplying the signals of political protest. Nevertheless, no innocent explanation for the story's inclusion is provided; and given the topicality of the issue concerned, one imagines that its meaning would have been clear to most contemporary readers.

It is also noticeable that Heine's most explicit challenges to official ideology in this first letter do not involve direct criticisms of Prussian government policy. As the narrator and his companion ride in a carriage, for example, the former abruptly initiates a metaphysical discussion: "Was halten Sie von der Unsterblichkeit der Seele? Wahrhaftig, es ist eine große Erfindung, eine weit größere als das Pulver. Was halten Sie von der Liebe? Schnell, Kutscher. Nicht wahr, es ist bloß das Gesetz der Attrakzion" (DHA 6:16). This clear denial of the soul's immortality and the spiritual dimension of love is in direct contradiction to the teachings of both Christian churches; and as such it represents an assault on the basis of religion and morality protected by Prussian censorship legislation.[50]

Yet at the same time, the passage's formulation mitigates its appearance as a challenge to the contemporary moral and religious order. Like similar contradictions of religious orthodoxy in Grabbe's early plays, this is achieved partly through the use of only abstract terms: the section contains no mention of existing religious institutions, figures, or practices. In addition, however, the flight into philosophy is intensified by an interruption of the narrative flow, which abruptly switches to a dialogic form. Moreover, this passage too is free from the verbal gestures usually associated with dissent. The critical comments are delivered in a light-hearted tone, without employing negative or aggressive vocabulary. A dispassionate stance is suggested by the narrator's swift progress from one subject to another (his provocative comments are themselves followed by an abrupt return to the theme of Berlin's external appearance); and by using the words "wahrhaftig" and "nicht wahr" to indicate the expected agreement of his companion, the narrator signals that nothing provocative is being said. Therefore, although the heretical content of this passage is clearly accessible, it gives the superficial impression of a blithe confirmation of widely held beliefs.

While Heine's first letter from Berlin uses a tight narrative framework to disguise many of its critical messages, this does not prove necessary in all cases. As we have seen, at several points the logic of this text clearly reveals challenges to official ideology. In such passages, the writer appears careful to combine these critical messages with phrasing and vocabulary that point away from both their link with political reality and his own dissatisfaction with that reality. The fact that all such examples were passed by official censorship indicates that such nonthreatening presentation could compensate for a degree of openly critical content. And as we will see, this success appears to have encouraged Heine to pursue this approach further in the second letter, and to present his criticisms of Prussian society and government with increasing boldness.

The Second Letter

Early in the second letter from Berlin, we are confronted with the following declaration of its purpose: "ich muß jetzt davon sprechen, was die Leute singen und sagen bey uns an der Spree. Was sie klingeln und was sie züngeln, was sie kichern und was sie klatschen" (DHA 6:20). By introducing this with "ich muß," Heine suggests an external obligation that appears to reduce his responsibility for the contents of the text. And at various points throughout the letter, he refers back to this duty, introducing new topics either with another "ich muß," or by explaining that Berliners are talking about the subject concerned. On the whole, however, it is clear that this textual purpose grants the writer far more freedom than the tour of Berlin that structures the first letter. For although the letter proceeds more or less along thematic lines, the absence of a chronological frame and intrusions from the physical world means that the writer's responsibility for selecting and organizing the text's material is obvious to the reader.[51]

This flexible structure represents a step toward the open construction of Heine's later *Reisebilder* works[52] and allows the writer to signal his disapproval of government policies more clearly. This can be seen particularly in the letter's presentation of acts of censorship. As we have seen, in the first letter from Berlin, these were limited to brief, factual statements and attributed to the *Kammermusikus*. In the second letter, however, the narrator reports on such matters directly and indicates where his own sympathies lie. For example, after describing how the publisher Friedrich Arnold Brockhaus had failed to persuade the authorities to lift restrictions it had imposed on his firm, Heine delivers the following account of his character:

> Brockhaus ist ein Mann von angenehmer Persönlichkeit. Seine äußere Repräsentazion, sein scharfblickender Ernst und seine feste Freymüthigkeit lassen in ihm jenen Mann erkennen, der die Wissenschaften und den Meinungskampf nicht mit gewöhnlichen Buchhändler-Augen betrachtet. (DHA 6:31)

Such praise for Brockhaus's approach to publishing implies a disapproval of the government action against him. In particular, the commendation of Brockhaus's "Freymüthigkeit" suggests an endorsement of the political liberalism that Prussian censorship policy aimed to thwart. However, the formulation of the passage that delivers these subversive implications shares many characteristics with overt critical utterance in the first letter. Positive in tone, it is devoid of negative vocabulary and explicit criticism of the government. As we will see, the importance of such presentational aspects is confirmed by other cases in which the text's logic points firmly toward a critical intention. Although Heine often reveals his opposition to government policy, he is also careful to express this opposition in an ostensibly harmless manner.

Further effects of this strategy on the *Briefe aus Berlin* are illustrated by the text's treatment of the Spontini-Weber affair. Gasparo Luigi Pacifico Spontini and Carl Maria von Weber were both operatic composers, but while the Prussian king had summoned the Italian Spontini to Berlin to create lavish works of homage,[53] the German-nationalist works of Weber were far more popular among the general population, and particularly those of a liberal persuasion. Frederick William III, however, had a strong antipathy toward German nationalism and rejected the repeated attempts of the director of court theater in Berlin, Graf von Brühl, to engage Weber.[54] The affair soon acquired a political dimension, and by May 1821, it was reported that the king had forbidden Berlin newspapers from printing negative reviews of Spontini's latest opera.[55]

Although Heine's second letter from Berlin does not criticize Spontini's work explicitly, it cleverly reveals the author's preference for that of Weber. While the latter's most recent opera, *Der Freischütz*, is praised as "vortrefflich" (DHA 6:24), the narrator simply emphasizes the loudness of Spontini's *Olympia* (DHA 6:25). We can also read that the Italian has a detrimental effect on opera in Berlin, and that Spontini's supporters include only a handful of genuine admirers (DHA 6:25). Such opinions imply a clear disapproval of the favor granted to Spontini by the Prussian king, and as such constitute a taking of sides in a political debate of the day.

While stating such views directly, Heine also uses a variety of techniques to render them more palatable to the authorities. First, he repeatedly dissociates himself from the issue by focusing on the reactions of others to Spontini's work. He also grants space to content that mirrors government sympathies. The report of the operatic dispute in Berlin, for example, is preceded by a long episode (DHA 6:21–24) in which the narrator complains about hearing the *Jungfernkranz*, a song from Weber's *Freischütz*, wherever he goes. Although this anecdote also reveals the opera's popularity, the comments of the narrator express only unrestrained irritation: "Und nun den ganzen Tag verläßt mich nicht das vermaledeite Lied. Die schönsten Momente verbittert es mir" (DHA 6:23). Later on, Heine devotes much of a paragraph to a quotation of praise for Spontini's work (25); and his skepticism about the Italian's influence on the Berlin opera is immediately preceded by commendation of the institution as a whole: "Genug, es ist unbestritten, daß man die Oper hier auf eine erstaunliche Kunsthöhe gebracht hat, und daß sie keiner andern deutschen Oper nachzustehen braucht" (DHA 6:24).

The amount of text in obvious opposition to official sympathies is further diminished by the introduction of critical comments by words or phrases that promise a pro-government opinion. After stating his belief that Spontini's leadership has been detrimental to opera in Berlin, for instance, the narrator begins the next sentence with "aber," signaling a qualification of the initial judgment. However, he then continues in the same critical vein: "Aber ich behaupte durchaus, daß seit der völligen Trennung der Oper von dem Schauspiel, und Spontinis unumschränkter Beherrschung derselben, diese täglich mehr und mehr Schaden erleiden muß [. . .]" (DHA 6:25). Similarly, Heine's report on Spontini's *Olympia* contains a series of anecdotes emphasizing the loudness of the work. After suggesting that Berlin's deaf enjoyed the opera because they were able to feel the vibrations it caused, the following sentence begins with "Die Enthousiasten aber riefen," indicating a switch in gear to unadulterated admiration. Yet although it begins with a promising "Hosiana," the terms of their praise are distinctly ambivalent: "Hosiana! Spontini ist selbst ein musikalischer Elephant! Er ist ein Posaunenengel!" (DHA 6:26). Such intricate phrasing does not conceal the author's opinion from attentive readers, but they do reduce the intensity of his critical utterance.

The same effect is generated by Heine's repeated efforts to align vocabulary, phrasing, and perspective with state sympathies. His account of the confiscation of E. T. A Hoffmann's novel *Meister Floh* provides one example of such techniques. This book had been prohibited because it satirized the government investigation into liberal-nationalist agitation following the wars of liberation. In his account of the affair, however, Heine points out that *Komet,* a work by Jean Paul that made fun of the same process, had been printed with the censors' permission (DHA 6:32). He also indicates that the authorities treated *Meister Floh* more severely because Hoffmann himself had taken part in the *Demagogenverfolgung* and those involved felt betrayed by the satire presented in his novel.

While the information conveyed reveals that the actions against Hoffmann were unjust, it is delivered in a paragraph that contains many superficial indications of government sympathy. The narrator downplays his own interest in the affair by introducing the topic with the phrase: "Es wurde hier viel darüber geschwatzt [. . .]" and suggests closeness to the Prussian government by calling it "unsere Regierung." On the surface, the account appears to adopt the authorities' perspective: it refers to the "gegründetes Recht" of the government to treat Hoffmann more severely as a result of his previous affiliation, and describes the novel's presentation of the *Demagogenverfolgung* as a "tadelhafte Unziemlichkeit." Although the facts reported indicate that the writer has been treated unfairly, Heine nonetheless manages to convey this information while maintaining a perspective and vocabulary that suggest sympathy for the state (DHA 6:31–32).

While all manifest dissent in *Briefe aus Berlin* is expressed with considerable caution, Heine frequently dares to attack government and royal actions more emphatically in passages that do not make their official dimension explicit. One example is his denunciation of the "Gesellschaft zur Beförderung des Christenthums unter den Juden." This society, which aimed to convert Jews to Christianity, was under the protection of the king and dominated by conservatives.[56] The second letter does not mention the society's royal connection, but does express open disapproval of its activities. The letter's author refers to the purpose of the society disparagingly as the "alte[s], neu aufgewärmte[s] Projekt[. . .] der Judenbekehrung," before deciding that it is a "zu trauriger Gegenstand" (DHA 6:30) for discussion.

The treatment of the "Neue Liturgie" issue in this second letter similarly combines relatively bold expression with silence regarding the government's connection with the issue. There are some signs of caution: Heine reveals his opposition to the new rites indirectly, by praising the rhetorical talents of Friedrich Schleiermacher, who as a liberal theology professor preached against the "Neue Liturgie." However, in contrast to his tentative allusions in the first letter, the author here refers to the new rites by name and states explicitly that many people are opposed to them. Moreover, his enthusiastic final verdict on Schleiermacher's sermons leaves little doubt as to his own sympathies: "aber ich finde mich im bessern Sinne dadurch erbaut, erkräftigt, und wie durch Stachelworte aufgegeißelt vom weichen Flaumenbette des schlaffen Indifferentismus. Dieser Mann braucht nur das schwarze Kirchengewand abzuwerfen, und er steht da als Priester der Wahrheit" (DHA 6:30).

The association between the Prussian government and both the "Gesellschaft zur Beförderung der Wissenschaften unter den Juden" and the "Neue Liturgie" was well-known. However, not making this link explicit seems to have allowed Heine to employ vocabulary and syntax more reflective of his own critical views than in passages that mention the Prussian government directly. That freedom of expression could be won by shifting attention away from Prussian institutions confirms the findings of the first letter from Berlin. There, the narrator does not mention the Prussian government's connection with acts of political repression; and he expresses bold materialist views in exclusively abstract terms. And indeed, this pattern is also continued by the second letter's most daring challenge to religious orthodoxy. At a masked ball described toward the end of the report, the narrator experiences a rush of exhilaration, which leads him to the blasphemous deduction that God is pure merriment: "Die reinste Lustigkeit ist die Liebe, Gott ist die Liebe, Gott ist die reinste Lustigkeit" (DHA 6:37). This statement — which also contains a notable hint of Heine's later sensualism — is in clear contradiction to the teachings of the Christian churches.

Not stating sensitive political implications directly also allows Heine to address extremely controversial issues, even when the significance of his comments would have been clear to his readers. One such topic was the convening of the estates for negotiations with central government. These assemblies were contentious because they represented a substitute for the promised Prussian constitution; and they were closely associated with the monarch's refusal to fulfil his earlier pledge. As mentioned in the introduction, the *Anzeiger* was almost banned in 1820 after publishing an article reminding the Prussian king of this promise. The summoning of the estates in early 1822 was supposed to be kept secret; and Heine was evidently the first writer to report on them in the *Anzeiger*.[57]

As with his treatment of other political issues, Heine uses a variety of stylistic devices to generate an impression of casual approval. In addition, he does not allow the text itself to reveal any criticism of the assemblies and omits to mention both their contentious nature and their relationship with the promised Prussian constitution. Yet, given the notoriety of the constitution issue, Heine's account of the meetings would have been sufficient to alert his readers to their significance. In particular, his description informs us that "[v]on den Verhandlungen der Notablen mit der Regierung erfährt man nichts, da sie, wie man sagt, *Juramentum silentii* abgelegt haben" (DHA 6:34), which both reminds us of the assemblies' contentious nature, and hints at double-dealing on the part of the government.

Heine pursues a similar strategy when alluding to chancellor Hardenberg's affair with Friederike Hähnel. Such references are as close as he comes to criticizing individual government members; given explicit protection granted to both personal honor and government dignity in Prussian censorship law,[58] it is likely that such attacks were a particularly dangerous undertaking. Indeed, when referring to the chancellor's affair, the text does not address the topic explicitly: superficially harmless details are used to activate the reader's background knowledge instead. Toward the end of the second letter, for example, we read the following: "Unser Staatskanzler befindet sich jetzt ganz hergestellt, und ist theils hier, theils in Glienicke" (*HKG* 6:34). Yet despite the innocent appearance of this comment, its ramifications would have been clear to most Berliners, at least: Hähnel resided at the chancellor's estate in Glienicke and their relationship was the subject of much gossip.[59]

Despite the impossibility of stating directly the full implications of his political views, Heine nevertheless developed alternative means of communicating them. One such technique, which first appears toward the end of the second letter, is particularly significant because it prefigures a distinctive aesthetic element of his main *Reisebilder* series. This strategy involves the creation of links between a series of passages that each delivers a limited measure of nonconformist meaning. As a result, the heretical elements contained within each section of text can be combined and Heine's revolutionary political principles communicated.

The author's desire for freedom and equality, for instance, is articulated most explicitly during a description of a masked ball. The hostility of Prussian censorship authorities to the vocabulary associated with liberal ideology is well established: one set of censorship instructions from 1820 requires the word "Liberale" to be preceded by the adjective "sogenannte."[60] In the following passage, the writer's enthusiasm for freedom and equality is associated with an absence of social barriers in a way that points toward the political implications of his remarks. Yet, like most of the writer's boldest expression, these comments also appear free from critical intentions and dissociated from political life. As we can see from the following, the celebration of liberal ideals is immediately followed by a reminder of their social context:

> Und Mensch ist man erst recht auf dem Maskenballe, wo die wächserne Larve unsere gewöhnliche Fleischlarve bedeckt, wo das schlichte Du die urgesellschaftliche Vertraulichkeit herstellt, wo ein alle Ansprüche verhüllender Domino die schönste Gleichheit hervorbringt, und wo die schönste Freyheit herrscht — Maskenfreyheit. Für mich hat eine Redoute immer etwas höchst Ergötzliches. (DHA 6:37)

However, while this exaltation of liberal principles appears apolitical, another passage later on in the same account links the removal of social barriers with political concerns. When a patriot scolds Heine for speaking French, the writer's response both rejects German nationalism and reveals sympathy for the oppressed peoples of Africa. Although he avoids provocative ideological terminology here, the idea of universal brotherhood completes the trio of revolutionary ideals initiated by Heine's celebration of freedom and equality in the earlier passage:[61]

> O deutscher Jüngling, wie finde ich dich und deine Worte sündlich und läppisch in solchen Momenten, wo meine Seele die ganze Welt mit Liebe umfaßt, wo ich Russen und Türken jauchzend umarmen würde, und wo ich weinend hinsinken möchte an die Bruderbrust des gefesselten Afrikaners! (DHA 6:37)

And while the political concerns revealed here may not be a threat to the Prussian state, a third passage links the theme of social barriers to the behavior of elite groups in contemporary Berlin. This section appears a little earlier in the text than the other two, and presents the author's complaints about the fragmented social life in Berlin. Although critical, it mentions neither liberal principles nor political reality. Yet, like the other passages, this one also addresses the theme of balls; and by characterizing wider Berlin society as the opposite of the ideal found at the masked ball, it creates a negative association between his political principles and the conduct of the establishment in Berlin:

> Es ist hier ungemein viel geselliges Leben, aber es ist in lauter Fetzen zerrissen. Es ist ein Nebeneinander vieler kleinen Kreise, die sich immer mehr zusammen zu ziehen als auszubreiten suchen [...]. Der Hof und die Minister, dasdiplomatische Corps, die Civilbeamten, die Kaufleute, die Offiziere etc. etc., alle geben sie eigene Bälle, worauf nur ein zu ihrem Kreise gehöriges Personal erscheint. (DHA 6:35)

Read separately, none of these passages contains enough information to reveal a threat to the Prussian status quo. The first praises liberal ideals within a nonpolitical context and with an approving tone that suggests contentment with existing society; the second retains this affirmative character and avoids ideological language, but hints at the political relevance of liberal ideals; and the third refrains from political language or references, but expresses dissatisfaction with the structure of Berlin social life. These statements, however, all appear within a discussion of Berlin balls and are linked thematically by the author's dislike for social barriers. This encourages readers to associate the critical elements contained within each of them and detect a democratically tinged, politically committed rejection of Prussia's social hierarchy.

The result of this strategy is a series of passages in which different aspects of the same idea are presented to the reader. This pattern prefigures the organization of later *Reisebilder* texts, in which a sequence of descriptions and anecdotes also reveal different manifestations of a central concept. In the later texts, the passages that communicate the recurrent idea are more diverse in both theme and context than is the case for the *Briefe aus Berlin*. As a result, a wide spectrum of reality serves to illustrate a central precept, an effect that contributes significantly to the distinctive aesthetic quality of the *Reisebilder* texts.[62] Although this approach is not pursued on such a large scale in the *Briefe aus Berlin,* the technique of repeatedly describing different manifestations of an idea is the same in both cases. The role of censorship pressure in stimulating the development of this distinctive style of composition is suggested by the fact that, both here and in later works, it allows Heine to hint powerfully at subversive opinions without expressing them directly.[63] In the third letter from Berlin, too, we will see the writer using this approach to address a highly sensitive theme while avoiding open criticism.

The Third Letter

Unlike the first two letters from Berlin, Heine's third report from the Prussian capital does not attempt to suggest that its composition was subordinated to an externally imposed purpose. Although the letter begins with a lengthy account of the wedding between the Prussian princess Alexandrine and Paul Frederick of Mecklenburg-Schwerin, directly after this report, the narrator informs us of the role played by his mood in structuring the text: "Ich habe längst bemerkt, daß über die Rangordnung, womit ich Ihnen die hiesigen Begebnisse melde, bloß meine Laune entscheidet, und nicht die Anciennität" (DHA 6:43). This narrative freedom points toward the pronounced subjectivity of the *Reisebilder*[64] and is reinforced later on in the letter by passages in which the author discusses his own opinions, as well as the absence of a bulletin from the *Kammermusikus*.

Signals of authorial indifference toward contentious issues are far less frequent in this final letter than in the other two; and Heine's greater willingness to reveal his own responsibility for the contents of his report can be linked to the successful publication of recognizably critical passages in the second letter. In particular, the printing of his celebration of freedom within the previous text seems to have encouraged the composition of bolder passages on the same topic. After mocking the activities of certain patriotic groups, for example, the narrator briefly apologizes to his readers and then explains: "Meine Seele glüht zu sehr für die wahre Freyheit, als daß mich nicht der Unmuth ergreifen sollte, wenn ich unsere winzigen, breitschwatzenden Freyheitshelden in ihrer aschgrauen Armseligkeit betrachte [. . .]" (DHA 6:44). In addition to its passionate tone, it is striking that this statement endorses the ideals of freedom within the context of a discussion of Prussian political affairs. Indeed, although the Prussian government shared Heine's antipathy toward the liberal nationalism of the "Freyheitshelden," they would not have welcomed the other implication of these comments. For by contrasting the victory celebrated by the "Freyheitshelden" — which restored Prussian autonomy — with the ideal of "wahre Freiheit," Heine also reminds us of the oppressive measures imposed by the then current government.

Shortly afterwards, Heine links the ideal of freedom even more concretely with contemporary society. Like many other commentators at the time, the writer includes in his report on the case of Peter Anton Fonk, a Cologne man sentenced to death for murder, a discussion of the system of trial by jury instituted by Napoleon in the Rhineland.[65] Less typically, however, his account climaxes in an equation of this institution's continuation with Rhinelanders' love of freedom; and his vehement defense of the "Fesseln" brought to the region by the French clearly implies the inferiority of the Prussian legal and political system: "Möge das geliebte Rheinland noch lange diese Fesseln tragen, und noch mit ähnlichen Fesseln belastet werden! Möge am Rhein noch lange blühen jene ächte Freyheitsliebe, die nicht auf Franzosenhaß und Nazionalegoismus basirt ist [. . .]"

(DHA 6:48). Despite the critical implications and energetic mood of such statements, the manner of their presentation nevertheless confirms several of the principles suggested by the formulation of previous subversive messages. Predominantly enthusiastic in tone, such passages avoid explicit attacks on Prussian institutions; indeed, like the bolder comments contained within the first two letters, they do not mention these institutions at all. Moreover, in both cases the ideal of freedom is used to attack German nationalist groups, to which the government itself was opposed. On a superficial level, therefore, Heine's commitment to freedom was aimed away from the Prussian authorities.

Other critical passages in the third letter follow a similar pattern. Although Heine does not venture any open condemnations of government policy, he does articulate many oppositional views more vigorously and at greater length than in the previous texts. In particular, it is noticeable that Heine's use of vocabulary in such statements is frequently bolder than in the first two letters. At the same time, however, such critical opinions are in many cases juxtaposed with other statements that indicate sympathy for the Prussian establishment. Early on in the letter, for instance, the narrator tells us that he was given free tickets to see the opera Spontini had composed in honor of the royal wedding: *Nurmahal, oder das Rosenfest in Kaschimir.* He opts not to attend and justifies his decision with an energetic swipe at Spontini's previous opera, *Olympia:* "glauben Sie, daß ich mich für meine Korrespondenz aufopfern soll? Mit Grausen denke ich noch an die Olympia, der ich kürzlich, aus einem besonderem Grunde, nochmals beywohnen mußte, und die mich mit fast zerschlagenen Gliedern entließ" (DHA 6:41). Although Heine again avoids an explicit condemnation of the opera, the evocative word "Grausen" and the reference to "fast zerschlagenen Gliedern" contribute to a far more emphatic attack on the composer's work than was ventured in the second letter. Yet immediately afterwards, the narrator switches into a more dispassionate mode and expresses skepticism about the *Kammermusikus*'s negative judgment of the new work: "Doch kann ich mich hierin auf den Kammermusikus nicht verlassen, denn erstens komponirt er auch, und nach seiner Meinung besser als Spontini [...]" (DHA 6:41). This method of presentation also allows Heine to express sympathy for the victims of government repression for the first time in the work. Following a report that thirty-two students had been expelled from the university due to membership of an illegal organization, the narrator's first comment points out the severity of this punishment: "Es ist eine fatale Sache relegirt zu werden; sogar das bloße Konsilirtwerden soll sein Unangenehmes haben" (DHA 6:48).

Heine himself had been suspended from Göttingen university and the reference to "das bloße Konsilirtwerden" was a private joke for his friends. Yet his adoption of the expelled students' perspective is quickly followed by professions of faith in the authorities' judgment. For in addition to not mentioning the government agencies involved in the expulsions, Heine also suggests that higher powers will prevent them from being carried out: "Ich glaube aber, daß jenes strenge Urtheil gegen die 32 noch gemildert wird" (DHA 6:48).

Although such techniques allowed Heine to express open disapproval of many government policies, it is interesting that this confidence did not extend to all thematic areas. For, if we examine the discussion of social relations within *Briefe aus Berlin*, it soon becomes clear that the writer felt obliged to express his views on the subject with particular caution. A first indication of this topic's sensitivity is the presentation of poverty in the second letter. Despite the author's growing audacity in other areas, his only reference to poverty in the second report appears to originate from the *Kammermusikus,* and is brief, factual, and apparently incidental: "Mehrere Menschenfreunde wollen hier eine Anstalt für verwahrloste Knaben stiften, ähnlich der des Geheimrath Falk in Weimar" (DHA 6:33). In the third letter, too, Heine's treatment of social relations is far more restrained than his discussion of both government repression and political ideals; and it does not include even the cautious articulation of opinion. However, as at the end of the second letter, the writer uses a series of restrained comments to suggest a serious attack on the Prussian social hierarchy. Although his description of the royal wedding appears to be neither critical nor political, it contains a network of references that together reveal the inequality inherent in Berlin society.

An important part of this suggestion is Heine's emphasis on the material extravagance of the marriage celebrations. Although he does not speculate on the cost involved in these, an indication is given by descriptions of the luxurious coaches and clothes of the guests, as well as the newlyweds' diamonds and the "Pracht" of the opera composed for the occasion. And while the narrator does not criticize the riches on parade, his detached amusement at the trappings of wealth often seems incompatible with respect for the social elite. This can be seen most clearly in his description of the wedding guests' servants. By concentrating on the guests' personnel, Heine is able to ridicule their extravagant tastes while remaining focused on a safe target. He exercises further caution by beginning many comments in a manner that signals admiration rather than mockery. One statement, for example, begins with the apparently loyal announcement that the servants were in their best livery and ends by comparing them to Dutch tulips. Later in the same passage, Heine again avoids vocabulary associated with mockery in a sketch of the personnel belonging to one particular guest.[66] Instead, he attaches the positive attribute of brotherliness to the servants; and, beginning with the coachman, he leaves their headwear to provide grotesque visual comedy:

Sein edles Haupt, kreideweiß gepudert, und mit einem unmenschlich großen schwarzen Haarbeutel geziert, war von einem schwarzen Sammtkäppchen mit langem Schirm bedeckt. Ganz auf gleiche Weise waren die vier Bedienten gekleidet, die hinten auf dem Wagen standen, sich mit brüderlicher Umschlingung einer an dem andern festhielten, und dem gaffenden Publikum vier wackelnde Haarbeutel zeigten. (DHA 6:38–39)

While Heine treats the royals' finery with more respect, he does not express admiration for it. Although he emphasizes the opulence of their clothing, jewelry, coaches, and celebratory opera, he at no stage offers praise for these items themselves. Indeed, his observation that, at the celebratory ball, the new bride "glänzte mehr durch ihre Liebenswürdigkeit als durch ihren reichen Diamantenschmuck" (43) suggests a certain distaste for ostentatious wealth. And while the writer does not attempt a humorous depiction of the royal entourage itself, he does follow a description of the young couple's lavish coach with a reminder of the amusing "Haarbeutel" discussed in the previous paragraph: "Sie fuhren in der achtspännigen goldnen Kutsche mit großen Glasfenstern, und wurden von einer gewaltigen Menschenmenge bestaunt. Wenn ich nicht irre, trugen die obigen Bedienten an diesem Tage keine Haarbeutel" (DHA 6:41).

Although cautiously expressed, these hints of disapproval are closely linked to a series of references to the theme of inequality. Immediately before his description of the servants' costume, Heine informs his readers that he cannot attend the marriage ceremony because "Ich bin kein Adeliger, kein hoher Staatsbeamte und kein Offizier" (DHA 6:38). Although this revelation is delivered in a calm tone and appears motivated by a desire to explain the nature of his report, its reference to social inequality connects it to a more overtly political comment only a few lines later. This is Heine's observation that, among the servants in attendance, "Mancher [. . .] trug mehr Gold und Silber am Leibe als das ganze Hauspersonal des Bürgermeisters von Nordamerika" (DHA 6:38). The avoidance of political language and the use of a fictional title may give this allusion a jovial air. However, the young American republic was seen by many as a model of freedom and equality;[67] and the suggestion that its ruling class was much less extravagant than Prussia's therefore had potentially serious political implications.

Other passages within the wedding report contain even more restrained hints at the gap between rich and poor. We are told, for example, that, as the royal couple drove to the Domkirche in a large golden coach, they "wurden von einer gewaltigen Menschenmenge bestaunt" (DHA 6:41). The word "bestaunt" suggests that the peoples' reaction to this luxury was astonishment rather than the enthusiasm expected of loyal subjects. Earlier on, we read that, after twelve cannons had been fired to announce that the couple had exchanged rings, clouds of dust and steam appeared in the air (DHA 6:41). Placed within an account of the royal wedding, this reminder of the presence of filth and industrial production in Berlin also highlights the gap in living conditions between the aristocracy and masses.

In addition, bolder references to the lower classes' situation can be found in passages that do not address the extravagance of the wedding celebrations. When setting the scene for his account, for instance, Heine provides the following sketch: "Herumlaufende Bedienten, Friseure, Schachteln, Putzmacherinnen u.s.w. Ein schöner Tag, nicht sehr schwül; aber die Menschen schwitzten" (DHA 6:38). Here, a description of people sweating despite mild weather conditions immediately follows an account of the hectic preparations of court personnel. The juxtaposition reminds us of the strenuous labor required to put on such lavish festivities. Later, a considerably more explicit reference to poverty is made during a report of the "Freyredoute" held to celebrate the wedding. Those in attendance gorged themselves on the free refreshments, causing Heine to comment:

> wenn ich mich nicht bey vielen Gelegenheiten überzeugt hätte, daß der poverste Berliner es im anständigen Hungerleiden sehr weit gebracht hat, und meisterhaft darauf eingeübt ist, den schreienden Magen in die Formen vornehmer Konvenienz einzuzwängen: so hätte ich von den Leuten hier sehr leicht eine ungünstige Meinung fassen können [...]. (DHA 6:42)

As for most of Heine's critical comments, his tone here is calm and his remarks appear to be motivated by a nonpolitical purpose: in this case, that of excusing the Berliners' behavior. Nevertheless, he is able to make it clear that he has encountered poverty "bey vielen Gelegenheiten"; and his description of impoverished Berliners' "schreienden Magen" is a vivid suggestion of their hardship.

Despite his boldness in other areas, Heine evidently felt unable to voice explicit criticisms of inequality within Prussian society. However, repeated descriptions of different aspects of Prussian social relations did allow him to suggest disapproval. Although the writer was unable to state his views directly, continual references to various facets of inequality provided an alternative means of sensitizing his readers to the theme. As at the end of the second letter, instead of stating his views in a direct and abstract manner, Heine was forced to present his readers with different manifestations of his subversive idea. The impossibility of discussing Prussian social equality directly therefore seems to have impelled its replacement by presentations of reality that were permeated by a critical awareness if the issue. While less forceful than explicit comment, such indirect presentation also offered a means of addressing political matters in an intricate and aesthetically sophisticated manner.

Conclusion

During the course of *Briefe aus Berlin,* Heine grew increasingly bold in articulating his criticisms of Prussian government policy. We have seen that, at the beginning of the first letter, the young writer was reluctant to name political issues explicitly, tried to conceal his critical intentions, and only occasionally hinted at disapproval for government actions. Within subsequent reports, however, Heine allows the logic of his texts to reveal his oppositional views more and more clearly. Among other things, the third letter expresses a passionate commitment to the ideal of freedom, reveals a belief in the superiority of the Napoleonic legal code over the Prussian, and clearly implies opposition to repressive government actions. The letters attracted a fair amount of interest, both in Berlin and in Westphalia; and their critical content was noticed by many in Berlin: in March 1822, a rumor was circulating according to which Heine was to be expelled from the city.[68] It is therefore almost certain that the authorities in Berlin had some awareness of the texts' oppositional character.

The content of *Briefe aus Berlin* demonstrates that Prussian state censorship did not prevent the publication of all politically oppositional expression. Yet it is also clear that a number of principles restricted the nature of this dissent. Although Heine suggests criticisms of many state actions in *Briefe aus Berlin,* he does not allow the work to attack either the Prussian government itself, its institutions, or its members. It is striking that, just as the blasphemous sections in Grabbe's early plays mention neither churches nor contemporary religious practices, Heine's clearest statements of oppositional thought either do not refer to the state or are accompanied by gestures of sympathy for the authorities. This particular caution with regard to the portrayal of the Prussian state can be related to censorship legislation protecting the "Würde und Sicherheit [. . .] des preußischen Staates." Prussian censorship law also forbade challenges to monarchical authority,[69] and this explains both Heine's tentative treatment of the Prussian constitutional question and the absence of any discussion of different forms of government, despite the writer's manifest dissatisfaction with Prussian institutions. In addition, Heine's careful treatment of Prussian political structures seems to have extended to the social order upon which these institutions were based. The writer's restrained portrayal of the gap between rich and poor is one example of this; and although the depiction of the nobility in *Briefe aus Berlin* reveals a lack of respect for their status, it is noticeable that he steers clear of passing an explicit moral judgment upon either their behavior or their privileged position.

Where censorship pressure did not prevent the appearance of accessibly subversive material, it nonetheless affected the formulation of such content. Despite the increasing clarity of Heine's subversive messages, their intensity is consistently diminished by a variety of presentational factors. The author avoids making the political implications of his texts explicit, for example, and, during the first two letters in particular, is careful to generate an impression of nonchalance when discussing controversial matters. Even when this is not the case, he maintains a positive, good-humored tone that removes any suggestion of anger or protest from the text. Also important in softening the mood of the letters is Heine's skilful use of vocabulary, which in the first letter avoids political terminology, and in later passages is often aligned with government perspectives. In many instances, proscribed content is either introduced by signals of pro-state opinion or juxtaposed with expressions of sympathy for the government. These strategies parallel Grabbe's efforts to diminish the impact of illicit elements within his early plays: Heine's avoidance of political terminology has a similar effect to Grabbe's selective removal of exclamation marks, while his misleading pro-government gestures are reminiscent of the forewords and anti-blasphemous footnotes within *Dramatische Dichtungen,* both of which were intended to generate an impression of respectable conformity.

Yet while such techniques allow Heine to communicate oppositional ideas, they also place other restrictions on the scope of his critical utterance. Most obviously, the simulation of a light-hearted mood prevents the expression of more threatening emotions such as anger or defiance. In addition, the alternation of critical statements with those suggesting sympathy for the state precluded the construction of a detailed, sustained discussion; and the writer's reluctance to mention government institutions placed considerable restrictions on the precision of his political analysis. At the same time, however, these limitations — and Heine's efforts to overcome them — also contributed to the development of his unique writing style. We have seen, for instance, that as the *Briefe aus Berlin* move toward the unrestrained subjectivity of the later *Reisebilder* texts, a distinctive and subtle form of irony is generated by the delivery of critical messages by syntax and vocabulary that signal approval. And in general, Heine's concern to diminish the intensity of his critical utterance stimulated the composition of many imaginative and intricate passages. Perhaps most significantly, the writer's innovative treatment of political freedom and inequality involved recourse to descriptions of reality that demonstrate the wide implications of his thought. While state censorship undeniably placed considerable restrictions on the composition of *Briefe aus Berlin,* it also helped to stimulate the development of a new style of prose.

Notes

[1] Heinrich Heine, *Historisch-kritische Gesamtausgabe der Werke*, Düsseldorfer Ausgabe, ed. Manfred Windfuhr and others, 16 vols. (Hamburg: Hoffmann und Campe, 1973–97) vol. 6:7–53 (edition subsequently as DHA).

[2] *Begegnungen mit Heine: Berichte der Zeitgenossen 1797–1846,* ed. Michael Werner, 2 vols. (Hamburg: Hoffmann und Campe, 1973), 1:74.

[3] See letter of 25 June 1827, Christian Dietrich Grabbe, *Werke und Briefe: Historisch-kritische Gesamtausgabe in sechs Bänden,* 5:162.

[4] See Brose, *German History 1789–1871,* 120.

[5] See, for example, Ronald Taylor, *Berlin and its Culture: A Historical Portrait* (New Haven: Yale UP, 1997), 115.

[6] See Taylor, *Berlin,* 138–39.

[7] See Walter Kanowsky, *Vernunft und Geschichte: Heinrich Heines Studium als Grundlegung seiner Welt- und Kunstanschauung* (Bonn: Bouvier, 1975), 175.

[8] See Sheehan, *German History 1770–1866,* 486.

[9] See Klaus Pabel, *Heines "Reisebilder": Ästhetisches Bedürfnis und politisches Interesse am Ende der Kunstperiode* (Munich: Fink, 1977), 63.

[10] See Nipperdey, *Deutsche Geschichte,* 220–21.

[11] See Nipperdey, *Deutsche Geschichte,* 47–48.

[12] See Nipperdey, *Deutsche Geschichte,* 56–62.

[13] See Sheehan, *German History,* 306.

[14] See Nipperdey, *Deutsche Geschichte,* 334.

[15] See Nipperdey, *Deutsche Geschichte,* 334.

[16] See Fritz Mende, *Heinrich Heine: Chronik seines Lebens und Werkes,* 2nd ed. (Stuttgart: Kohlhammer, 1981), 23–27, and DHA 6:361–62.

[17] See Jost Hermand, *Der frühe Heine: ein Kommentar zu den "Reisebildern"* (Munich: Winkler, 1976), 24.

[18] See Hermand, *Der frühe Heine,* 1:635.

[19] See Hermand, *Der frühe Heine,* 10:497 and 509–10.

[20] See Hermand, *Der frühe Heine,* 6:362–63.

[21] See Gerd Heinemann, *Die Beziehungen des jungen Heine zu Zeitschriften im Rheinland und in Westfalen: Untersuchungen zum literarischen Leben der Restaurationszeit,* Geschichtliche Arbeiten zur Meinungsbildung und Kommunikationsmitteln in Westfalen 1 (Münster: Aschendorff, 1974), 113.

[22] See Heinemann, *Die Beziehungen des jungen Heine,* 136.

[23] See Heinemann, *Die Beziehungen des jungen Heine,* 144.

[24] See DHA 6:364–65.

[25] See Heinemann, *Die Beziehungen des jungen Heine,* 144.

[26] See, for example, Manfred Windfuhr, *Heinrich Heine: Revolution und Reflexion* (Stuttgart: Metzler, 1969), 57.

[27] See, for example, Bernd Kortländer, *Heinrich Heine* (Stuttgart: Reclam, 2003), 160.

[28] See Heinemann, *Die Beziehungen des jungen Heine*, 144–46.

[29] See DHA 6:367–69.

[30] This assessment is shared by most recent studies of the *Briefe aus Berlin*. For other ways in which this work anticipates the later *Reisebilder*, see Alfred Betz, *Ästhethik und Politik: Heinrich Heines Prosa* (Munich: Hanser, 1971), 109–10; and Klaus Briegleb, "Heine und Preußen: Notierungen zur "Vorrede" vom 18. Oktober 1832," in Klaus Briegleb, *Opfer Heine? Versuche über Schriftzüge der Revolution* (Frankfurt: Suhrkamp, 1986), 45–70; here 46.

[31] Three short extracts from *Briefe aus Berlin* were included in the first edition of *Reisebilder* II so that the volume's length would exceed the twenty-Bogen limit required to escape pre-publication censorship. See DHA 6:370–71.

[32] See letter of 1 September 1822, Heinrich Heine, *Werke, Briefwechsel, Lebenszeugnisse: Säkularausgabe*, ed. Nationale Forschungs- und Gedenkstätten der klassischen deutschen Literatur in Weimar and Centre National de la Recherche Scientifique in Paris, 27 vols. (Berlin and Paris: Akademie Verlag and Editions du CNRS, 1970 ff.), vol. 20, ed. Fritz H. Eisner, 1970, 58–59 (edition subsequently cited as HSA). The censored form in which the passage appeared is given in DHA 6:378.

[33] See DHA 6:364. "Zensurstriche" were forbidden by a federal decree in 1834. See "Die Sechzig Artikel vom 12. Juni 1834" in *Dokumente zur deutschen Verfassungsgeschichte*, ed. Huber, 1:123–135; here 128.

[34] See DHA 6:373–74.

[35] For the full text of this decree, see *Dokumente zur deutschen Verfassungsgeschichte*, 1:95–98.

[36] The dignity and security of the Prussian state is explicitly protected in article two of the "Preußische Zensur-Verordnung vom 18. Oktober 1819." See *Dokumente zur deutschen Verfassungsgeschichte*, 1:95–96. For a detailed account of Vincke's instruction to Landrat Wiethaus, the censor responsible for the *Anzeiger* at the time, see Heinemann, *Die Beziehungen des jungen Heine*, 97–98.

[37] See Heinemann, *Die Beziehungen des jungen Heines*, 94–100.

[38] See Heinemann, *Die Beziehungen des jungen Heines*, 94.

[39] See Friedrich Kapp, "Die preußische Preßgesetzgebung unter Friedrich Wilhelm III. 1815–1840: nach den Akten im Königlich Preußischen Geheimen Staatsarchiv," *Archiv für die Geschichte des Deutschen Buchhandels*, 6 (1881): 185–249.

[40] See Kapp, "Die preußische Preßgesetzgebung," 205–6.

[41] See Kapp, "Die preußische Preßgesetzgebung," 202–3.

[42] See Kapp, "Die preußische Preßgesetzgebung," 219.

[43] An extract from a letter to Karl Immermann, in which Schulz discusses his fears that the publication of certain material in the *Anzeiger* will provoke punitive action from the Berlin censorship authorities, is reprinted in Heinemann, *Die Beziehungen des jungen Heine*, 106.

[44] See DHA 6:373–74.

[45] For more on Heine's use of association as an evasive strategy in *Briefe aus Berlin*, see Pabel, *Heines "Reisebilder,"* 52–56.

[46] For the full text of this instruction, see Kapp, *Die preußische Gesetzgebung*, 211.

[47] It has been pointed out by various critics that such lists of trivia offered the hope of exhausting the censor's patience before he reached the dangerous material. See, for example, Wulf Wülfing, "Reisebericht im Vormärz. Die Paradigmen Heinrich Heine und Ida Hahn-Hahn," in *Der Reisebericht*, ed. Peter J. Brenner (Frankfurt: Suhrkamp, 1989), 333–62; here 338–39.

[48] Over twenty years later, Heine referred to his use of an indifferent tone as an evasive strategy in the foreword to the French edition of his collected articles on Paris for the *Augsburger Allgemeine Zeitung*. See Michael Werner, "Der politische Schriftsteller und die Selbstzensur. Zur Dialektik von Zensur und Selbstzensur in Heines Berichten aus Paris 1840–1844 (*Lutezia*)," *Heine-Jahrbuch* 26 (1987): 29–53; here 34. Werner's analysis of Heine's use of this strategy (Werner, "Der politische Schriftsteller," 41–43) concentrates on his efforts to appear impartial as opposed to lacking in interest.

[49] See DHA 6:432–33.

[50] See article 2 of the "Preußische Zensur-Verordnung von 18. Oktober 1819," in Huber, *Dokumente zur deutschen Verfassungsgeschichte*, 1:95–98; here 95–96.

[51] Jost Hermand (*Der frühe Heine*, 28) describes the structure of each letter as an anecdotal core followed by a series of news items. This is basically correct, but obscures the fact that, in the second and third letters, the central anecdotes (in the second letter, the "Jungfernkranz" song, and in the third, the royal wedding) only account for a small proportion of the text. In addition, as we will see, the news coverage in the later letters becomes more reflective and subjective, and is occasionally interrupted by personal and discursive passages.

[52] The fragmented, open form of the *Reisebilder* is universally recognized as one of the works' defining characteristics. See, for example, Kortländer, *Heinrich Heine*, and Slobodan Grubačić, *Heines Erzählprosa: Versuch einer Analyse* (Stuttgart: Kohlhammer, 1975), 9.

[53] See DHA 6:388–89.

[54] See DHA 6:418.

[55] See DHA 6:422.

[56] See DHA 6:432.

[57] See DHA 6:447.

[58] For both of these stipulations, see article 2 of the "Preußische Zensur-Verordnung von 18. Oktober 1819," in Huber, *Dokumente zur deutschen Verfassungsgeschichte*, 1:95–98; here 95–96.

[59] See DHA 6:448.

[60] See Kapp, *Die preußische Gesetzgebung*, 216.

[61] See also Pabel, *Heines "Reisebilder,"* 73.

[62] See, for example, Wolfgang Preisendanz, *Heinrich Heine: Werkstrukturen und Epochenbezüge*, 2nd ed. (Munich: Fink, 1983), 54–57.

[63] In *Reise von München nach Genua*, for example, one such recurrent theme is the contrast between the impotence and suffering of contemporary Austrian-occupied northern Italy and the land's glorious classical past. See Preisendanz, *Heinrich Heine*, 54–56.

[64] See, for example, Peter Stein, "'Prototyp einer Denk- und Schreibweise': Heinrich Heines *Reisebilder* als Auftakt zur 'Julirevolution der deutschen Literatur,'" in *Heinrich Heine: Ästhetisch-politische Profile*, ed. Gerhard Höhn (Frankfurt: Suhrkamp, 1991), 50–65; here 52.

[65] See DHA 6:463–64.

[66] When this section of the text was reprinted in *Reisebilder I*, the guest concerned was identified as the Duke of Cumberland, who was related to the Prussian royal family through marriage (see DHA 6:451). In the *Anzeiger* version of the article, however, he is simply identified as "eine fremde Herrschaft" (DHA 6:378). Due to a lack of manuscript evidence, it is not clear whether Heine, Schulz, or the censor in Hamm decided not to identify him in the first version of the text.

[67] Instructions issued to Prussian censors in January 1820 forbade praise of the American government. See Kapp, *Die preußische Preßgesetzgebung*, 212.

[68] See DHA 6:366–67. In fact, Heine continued to live in Berlin until early 1823.

[69] For both of these stipulations, see article 2 of the "Preußische Zensur-Verordnung von 18. Oktober 1819," in Huber, *Dokumente zur deutschen Verfassungsgeschichte*, 1:95–98; here 95–96.

4: Smuggling or Stalemate?: Heinrich Heine's *Reise von München nach Genua*

THROUGHOUT THE 1820S, repressive government actions such as those described in *Briefe aus Berlin* continued to stifle political life throughout the German lands. The Carlsbad Decrees were renewed in 1824, and surveillance of universities, persecution of political dissidents, and censorship controls prevented the emergence of any serious threat to the status quo before 1830. The reactionary climate affected Heine directly: officially implemented anti-Semitism led him to become baptized as a Protestant shortly before receiving his doctorate in law in 1825; and when first published in the *Gesellschafter* in 1826, his poetic travelogue *Die Harzreise* suffered severe cuts due to censorship.[1] In January 1826, however, the writer met Julius Campe, the owner of the Hamburg publishing firm Hoffmann und Campe, a specialist in oppositional writings. Campe soon agreed to publish a first volume of Heine's *Reisebilder*, which included a reworked and extended version of *Die Harzreise*. *Reisebilder* I was very successful;[2] and a second, politically more daring, volume of *Reisebilder* appeared in April 1827.[3]

In November 1827, Heine moved to Munich to take up a job offer made to him by the south German publisher Johann Friedrich von Cotta, who wanted him as co-editor of a new political magazine, *Neue allgemeine politische Annalen*. The writer was at first enthusiastic about the project,[4] but soon faced various difficulties. He had trouble obtaining suitable material for the *Annalen*,[5] found the intellectual climate in Munich too reactionary,[6] and had a strained relationship with the journal's other editor, Friedrich Lindner.[7] During this time, Heine also applied for the post of professor of literature at the newly-founded university of Munich, but continued to feel isolated in the city.[8] At the beginning of August 1828, shortly after the suspension of the unsuccessful *Annalen*, he set off on a visit to Italy.

Reise von München nach Genua[9] is based on the first part of that journey. After leaving Munich, Heine traveled through the Austrian Tyrol to Habsburg-occupied northern Italy, where he visited Verona, Brescia, Milan, Pavia, Genoa, Livorno, and Lucca, before arriving in Bagni di Lucca in early September. Few letters remain from this period, but in Bagni di Lucca Heine began to develop notes made during the journey into longer fragments. This process continued during his subsequent extended stay in Florence, and it was from there, on 11 November 1828, that he sent to Cotta the first fourteen chapters of *Reise nach Italien*, which gave an account of his travels from Munich to Trento. These first instalments appeared in one of Cotta's newspapers, the *Morgenblatt für gebildete Stände*, during the first half of December.

Despite this brisk start, almost a year elapsed before the final version of *Reise von München nach Genua* appeared in print. At the same time as the first chapters of *Reise nach Italien* were published in the *Morgenblatt*, Heine returned to Munich, where he discovered that his bid to gain a professorship had failed. Shortly afterwards, he received news that his father, Samson Heine, was seriously ill, but he failed to reach his parents' home in Lüneburg before Samson's death. He stayed with his mother for the next two months; several accounts describe him as deeply affected by the bereavement, and it seems that he ceased writing during this period.[10] At the end of February 1829, Heine returned to Berlin, where he concentrated his attention on *Die Bäder von Lukka*,[11] a humorous work set in Bagni di Lucca. It was only in the middle of May, after moving to the relative solitude of Potsdam to escape distractions, that he finally set about completing the *Reise von München nach Genua*.[12]

Once started, work proceeded swiftly. In June, Heine sent Cotta a second selection of chapters from the text for publication in the *Morgenblatt*; and by the end of September, Campe wrote that *Reisebilder* III was eleven days away from being printed.[13] Publication was delayed, however, by Heine's determination to retaliate against anti-Semitic jibes made about him by Graf August von Platen in his recently-published comedy, *Der romantische Oedipus*.[14] The writer eventually decided that *Die Bäder von Lukka*, which was to appear alongside the *Reise von München nach Genua*, would be the best place for his revenge.[15] Regarding his conflict with Platen as a "Vernichtungskrieg,"[16] the writer then spent much of the autumn working the brutally homophobic Platen polemic into *Die Bäder von Lukka*. *Reisebilder* III, which incorporated *Die Bäder von Lukka* and *Reise von München nach Genua*, finally appeared at the very end of December 1829.

The straightforward title of *Reise von München nach Genua* may appear to place the work within the popular contemporary genre of travelogue.[17] Yet, as mentioned in the previous chapter, Heine's *Reisebilder* works share a distinctive form that deviates in many ways from that of conventional travel writing. Like most of his prose writings, the *Reisebilder* have an open, frequently disjointed structure and combine political engagement with extreme subjectivity.[18] Thus, the text of *Reise von München nach Genua* repeatedly draws attention to Italy's suffering under its Austrian occupiers, but is nevertheless driven along by the subjective interests of its narrator: substantial sections of Heine's real journey are not reported on and the travel account provided is regularly interrupted by digressions, including dreams, reminiscences, fictional encounters, general philosophical and historical reflections, and descriptions of the narrator's state of mind.

The emphasis the *Reisebilder* place on the inner life of their narrator has led to comparisons with Laurence Sterne's novel *A Sentimental Journey through France and Italy* (1768); and their political engagement continues a tradition of critical German travel literature established in the late eighteenth century.[19] Yet despite these influences, the *Reisebilder* were regarded as highly original by Heine's contemporaries. During the 1830s and 1840s, his prose works were hailed by many radicals as art fit for the coming revolutionary era,[20] and widely imitated.[21] However, other commentators — both during Heine's lifetime and since — have been less enthusiastic. According to one recurring judgment, Heine's prose works do not possess the artistic qualities necessary to distinguish them from journalism. This opinion has been supported with reference to the texts' deviance from the demands of classical aesthetics, for example, in their failure to create a self-contained, coherent illusion of an alternative reality.[22]

Such verdicts fail to take into account the unmistakable literary qualities of Heine's *Reisebilder,* which are exemplified by *Reise von München nach Genua*. At several points in the text, for example, Heine plays with various motifs associated with the well-worn German genre of travel writing about Italy. In particular, his parodying of Goethe's *Italienische Reise* suggests a desire to compete with the dominant figure of contemporary German literature.[23] The work also employs the distinctive compositional technique that began to emerge in *Briefe aus Berlin,* using association to unite diverse realms of human experience so that the segments of reality depicted in the work point toward more fundamental, yet unspoken, connections.[24] Finally, other forms of indirect and poetic expression involved in the text's networks of references mean that it is too complex and multilayered to fit comfortably into the category of journalistic writing.[25]

While esoteric forms are used to express subversive messages at several points within *Reise von München nach Genua,*[26] the text also contains many more accessible attacks on contemporary political conditions. The contrast between Italy's glorious classical past and oppressed present, for instance, is one recurrent theme. This anti-Restoration tendency is reinforced by jibes at the Catholic Church, and a provocative comparison between the Prussian state and a slave ship. Finally, an unusually explicit series of chapters set on the battlefield of Marengo express a forceful denunciation of the aristocracy, open approval for the French revolution, rejection of Christianity in favor of a new "Freiheitsreligion" (DHA 7:70), and Heine's notorious self-depiction as a "braver Soldat im Befreyungskriege der Menschheit" (DHA 7:74).

Censorship

The radical content of *Reise von München nach Genua* has led several critics to suggest that the text was unaffected by censorship pressure.[27] After failing to gain the professorship in Munich, so the argument runs, Heine no longer had any reason to fear the authorities' response to his writing. However, although the work's bold political statements may at first appear to support such a conclusion, a closer examination of the circumstances under which the text was written reveals it to be mistaken.

For one thing, the consequences of a ban were serious for both author and publisher. Both faced the prospect of possible police action, and the heavy financial losses suffered by Campe in the event of a prohibition would have damaged Heine's chances of getting his works published in the future.[28] Despite occasional statements from Heine indicating that he would have welcomed the increased publicity aroused by the prohibition of his works,[29] there is substantial evidence that both he and Campe were anxious to avoid such measures. In the weeks before *Reisebilder* II went to the printers, for example, Heine hastily cut several of its more dangerous passages;[30] and on the night before it was published, he set off for England in order to escape the reach of the Prussian authorities. Three and a half years later, in the repressive climate that soon followed the 1830 July Revolution, Heine and Campe were by again alarmed by warnings that the fourth *Reisebilder* volume might face a ban. In a letter to his friend Johann Detmold, of 30 November 1830, Heine wrote that he might have to leave Germany once again following the publication of his new book,[31] and Campe, for his part, hastily made arrangements for the entire print run to be sent away to avoid confiscation.[32]

By contrast, it is significant that Heine's correspondence from the period preceding the publication of *Reisebilder* III betrays no indication that he was expecting government action in connection with the work. While he wrote numerous letters discussing the volume's forthcoming appearance,[33] none mentions the possibility of a ban. The relatively untroubled anticipation of *Reisebilder* III's appearance is consistent with statements from Heine describing his cautious approach to the work's composition. In a letter to Karl Immermann of 17 November 1829, for example, the writer described his forthcoming *Reisebilder* volume as "zahm geschrieben, nicht im mindesten demagogisch, sogar gut russisch, was jetzt so viel ist wie ultrapreußisch."[34] Similarly, a letter to Heine's friend Friederike Robert, originating from the second stage of work on the text, reveals little appetite for risk-taking in the cause of ideology:

> Ach, krank und elend wie ich bin, wie zur Selbstverspottung, beschreibe ich jetzt die glänzendste Zeit meines Lebens [...], wo ich, berauscht vor Uebermuth und Liebesglück, auf den Höhen der Ap-

peninen umherjauchzte, und große, wilde Thaten träumte, wodurch mein Ruhm sich über die ganze Erde verbreite, bis zur fernsten Insel, wo der Schiffer des Abends am Herde von mir erzählen sollte; jetzt, wie bin ich zahm geworden, seit dem Tode meines Vaters! Jetzt möchte ich auf so einer fernen Insel nur das Kätzchen seyn, das am warmen Heerde sitzt und zuhört, wenn von berühmten Thaten erzählt wird.[35]

While Heine's reference to "große, wilde Thaten" here confirms the importance of political themes to the work, the writer's professions of timidity when composing *Reise von München nach Genua* clearly point toward the role of censorship pressure in the work's composition.

Further evidence that *Reise von München nach Genua* was not written with complete disregard for censorship controls is the fact that *Reisebilder* III was tolerated in most German states for several years. The volume was printed at the Conrad-Müller Druckerei in Hamburg and, at twenty-five and a half Bogen, easily exceeded the twenty-Bogen length required to escape pre-publication censorship there.[36] Prussia, whose dominant book market made it a primary concern for most writers,[37] did not take any action against the volume until 1833. In that year, the Prussian government ordered the confiscation of the second editions of the third and fourth *Reisebilder* volumes as part of a crackdown on opposition literature following the July Revolution of 1830.[38]

This delayed response cannot be attributed to difficulties in detecting the book's political messages. Although the Preußisches Oberzensurkollegium was under-resourced,[39] it is hard to imagine that the organization was ignorant of the work's political content. By this time, Heine was well known as an oppositional writer; and while most reviews of *Reisebilder* III were dominated by outrage at the Platen polemic, a significant number addressed the work's ideological content: indeed, in many cases, their reception was positive.[40] Furthermore, a general awareness of the political flavor of the first three volumes of the *Reisebilder* series is clearly implied by the reaction of a commentator in the *Morgenblatt* to the prohibition of the fourth *Reisebilder* book in 1831:

> Eben höre ich, daß die Polizei den Debit des vierten Bandes der Heineschen Reisebilder untersagt hat; eine große Gefälligkeit für den Verleger. Aber konnte noch etwas Stärkeres gesagt werden, als in den drei ersten Bänden? Und damals war man so klug, kein Aufhebens davon zu machen, und sie haben nichts geschadet.[41]

It may at first be difficult to reconcile the overt political engagement of *Reise von München nach Genua* with Heine's professed caution when writing the work and the toleration of *Reisebilder* III by the Prussian authorities. However, as we will see, there is clear evidence that the composition of the work was affected significantly by Heine's desire that it should not be prohibited. Indeed, the following discussion will reveal that the text's presentation of subversive content is consistently shaped by similar principles to those that molded political expression in *Briefe aus Berlin*. For, although *Reise von München nach Genua* is considerably bolder than the earlier work, it too avoids direct threats to the dignity and stability of the German states, and employs a variety of techniques to diminish the vigor and intensity of its critical expression. The result is a text that is openly hostile to the Restoration, but was nevertheless tolerated by the Prussian authorities.

"Das Schlachtfeld von Marengo"

Supposedly prompted by a visit to the battlefield of Marengo,[42] where Napoleon won a decisive victory in his Italian campaign of 1800, chapters 29–31 of *Reise von München nach Genua* contain a sustained discussion of political ideology and unmistakable expressions of opposition to the Restoration. The section begins with the narrator qualifying his admiration for the great military leader. He explains this judgment by referring to Bonaparte's aristocratic allegiances and, above all, to the betrayal of freedom represented by his coup d'état in 1799. The narrator then moves on to the central theme of the chapters, "die Emanzipazion der ganzen Welt," which, he tells us, is the great task of contemporary times. As well as speaking enthusiastically of the efforts made by the French Revolution in working toward this goal, the "Marengo" chapters look forward to the day when humanity is finally emancipated from the influence of the aristocracy and "geistliche Zöllner." As mentioned earlier, the section concludes with Heine's famous proclamation that he desires to be remembered as a "braver Soldat im Befreyungskriege der Menschheit" (DHA 7:68–74).

Although these sentiments are expressed with arresting clarity, signs of restraint become noticeable upon closer examination. The most obvious mark of censorship pressure on these ideologically committed chapters is the absence of any mention of the Restoration, absolutist monarchs, conditions in the German lands, or concrete political issues of the time. Indeed, although the chapter's emphasis on the fight for freedom could be seen as an obvious attack on contemporary German governments, the international character of this struggle, as well as its positioning within the sphere of "Geisterpolitik" (DHA 7:69), serve to shift the focus of this implied attack away from the German states. Only the occasional use of the vague term "Feinde" (DHA 7:72) to denote the enemies of emancipation points toward the existence of other adversaries that Heine refrained from naming. As in *Briefe aus Berlin,* here, too, the writer crafted his subversive utterance in a manner that mitigated its appearance as a threat to the German political establishment.

Evidence confirming the role of censorship pressure — rather than Heine's interests — in the chapters' thematic focus is provided by several peripheral references to the Restoration. Although these are intelligible to moderately attentive readers of the text, none of them identifies its theme explicitly, and all are too brisk or too vague to bring the issue concerned into focus. During the third chapter, for example, reflections on the likely inability of future generations to appreciate the suffering brought about by the Restoration may be heartfelt, but they are also nebulous and insubstantial: "O! sie werden eben so wenig ahnen, wie entsetzlich die Nacht war, in deren Dunkel wir leben mußten, und wie grauenhaft wir zu kämpfen hatten, mit häßlichen Gespenstern, dumpfen Eulen und scheinheiligen Sündern" (DHA 7:74). Similarly, during the second of the three Marengo chapters, it is only a subtle shift in tense that allows the text to hint briefly at the political subjugation within Restoration Europe. Here, Heine refers to the former role of England as a sanctuary for Europeans fleeing despotism and argues that this function has been usurped by America: "[W]ürde auch ganz Europa ein einziger Kerker, so gäbe es jetzt noch immer ein anderes Loch zum Entschlüpfen, das ist Amerika [. . .]" (DHA 7:73). Although the main thrust of this thought is in the conditional, Heine adds on to it as a seemingly frivolous exclamation: "Gottlob! Das Loch ist noch größer als der Kerker selbst" (DHA 7:73). The switch to the indicative within the final sentence allows the passage to imply that the first scenario is not merely a hypothesis. Yet the impact of this sentence that does not mention Europe by name remains severely limited.

To a lesser extent, the intensity of the narrator's enthusiasm for the French Revolution is diminished by similar devices. For, although his admiration for the Revolution is clear, he stops short of praising it explicitly. It is also striking that accounts of revolutionary violence in the Marengo chapters are accompanied by a slight distancing of the narrative voice. One reference to the guillotine avoids specifying those beheaded more precisely than "d[ie]jenigen, die durchaus hervorragen wollten" (DHA 7:70); and the following three lines of a bloodthirsty revolutionary song involve an unexplained interruption of the narrative flow:

Heida! Am Polterabend,
Zerschlug man statt der Töpfe
Aristokratenköpfe. (DHA 7:71)

While such presentation does not limit the intelligibility of Heine's message, it does render it less immediate. Evidence that these techniques were a response to censorship pressure is provided by the use of similar distancing devices in the presentation of revolutionary violence in *Ideen. Das*

Buch Le Grand. In that work, phrases relating to this theme are either given in French or quoted from a school book (DHA 6:191); and despite Heine's fears, *Reisebilder* II, within which *Ideen: Das Buch Le Grand* appears, was tolerated in most of Prussia during the 1820s. Although the meaning of Heine's text is in both cases quite clear, its slightly abstract presentation diminishes its energy and renders it less immediate. Given the shocked reaction of the German reading public to the Jacobin terror that followed the Revolution,[43] such restraint may have been enough to make the texts appear incapable of infecting readers with their revolutionary fervor and thus tolerable in the eyes of the authorities.

The emphasis placed on other elements of Heine's anti-Restoration ideology is also limited in various ways. In many cases, the writer's political sentiments are clearly revealed, but no space is devoted to their promotion. Instead, such opinions frequently occupy a position of secondary importance within another statement. This muted presentation allowed Heine to express his revolutionary ideals without recourse to the gestures of sympathy for the Prussian government that had seemed necessary in *Briefe aus Berlin*. The author's admiration of Napoleon, for example, is expressed within the context of its own qualification: "Ich bitte dich, lieber Leser, halte mich nicht für einen unbedingten Bonapartisten; meine Huldigung gilt nicht den Handlungen, sondern nur dem Genius des Mannes" (DHA 7:68). Later on in the following sentence, this train of thought is continued in a statement that also reveals Heine's commitment to freedom: "Unbedingt liebe ich ihn nur bis zum achtzehnten Brumaire — da verrieth er die Freyheit." Here it is apparently assumed that the reader shares the ideal of freedom and, rather than being advanced for its own sake, the concept is simply employed to explain the narrator's opinion of Bonaparte following his participation in the coup d'état. Similarly, later on in the same chapter, it is in support of Heine's call, "Laßt uns die Franzosen preisen!," that he mentions the nation's progress in the "zwey größten Bedürfnisse der menschlichen Gesellschaft, [. . .] Kochkunst und [. . .] bürgerliche Gleichheit" (DHA 7:70).

Another technique used by Heine to limit the intensity of anti-Restoration passages is the avoidance of provocative vocabulary within particularly energetic sections. During his forceful announcement of the great task of contemporary times, Heine abandons the inflammatory "Freiheit" in favor of "Emanzipation," which is more closely associated with the emancipation of the peasants from feudal bonds.[44] When we read of the author's eagerness for his enemies to be beaten, surrounding references to "Feudalismus," "Adlige in Siam," and "die englische Nobility" strongly indicate that he has the aristocracy in mind. Yet Heine refrains twice from identifying the nobility as the intended recipients of this "Prügel" (DHA 7:72). While the author of *Reise von München nach Genua* generally makes little effort to disguise his hostility toward the aristocracy, he evidently thought it wise to avoid making such aggressive thoughts explicit.

Other Chapters

Due to their sustained political focus and open enthusiasm for revolution, the "Marengo" chapters stand out from the rest of the *Reise von München nach Genua;* and, as suggested earlier, their audacity has been attributed to the period of their composition: namely, after Heine had failed to obtain the professorship in Munich.[45] Yet, although the chapters written during that period are undeniably bolder than those composed in Italy, it is important not to exaggerate the gulf between the Marengo section and the rest of the work. For one thing, we have seen that chapters 29 to 31 show clear signs of having been shaped by censorship pressure. Furthermore, these chapters were not the only ones written after Heine's Munich disappointment. The bulk of the work on chapters 3 and 17–33, the final version of chapters 9 and 10, and a substantial expansion to chapter 2 were all completed during his two-month stay in Potsdam from May to July 1829.[46] In addition, as we will see, the rest of the work also contains many overt expressions of opposition to the Restoration. The principles shaping such passages clearly reflect the concerns that molded the Marengo chapters. Here too, Heine communicates his radical ideology effectively while using a variety of techniques to lessen the vigor with which it is expressed. He also mounts more focused attacks on contemporary German governments, although — as in the Marengo chapters — such messages are advanced with particular caution.

Incidental Presentation

One similarity between chapters 29 to 31 and the rest of *Reise von München nach Genua* is Heine's incidental presentation of oppositional thought. In chapter 26, for example, the writer clearly reveals his enthusiasm for political liberty. As in the Marengo chapters, however, such principles are not linked to contemporary political issues and do not form the main focus of the statements within which they appear. Instead, the narrator uses these ideals to praise the authors of two liberal pieces of Italian travel literature. "Frau v. Morgan," the Irish-born writer of the Austria-critical *Italien,* is lauded as a "flatternde [. . .] Nachtigall der Freyheit," for instance, and "Frau von Staël," the author of *Corinne ou L'Italie,* is celebrated in similarly emphatic terms:[47]

> Eben so, wie männiglich bekannt ist, war Frau v. Staël eine liebenswürdige Marketenderinn im Heer der Liberalen, und lief muthig durch

die Reihen der Kämpfenden mit ihrem Enthusiasmusfäßchen, und stärkte die Müden, und focht selber mit, besser als die Besten. (62)

Although unmistakable in their ideological commitment, such statements do not grant any space for the promotion of such ideals in their own right. The central aim of the sentence appears to be the celebration of two fellow writers, and the emphasis granted to Heine's political principles is diminished as a result.

Vocabulary

The intensity of critical utterance in *Reise von München nach Genua* is also lowered by Heine's restrained use of vocabulary. Unlike *Briefe aus Berlin*, the later work includes few examples of vocabulary and phrasing aligned with government sympathies, and its anti-Restoration content is no longer accompanied by signals of authorial nonchalance. Here too, however, subversive comment is delivered in a predominantly enthusiastic, good-humored tone,[48] which renders it considerably less inflammatory. Evidence confirming the role of censorship in generating this tone is provided by early manuscripts revealing that Heine repeatedly discarded aggressive and provocative language when composing dangerous sections within *Reise von München nach Genua*.

The clearest examples of this can be found in passages relating to two important allies of the Restoration: the nobility and the Catholic Church. As we will see, the main chapters of *Reise von München nach Genua* advance far more substantial criticisms of the aristocracy than either the "Marengo" section or *Briefe aus Berlin*. However, these attacks are expressed in very general terms and make no reference to specific social realities, such as the privileges still enjoyed by aristocrats in the German lands at that time. Their confinement to isolated sentences diminishes their impact further, as does — as already indicated — Heine's careful use of language.

A comparison between the first and final versions of part of a discussion of Tyrolean servility in chapter 11 demonstrates the linguistic self-restraint exercised by Heine. While both forms of the passage deliver the same unflattering diagnosis of aristocratic psychology, the phrasing of the first draft highlights the gap between the nobility and the plebeians:

> [D]er starrste Aristokrat liebt es zuweilen mit dem Plebs [. . .] auf du u[nd] du zu konversiren wenn er nur sicher ist, daß dieser nie die Kluft vergißt, die Gott selbst zwischen die verschiedenen Stände gestiftet. (DHA 7:685)

The final version of this sentence, on the other hand, delivers exactly the same accusation of aristocratic condescension, but uses a significantly calmer tone. Although the message of the following statement is clear, Heine manages to avoid employing any term more negative than the moderate "starrsten":

> [D]ie starrsten Aristokraten sind froh, wenn sie Gelegenheit finden zur Herablassung, denn dadurch eben fühlen sie, wie hoch sie gestellt sind. (DHA 7:35)

Later on, we read that during his stay in Trento, the author dreamt that the city was inhabited only by flowers, and his account of the city's new society includes a description of its nobility. In an early draft of the flower chapter, the negative aspect of social divisions is emphasized by a description of the aristocratic lily nagging some "elender Graspöbel" (DHA 7:770). This aggressive language was removed from the final draft of the passage, which nevertheless effectively conveys an impression of aristocratic snobbery. Here, Heine writes of "jene Liljen, die nicht arbeiten und nicht spinnen und sich doch eben so prächtig dünken wie König Salomon in all seiner Herrlichkeit" (DHA 7:51).

The same combination of open disrespect and linguistic restraint characterizes Heine's treatment of the Catholic Church in *Reise von München nach Genua*. The text is clearly blasphemous: in addition to predicting the end of Christianity (DHA 7:75) and depicting a priest in a decidedly unflattering light (DHA 7:32), it also includes a passage in which the narrator compares himself with the redeemer (DHA 7:26). The first draft of this comparison involved the words "gekreuzigter Heiland," although Heine removed them from the manuscript, evidently realizing the provocation that such formulation would cause (DHA 7:659). Yet even in the final version, the content of this sentence is essentially unchanged. Although the explicit reference to the redeemer is removed, the adoption of his role — that of suffering for the sins of humanity — remains clear; and it is even followed by a clever, thinly veiled reference to the pleasures afforded by sinning: "ich leide für das Heil des ganzen Menschengeschlechts, ich büße dessen Sünden, aber ich genieße sie auch" (DHA 7:26).

A similar pattern is revealed by the composition of chapter 15, which describes the narrator's visit to the cathedral in Trento. At several points within the first draft of this chapter, Heine first wrote the provocative phrase "wollüstiger Andacht," but then crossed it out (DHA 7:712–14). This restraint did not prevent him from skillfully creating a cathedral scene with unmistakable sensual overtones, however. The narrator's account of his visit to the cathedral contains a report of how "große katholische Augen sahen mich an, halb neugierig, halb liebwillig, und mochten mir wohl rathen, mich ebenfalls hinzustrecken und Seelensieste zu halten." Then, the following paragraph describes Madonnas nodding forgiveness, "sogar, wenn man ihre eignen holden Züge in die sündigen Gedanken verflochten hat." The blasphemous character of the scene is finally sealed by a reference to a confessional chair as "ein brauner Nothstuhl des Gewissens" (DHA 7:42). Although the suppression of some religious key words may have disguised these thoughts from some readers, they are still clearly intelligible to those reading the text with a moderate degree of attention. Heine's avoidance of aggressive and provocative language when attacking both the nobility and the Catholic Church thus does not conceal such assaults from his readers, but it does ensure that they are delivered in a calm and controlled tone.

The Restoration

Due to close links between the aristocracy, Catholic Church, and Restoration, Heine's criticisms of the first two institutions represented an implied attack on the contemporary social and political order. As in *Briefe aus Berlin*, however, direct discussion of the Restoration itself was clearly more problematic. Like the "Marengo" chapters, the rest of the work combines a clear anti-Restoration tendency with a noticeable silence regarding the contemporary conditions and rulers of the German lands. Instead, Heine used indirect methods to convey his rejection of the Restoration as a whole.

In chapter 9, for example, Heine subtly draws attention to the link between nobility, church, and Restoration governments. Here, the narrator describes the unappealing behavior of an aristocrat and a clergyman taking a meal together at an inn. After fondling their waitress and embarrassing her with crude jokes, the two men are finally forced into propriety when she starts serving them with a young child in her arms. Their conversation then takes a political turn, which is related with derision: "[B]eide schwatzten jetzt das gewöhnliche Geschwätz von der großen Verschwörung gegen Thron und Altar, [. . .] und reichten sich mehrmals die heiligen Allianzhände" (DHA 7:32). The terms in which this conversation is described make it clear that the two men are intended to stand for the Restoration as a whole. This is achieved first by reporting their fears of a conspiracy against the throne, and then by the description of their "heiligen Allianzhände," which aligns them with the reactionary states of Russia, Prussia, and Austria. As a result, Heine's unflattering description of the priest and the aristocrat functions as an indirect, yet relatively open, expression of hostility toward the Restoration.

Heine's nervousness about addressing the question of absolutism directly, on the other hand, is underlined by changes made to an early draft of chapter 8. Here, the narrator tells the story of the English tourists in the Hofkirche in Innsbruck who read their guidebook the wrong way round. As a result, they become puzzled to see a statue of Rudoph von Habsburg apparently wearing women's clothes, and Queen Maria seemingly wearing iron trousers and a long beard. The narrator's response, we read, is to suggest to his fellow tourists that the personages concerned may have wanted to be depicted in this bizarre fashion. He then reflects, "So könne es ja dem jetzigen Kaiser einfallen, sich in einem Reifrock oder gar in Windeln gießen zu lassen" (DHA 7:30), and in an early draft continues with the words, "in absolut monarchistischen Staaten kann sich der Landesherr" (DHA 7:676), before breaking off and beginning the thought again. The absence of these words in the final version makes it clear that Heine did not want to risk referring to contemporary political forms directly.

Repressive Actions

As suggested by both the "Marengo" chapters and *Briefe aus Berlin*, the difficulty of discussing the Restoration as a whole extended to the criticism of contemporary rulers. Yet, while *Reise von München nach Genua* does not contain any explicit attacks on German governments, it uses a variety of techniques to imply negative judgments. One of these is to draw attention to repressive state deeds. Although it is always clear from the context which government is responsible for the measures in question, the authorities concerned are never named directly. As in *Briefe aus Berlin*, not presenting the state as a focus for dissatisfaction allows Heine to express his disapproval of government policies.

The importance of this strategy is suggested by successive versions of the report, in chapter 7, that Immermann's *Das Trauerspiel in Tyrol* is prohibited in the Tyrol. While the first draft of the passage states that the Austrian government banned the book (DHA 7:665), in *Reisebilder* III we simply read that "*Das Trauerspiel in Tyrol* [ist] in Tyrol verboten" (DHA 7:27). It is clear that, as the local rulers, the Austrian government must have been responsible for the ban. However, the fact that they are not identified allows Heine to call into question the efficacy of this action. In addition to stating his amusement at the prohibition, he also quotes Moses Moser's ironic acknowledgment of the popularity such measures could bring: "Die Regierung hätte aber das Buch gar nicht zu verbieten brauchen, es wäre dennoch gelesen worden" (DHA 7:27). Later on, by failing to mention the agents of their subjection, Heine is able to highlight the political repression suffered by the Italians, when he explains — "Dem armen geknechteten Italien ist ja das Sprechen verboten" (DHA 7:49).

This manner of presentation played an important role in the rewriting of an extremely dangerous section of chapter 10. The first draft of the chapter, which deals with promises made by rulers to their subjects during the wars of liberation and then later broken, was composed in Italy. This early draft was too controversial for publication in the *Morgenblatt,* from which it was simply omitted,[49] and had to be rewritten prior to its inclusion in *Reisebilder* III. The chapter refers to the successful Tyrolean uprising against Bavarian and French rule in 1805. Although led by the nationalist hero, Andreas Hofer, the rebellion was orchestrated by Austria, to whose rule the region consequently returned.[50] Heine's first sketch for the chapter begins with the direct question, "Hat Oestreich seine V[er]-sprech[ung]en gegen Tyrol gehalten?" (DHA 7:326). One of the few changes made to this sketch prior to its inclusion in *Reisebilder* III, however, involved obscuring the role of Austria in the Tyroleans' broken promises: "Die armen Tyroler haben nemlich auch allerley Erfahrungen machen müssen, und wenn man sie jetzt fragt, ob sie, zum Lohne ihrer Treue, Alles erlangt, was man ihnen in der Noth versprochen [. . .]" (DHA 7:33). The masterful phrasing of this final version does not in any way reduce the gravity of the betrayal, and a reference to the Kaiser later on in the sentence serves as a reminder of the Austrian ruler's involvement in this offense. Nevertheless, the replacement of "Oestreich" with "man" served to blur the Austrian government's role sufficiently for this controversial issue to be included in *Reisebilder* III. Although none of these passages conceal anything from the readers, Heine, by omitting to name the states in question, directs attention away from them, so that they are no longer present as a focus for discontent.

Links

Heine was also concerned not to make other critical links explicit. Yet, while the text does not articulate such connections directly, it frequently provides us with ample information to detect them ourselves. The role of censorship considerations in encouraging Heine to demand such active reading is demonstrated by another comparison between the earlier and later versions of chapter 10. Both drafts include the story of a slave ship in a fierce storm. Realizing the danger that he and his ship are in, the captain promises the slaves in his hold freedom if they help him to guide the ship through the storm. They do so, but as soon as the storm is over, the slaves are led down to the hold, where they are once again chained up as prisoners.

In the first version of the chapter, this story is clearly introduced as an allegory for the Prussian king's failure to grant his subjects a constitution following the wars of liberation. After relating the Tyroleans' understanding for Austria's broken promises, the text leads into the slave ship allegory with a number of specific references to other contemporary rulers and promises:

> Die Leute mögen mit Recht zufrieden seyn, Oestreichs Capitän war nicht in so große[r] Noth, wie seine Collegen und hat nicht so großes versprochen, nicht Unbedingtes, nicht Himmel und göttliche Freyheit. Anders verhält es sich mit anderen Leuten und mit anderen Schiffen. Ich kenne ein Sklavenschiff [. . .]. (DHA 7:326)

In *Reisebilder* III, on the other hand, this explicit link is replaced by a more general, associative introduction:

> Tröstet Euch, arme Schelme! Ihr seyd nicht die Einzigen, denen etwas versprochen worden. Passirt es doch oft auf großen Sklavenschiffen [. . .]. (DHA 7:33)

Yet although this second, publishable version does not articulate any direct connection between the slave ship allegory and the Prussian constitution, Heine's skillful composition of the section means that the link remains obvious enough. Merely the placing of the passage — straight after a discussion of promises made to the Tyroleans by the Austrian emperor and then broken — provides a strong hint of its real meaning. Further interpretative help is provided by the continuation of the passage. Directly after the slave ship paragraph, we read one of Horace's odes, which, as we are reminded by the narrator, compares the state with a ship. We also learn that, upon hearing news of the Battle of Leipzig, the narrator's schoolteacher shook his head in resignation, a gesture that receives the commentary, "Jetzt weiß ich was dieses Schütteln bedeutete [. . .]" (DHA 7:34).

The Prussian king's broken promise of a constitution remained a sensitive issue throughout the Restoration period.[51] After so many hints from Heine, it is therefore unlikely that he expected the meaning of the slave ship allegory to escape the attention of censorship authorities. Indeed, as this passage was one of the few mentioned by the Preussisches Zensurkollegium when justifying their 1833 ban of the work,[52] it is hard to imagine that they missed it the first time round. Nevertheless, although the final version of the slave ship story remains accessible, without an introduction that directly links it to the Prussian king's promise of a constitution, it becomes less sharply focused and as a result, less provocative.

Similar principles apply to Heine's portrayal of the effects of Austrian occupation on the Italians. *Reise von München nach Genua* contains many clear references to the oppression and hardship suffered by the Italians. Toward the end of chapter 27, for example, we read that "Der leidende Gesichtsausdruck wird bey den Italienern am sichbarsten, wenn man mit ihnen vom Unglück ihres Vaterlandes spricht" (DHA 7:65). The political dimension of this suffering is made clear by Heine's explanation of the esoteric meaning of the Opera Buffa, which, we are told, expresses the Italians' "Groll gegen fremde Herrschaft, [. . .] Begeisterung für die Freyheit, [. . .] Wahnsinn über das Gefühl der Ohnmacht [. . .]" (DHA 7:49). Although Heine avoids using inflammatory words such as *Besatzer,* the identity of this "fremde Herrschaft" is perfectly clear: references to Austrian soldiers punctuate his descriptions of Italian cityscapes. However, the absence of a directly articulated link between the Austrians' presence and the oppression suffered by the Italians renders this connection less prominent. While the text clearly reveals the harmful effects of Austrian occupation, it stops short of announcing them explicitly.

Indeed, Heine's presentation of the Austrian occupation exemplifies — even more than does the treatment of freedom and inequality in *Briefe aus Berlin* — his technique of using different aspects and levels of reality to point toward a central precept. As already suggested, *Reise von München nach Genua* describes diverse manifestations of the repressive Austrian occupation and includes metonymic representations of the same relationship in his text.[53] As a result, the reader is confronted with the reality of Austrian rule in Italy in a wide range of spheres. This innovative literary strategy compensates — at least partially — for the impossibility of condemning the occupation directly and provides further evidence of how one of the distinctive features of Heine's *Reisebilder* prose[54] offered a way of circumventing censorship controls. Although the writer is unable to elucidate the destructive influence of the Austrians in Italy, he provides a description of reality that leads his readers to an awareness of the issue.

Separation

In both of the previous examples, the intensity of Heine's critical messages is further reduced by the fragmentation of their constituent elements and by the dispersal of these elements over a longer section of text. In the case of the slave ship allegory in chapter 10, for example, the concise two-sentence introduction linking this passage with German rulers in the first version (DHA 7:326) is replaced by a series of hints that are scattered over several paragraphs in *Reisebilder* III (DHA 7:33–34). On a larger scale, a few pages separate each reference to Italy's oppression from the nearest description of Austrian soldiers.

A conscious effort to limit the concentration of sensitive information is also indicated by the composition of a section in chapter 27 which had extremely threatening implications for the Austrian government. This passage begins by reporting that the state of their country is "die schmerzlichste Wunde in der Brust der Italiener." We then go on to read Heine's report of the observations of a British companion: "Einer meiner Briten hielt die Italiener für politisch indifferent, weil sie gleichgültig zuzuhören schienen, wenn wir Fremde über die katholische Emanzipazion und den Türkenkrieg politisierten [. . .]" (DHA 7:65). The story continues with an account of how this same man had confronted an Italian with his compatriots' alleged political indifference. The accusation, however, was rejected by the man concerned with reference to the Italians' passionate reaction to music:

> Ach! Seufzte er hinzu, Italien sitzt elegisch träumend auf seinen Ruinen, und wenn es dann manchmal bey der Melodie irgend eines Liedes plötzlich erwacht und stürmisch emporspringt, so gilt diese Begeisterung nicht dem Liede selbst sondern vielmehr den alten Erinnerungen und Gefühlen, die das Lied ebenfalls geweckt hat. (DHA 7:65)

Since this passage is used to refute an accusation of political indifference, it follows that the Italians' enthusiasm for music is a result of their political fervor. And given the revolutionary terms in which this excitement is described — "erwacht and stürmisch emporspringt" — as well as the Italians' sensitivity to the unhappy state of their homeland, the rebellious intent of this fervor is clear.

The logic of the passage clearly suggests a significant threat to Austrian authority in Italy. However, Heine's literary virtuosity enables the stages of the argument that lead to such a conclusion to be kept far apart. The only explicit reference to the "Unglück" of the Italians' "Vaterland" comes four lines before the accusation of political indifference. That insinuation, in turn, is followed by two lines putting the encounter into context, before being rephrased in a manner that makes no reference to politics — "Ihr Italiener [. . .] scheint für alles abgestorben zu seyn, außer für Musik, und nur noch diese vermag Euch zu begeistern" (DHA 7:65). It is only then — seventy-six words after the original accusation — that we read of the real significance of the Italians' enthusiasm for music.

In chapter 32, the same considerations shaped the intricate construction of Heine's announcement of the end of the Catholic Church. While resting in a Franciscan monastery, the narrator reflects upon the religious buildings he has seen during his travels. At first, he appears to admire the dedication of all of those who built these structures, knowing that they would not be completed for several generations to come. He then uses a description of the builders' beliefs to equate the construction of such structures with the continuity of the Catholic Church: "alle im festen Glauben an die Ewigkeit der katholischen Religion und im festen Vertrauen auf die gleiche Denkweise der folgenden Geschlechter, die weiter bauen würden, wo die Vorfahren aufgehört" (DHA 7:75).

In the following paragraph, the narrator expresses the wish that such pious souls should rest in peace, especially those who had worked on religious buildings that were never completed. It is only at the end of the paragraph that he remarks that, should they wake up, this latter group would realize that their lives had been "nutzlos [. . .] und dumm," before suggesting more forcefully the implications of such uncompleted structures for the Catholic faith: "So spricht die jetzige neue Zeit, die eine andere Aufgabe hat, einen anderen Glauben" (DHA 7:75). Despite the clear logic of this passage, it is striking that the announcement of a new faith comes a full thirteen lines and two paragraphs after the last mention of the Catholic religion, which, we are told, it is replacing. When composing this chapter, Heine left a safe distance between the old faith in the permanence of the Catholic Church and announcement of the new beliefs that belong to contemporary times. While his predictions of the end of Christianity remain intelligible, their vigor and intensity is considerably limited by this diluted presentation.

The influence of this consideration can also be detected in the formulation of some of Heine's longer subversive sentences. In such statements, critical information is gradually introduced in measured dosages throughout a series of clauses, so that the concentration of dangerous terms is limited. As a result, the pace of communication is slowed down, and in some cases, the dangerous message is only revealed after several clauses when all of its constituent parts can be pieced together. This technique is exemplified by the following prediction of aristocratic decline:

> Auch in Betreff des Adels werden wir im Laufe einiger Zeit die Erfahrung machen, daß die *bonne société* aufhören wird, die *bonne société* zu sein, sobald der gute Bürgersmann nicht mehr die Güte hat, sie für die *bonne société* zu halten. (DHA 7:31)

Here, Heine's carefully measured expression reduces the sentence's energy and enables him to avoid the emotive vocabulary of dependence and downfall in favor of the more sedate "aufhören" and "halten." In addition, using a large number of clauses means that Heine can replace sensitive keywords with less striking alternatives — in this case "Adel" with *bonne société* — at the most critical points in his sentence. Consequently, the explicit mention of nobility is kept far apart from the announcement of its dependence on common citizens.

Conclusion

Until now, research into the influence of censorship on Heine's literary work has concentrated on his efforts to conceal subversive content from the censors; and in particular, serious attention has been given to the search for hidden layers of meaning within his texts.[55] Some of these studies have yielded important interpretative insights, but in general this approach has been accompanied by a neglect of other ways in which state censorship determined the formulation of Heine's critical utterance. As this chapter has shown, the version of *Reise von München nach Genua* published in *Reisebilder* III openly expresses many subversive ideas, including a commitment to the principles of political radicalism, criticisms of the nobility, enthusiasm for the French revolution, disrespect for the Catholic Church, and an obvious disdain for the repressive actions of the Austrian army in Italy. Given the accessibility of these messages, it is hard to imagine that the Prussian Oberzensurkollegium — under-resourced though it may have been — was not aware of them. As we have seen, the political content of *Reisebilder* III was remarked upon in several contemporary reviews, and one imagines that Heine's notoriety as an oppositional writer would have made the screening of his works a priority for censorship authorities.

While the initial toleration of *Reisebilder* III in Prussia may therefore appear puzzling, it is also clear that prohibition was not the automatic response of the authorities to all oppositional writings. In 1827, for example, the revolutionary character of Heine's *Ideen: Das Buch Le Grand* was brought to the attention of the Oberzensurkollegium, but despite this knowledge, its members decided against a ban of the *Reisebilder* II volume within which it was published.[56] This policy can be linked to the widespread awareness that prohibition could increase public interest in literary writings. The threat posed by subversive volumes had therefore to be weighed against the risk of drawing additional attention to them through a ban.

Indeed, in the case of *Reise von München nach Genua*, one imagines that the risks associated with tolerating the work in Prussia were relatively low due to the principal targets of its critical messages. As we have seen, much of these are directed against the Catholic Church and the Austrian occupation of northern Italy, neither of which were closely linked with the Prussian government. We also know from the chapter on *Scherz, Satire, Ironie und tiefere Bedeutung* that the Prussian authorities did not always live up to their pledge to protect the Catholic Church;[57] moreover, one study of censorship in Restoration Austria reports the Austrian authorities' view that Prussian censorship failed to protect the Catholic Church adequately.[58] Given these tendencies, it is possible that the Austrian occupation of northern Italy was considered a similarly remote concern.

In addition, one imagines the threat posed by *Reise von München nach Genua* to the Prussian political establishment appeared lower due to the manner in which Heine expressed the critical thoughts contained within the work: as we have seen, these were consistently communicated in a fashion that limited their vigor and intensity, and, consequently, their propagandist potential. Indeed, while the text is considerably bolder than *Briefe aus Berlin*, the open dissent contained within it is constrained by similar principles as those that molded the articulation of subversion in the earlier text. The most obvious example is Heine's consistent avoidance of both direct attacks on contemporary states and the explicit discussion of different forms of government. It is striking that, in *Reise von München nach Genua,* the writer's implied criticisms of state actions are kept well apart from the bold proclamation of his political ideals in the "Marengo" chapters. Similarly, the work's few accessible references to the Restoration itself are both brief and vague. While conveying unmistakable hostility, they offer only a blurred glimpse of Heine's sentiments.

As with *Briefe aus Berlin,* the impossibility of providing explicit, sustained discussion of many other issues, too, is strongly suggested by the techniques employed by the writer to prevent his most critical messages from coming into sharp focus. These include the incidental presentation of ideological convictions, the distancing of the narrative voice, and the withholding of argumentative links. In such cases, Heine provides enough information to enable the comprehension of subversive meanings, but the implications of the text's content are not made explicit. The result is an intricate, multilayered text that encourages an active mode of associative reading, but lacks the intensity and immediacy common to most forms of political agitation.

This combination of diminished propagandist potential and increased expressive virtuosity is also achieved by other facets of Heine's response to censorship pressure. When composing *Reise von München nach Genua,* the writer no longer felt the need to include within his critical passages signals of authorial indifference or vocabulary aligned with government sympathies, as in *Briefe in Berlin.* However, his avoidance of aggressive vocabulary and sensitive religious key words in explicitly subversive passages both softens the mood of such sections and results in their replacement by more subtle and skillful phrasing. Similarly, the separation of subversive elements by more innocuous material slows down the pace of communication and decreases the intensity of Heine's critical messages, while at the same time necessitating sophisticated and imaginative patterns of textual development. While none of these responses to censorship pressure obscured oppositional content in *Reise von München nach Genua* from its readers, they had a decisive impact on the text's tone, precision, and vigor. The result is a complex and fascinating literary work that communicates opposition to restoration politics effectively but was not threatening enough to provoke an immediate ban.

Notes

[1] See Heinrich Heine, *Historisch-kritische Gesamtausgabe der Werke,* 6:529–30 (edition subsequently cited as DHA).

[2] See DHA 6:533–39.

[3] See DHA 6:714.

[4] Heinrich Heine, *Werke, Briefwechsel, Lebenszeugnisse: Säkularausgabe*, ed. Nationale Forschungs- und Gedenkstätten der klassischen deutschen Literatur in Weimar und Centre National de la Recherche Scientifique in Paris, 27 vols. to date (Berlin and Paris: Akademie Verlag and Editions du CNRS, 1970 ff.), vol. 20, ed. Fritz Eisner, 1970, 315 (edition subsequently cited as HSA).

[5] See HSA 20:329.

[6] See HSA 20:331.

[7] Werner, *Begegnungen mit Heine*, 1:160–63.

[8] HSA 20:319.

[9] DHA 7:13–80.

[10] Werner, *Begnungen mit Heine*, 1:172–73.

[11] See DHA 7:604.

[12] HSA 20:358.

[13] Werner, *Begegnungen mit Heine*, 1:184.

[14] August von Platen, *Sämtliche Werke: Historisch-kritische Ausgabe mit Einschluß des handschriftlichen Nachlasses*, eds. Max Koch and Erich Petzet, 12 vols. (Hildesheim: Georg Olms, 1969), 10:89–176.

[15] See DHA 7:610–11.

[16] See Heine's letter to Karl Immermann from 26 December 1829, HSA 20:372–74.

[17] Travel literature was frequently used to provide an innocuous cover for political material during the Restoration period. See Wulf Wülfing, "Reiseliteratur," in *Deutsche Literatur: Eine Sozialgeschichte*, ed. Horst Albert Glaser, 10 vols. (Reinbek: Rowohlt, 1980–97), vol. 6, *Vormärz. Biedermeier, Junges Deutschland, Demokraten. 1815–1848*, ed. Bernd Witte, 1980, 180–94; here 183.

[18] For a detailed analysis of the form and structure of *Reise von München nach Genua*, see Grubačić, *Heines Erzählprosa*, 25–40.

[19] For more details of these influences, see Karol Sauerland, "Gattungsgeschichtliche Reflexionen zu Heine's *Reisebildern*," in *Zu Heinrich Heine*, eds. Luciano Zagari and Paulo Chiarini (Stuttgart: Klett, 1981), 79–88.

[20] See comments of Arnold Ruge, Georg Herwegh, and Ludolf Wienbarg quoted in Wolfgang Preisendanz, "Der Funktionsübergang von Dichtung und Publizistik," in *Heinrich Heine: Werkstrukturen und Epochenbezüge*, 2nd ed. (Munich: Fink, 1983), 21–68; here 21–23.

[21] See Kortländer, *Heinrich Heine*, 147.

[22] See Preisendanz, "Der Funktionsübergang von Dichtung und Publizistik," 25–28.

[23] For details of these influences, see Norbert Altenhofer, *Die verlorene Augensprache: über Heinrich Heine* (Leipzig: Insel, 1993), 233–55; Stefan Oswald, "Heinrich Heine: *Reise von München nach Genua:* Ironisierung eines Genres," in *Italienbilder: Beiträge zur Wandlung der deutschen Italienfassung 1770–1840*, ed.

Stefan Oswald (Heidelberg: Winter, 1985), 136–142; and Michael Werner, "Heine's *Reise von München nach Genua* im Lichte ihrer Quellen," *Heine-Jahrbuch* 14 (1975): 24–46. On the influence of Goethe specifically: Hanna Spencer, *Dichter, Denker, Journalist: Studien zum Werk Heinrich Heines* (Bern: Lang, 1977), 37–51.

[24] Cf. Preisendanz, "Der Funktionsübergang von Dichtung und Publizistik," 41.

[25] Cf. Preisendanz, "Der Funktionsübergang von Dichtung und Publizistik," 66.

[26] See, for example, Anglade, "Die Engländer in der Hofkirche," 415–34.

[27] See, for example, Stein, "'Prototyp einer Denk- und Schreibweise,'" 50–65; here 60.

[28] As suggested earlier, Campe's skill in publishing oppositional writings was unusual at the time. See Kortländer, *Heinrich Heine*, 35.

[29] See, for example, Campe's annoyed report of Heine's reaction to the prohibition of *Reisebilder* II in the Prussian Rhineland province, in Werner, *Begegnungen mit Heine: Berichte der Zeitgenossen 1797–1846*, 1:157.

[30] See DHA 6:787.

[31] HSA 20:424.

[32] See DHA 7:1440–41.

[33] See, for example, his letters to Julius Campe of 25 November 1829 (HSA 20:368–69); to Karl Immermann of 26 December 1829 (HSA 20:372–74); to Friederike Robert of 26 December 1829 (HSA 20:375); and to Moses Moser from 30 December 1829 (HSA 20:376–77).

[34] HSA 20:367.

[35] HSA 20:358–59.

[36] See DHA 7:547–49.

[37] As mentioned in the introduction, it has also been shown that Prussia's political importance enabled it to exert considerable pressure on censorship policy in other German states. For details of Prussian influence on censorship policy in Hamburg see Kramer, *Die Zensur in Hamburg 1819 bis 1848*, 247–53; and for information on Prussia's influence on censorship in Hesse, see Ohles, *Germany's Rude Awakening*, 105–7.

[38] See DHA 7:1465–66.

[39] See Kapp, "Die preußische Preßgesetzgebung unter Friedrich Wilhelm III.," 6:185–249; here 205–6.

[40] For reviews that welcome Heine's political engagement, see *Heinrich Heines Werk im Urteil seiner Zeitgenossen*, eds. Eberhard Galley and Alfred Estermann, 6 vols. (Hamburg: Hoffmann und Campe, 1985), 2:361, 401, 405–7, 411–15, and 417–19.

[41] Galley and Estermann, *Heinrich Heines Werk*, 2:39–40.

[42] Michael Werner has shown that this visit was almost certainly fictitious. See Werner, "Heine's *Reise von München nach Genua* im Lichte ihrer Quellen," 39.

[43] See Nipperdey, *Deutsche Geschichte*, 287–88.

⁴⁴ Most German governments tried to encourage this process during the first half of the nineteenth century. For more details, see Nipperdey, *Deutsche Geschichte*, 160–63.

⁴⁵ See Eberhard Galley, "Politische Aspekte in Heines italienischen Reisebildern," in *Internationaler Heine-Kongreß Düsseldorf 1972*, ed. Manfred Windfuhr (Hamburg: Hoffmann und Campe, 1973), 386–98; here 389.

⁴⁶ See DHA 7:603–10.

⁴⁷ This praise for Mme de Staël may seem odd, given Heine's later attacks on her in *Die Romantische Schule* (DHA 8:123–243). However, Heine also praises *Corinne ou L'Italie* in letters to Moses Moser (HSA 20:129) and Ludwig Robert (HSA 20:125). The enthusiasm expressed here can be attributed to the novel's condemnation of the political repression suffered by the Italians (see Werner, "Heines Reise von München nach Genua," 31–32).

⁴⁸ The sensitivity of some Restoration newspaper censors to tone has been noted in Siemann, "Ideenschmuggel," 102.

⁴⁹ See DHA 7:594–95, which, along with DHA 7:610–11, gives examples of specific phrases that were either removed or replaced by less offensive alternatives in the *Morgenblatt* articles. Some of these changes were evidently implemented by Heine, but in other cases, the journal's editors may have been responsible. There are no indications that any sections of the text were subsequently removed or altered by the censors (see also "Lesarten," DHA 7:634–820).

⁵⁰ See Nipperdey, *Deutsche Geschichte*, 24–25.

⁵¹ See Nipperdey, *Deutsche Geschichte*, 397–98.

⁵² See DHA 7:1466.

⁵³ As Heine describes passing the mountains that mark the beginning of Italy, for example, he writes how "über dem Hause selbst ragten hinten die hohen Berge, deren Schneegipfel die Sonne beschien, daß sie aussahen wie eine Schutzwache von Riesen mit blanken Helmen auf den Häuptern" (DHA 7:39).

⁵⁴ Cf. Grubačić, *Heines Erzählprosa*, 31.

⁵⁵ See, for example, Norbert Altenhofer, *Harzreise in die Zeit: Zum Funktionszusammenhang von Traum, Witz und Zensur in Heines früher Prosa* (Dusseldorf: Heinrich-Heine-Gesellschaft, 1972); Anglade, "Die Engländer in der Hofkirche," 415–34; Grözinger, "Die 'doppelte Buchhaltung,'" 65–83.

⁵⁶ See DHA 6:715–16.

⁵⁷ The Prussian "Allerhöchste Kabinettsorder" of 28 December 1824 includes an article that expressly forbids all "unanständige, zur Vertheidigung der eigenen oder ruhigen Widerlegung entgegen gesetzter Meinungen nicht unmittelbar gehörende, verletzende Angriffe auf andere Glaubens-parteien." For the full text of this order, see *Preussische Gesetz-Sammlung 1824* (Berlin: Staatsministerium, 1824), 2–3.

⁵⁸ See Marx, "Die amtlichen Verbotslisten," 11:412–66; here 432.

5: Too Nice a King for the People?: Franz Grillparzer's *König Ottokars Glück und Ende*

FRANZ GRILLPARZER'S OWN ACCOUNT of the painful passage of *König Ottokars Glück und Ende*[1] through Viennese censorship mechanisms has become one of the most celebrated anecdotes of Austrian censorship history. According to the playwright's "Selbstbiographie" (written in 1853), when he handed his historical drama over to the censors in 1823, neither he nor Josef Schreyvogel, the Theatersekretär at the Burgtheater, expected any problems, "da, wenn das regierende Haus eigens einen Schmeichler bezahlt hätte, dieser der Handlung keine günstigere Wendung geben konnte, als die dramatische Notwendigkeit von selber aufgedrungen hatte."[2] Despite this confidence, however, nothing was heard about the manuscript for two years.

Then — so the story goes — Empress Karoline fell ill and wanted something to read. She instructed the poet Matthäus Collin to go to the Burgtheater and see what they could offer her. There, he was told that they had nothing more interesting than Grillparzer's *König Ottokar*, which, however, had not been seen since its submission to the censors. Collin managed to retrieve the play and read it to the empress. She was so impressed — and so surprised that it had not been passed for performance — that she told the emperor, who duly instructed the censors to authorize it. A few years later, Grillparzer happened to meet one of the censors involved in the case, and asked him what had been considered so dangerous about his play. "Gar nichts," replied the man, "aber ich dachte mir: man kann doch nicht wissen."[3]

Although undeniably entertaining, the playwright's version of events is inconsistent with both surviving censorship documents and the accounts of a number of his contemporaries. According to sources assembled in the "Zeugnisse" section of the *Historisch-kritische Ausgabe* of Grillparzer's works, the play was initially prohibited in January 1824, before a year of campaigning by Grillparzer's allies eventually persuaded the emperor to overturn the ban. The drama ran at the Burgtheater for about a year, before it was again prohibited in the spring of 1826, and it was not performed again for another thirteen years.[4]

Perhaps the most surprising element of Grillparzer's story is his claim that neither he nor Schreyvogel was expecting any problems with *König Ottokar*. Both men had considerable experience with the Viennese censorship system. Grillparzer's fate tragedy, *Die Ahnfrau*, had been banned twice in 1817,[5] and the young writer came into conflict with the authorities again in 1819 as a result of "Campo Vaccino," a poem that contrasts the glories of antiquity with an insipid Christian present.[6] In addition to regularly preparing manuscripts for censorship as part of his job at the Burgtheater, which he had held since 1814, Schreyvogel had himself worked as a part-time censor of theatrical newspapers since 1817.[7]

The controversial elements in *König Ottokar* are directly related to the play's storyline. Based on sources from the thirteenth century, Grillparzer's drama traces the rise of the first Habsburg emperor, Rudolf, and the fall of the powerful Czech King Ottokar. While Rudolf is depicted in saintly colors,[8] Ottokar was loosely based on Napoleon, and, for much of the drama, displays an unreflective dynamism that results in excessive pride and self-deception. Toward the end of the play, Ottokar's humiliation at the hands of Rudolf leads him to become more reflective and morally sensitive, but also incapable of decisive action.[9]

Although the play's patriotic credentials are secured by its ending and the characterization of Rudolf, it clearly contains a number of problems. For one thing, the play ends with the decline and death of a monarch, an issue that had already forced Schreyvogel to "correct" the tragic ending of *King Lear* in a Burgtheater production of 1822.[10] In addition, obvious and embarrassing parallels exist between Ottokar's politically motivated second marriage to Princess Kunigunde of Hungary and Napoleon's union with Marie-Luise of Austria. Once she has become Czech queen, Kunigunde's affair with the devious Bohemian nobleman Zawisch Rosenberg is a further source of potential controversy. Finally, the plot turns on conflict between nations then united within the Habsburg Empire and — as already suggested — contains unattractive Hungarian and Czech characters as well as the humiliating downfall of the Czech hero, Ottokar. Ethnic relations and the Napoleonic parallel were named in official documents as the main reasons for the 1824 prohibition,[11] and the second banning of the play in March 1826 has been attributed to the agitations of the Czech aristocrat Baron Bretfeld.[12]

Theater Censorship in Restoration Austria

Censorship was originally introduced into Viennese theater in 1770 in response to Enlightenment concerns about the vulgarity of popular dialect plays. Extemporization had been outlawed for the same reason in 1769, and the first two Viennese theater censors, Joseph von Sonnenfels and

Franz Carl Hägelin, were both committed to upholding Enlightenment standards of language and morality. Protection of both the state and religion were also within the remit of theater censors from the beginning,[13] but the enforcement of political conformity became considerably stricter after the French Revolution of 1789 and the death of the enlightened monarch Joseph II, in 1790.[14] As elsewhere in Europe during these years, the fear of revolution generated a reactionary climate in Austria, and the political dimension of all public utterance became subject to increased official scrutiny.

As mentioned in the introduction, this repressive spirit manifested itself in a series of measures designed to increase the stringency of censorship controls. In 1795, for instance, a new set of censorship instructions established more rigorous procedures for the censorship of the written and printed word.[15] In 1801, responsibility for censorship administration passed into the hands of the newly formed Polizei- und Zensurhofstelle; and two years later, so-called *Theaterkommissäre* were given the task of visiting dress rehearsals at commercial theaters to check that the censors' decisions were implemented.[16] A set of censorship instructions issued in 1810 reiterated the importance of preventing challenges to the established political order;[17] and when the Carlsbad Decrees were introduced elsewhere in the German Confederation in 1819, they were not even announced in the Habsburg Empire, as they would have involved a relaxation of existing practices.[18]

Following the establishment of the Polizei- und Zensurhofstelle and the introduction of *Theaterkommissäre* in the first years of the nineteenth century, procedures for theater censorship in Vienna remained essentially unchanged until 1848. All texts intended for performance had to be approved in advance by the censor. The theater would submit a specially prepared manuscript written out by a copyist; from this the censor would cross out all offensive words or passages, before submitting the manuscript to the Zensurhofstelle for final screening. If authorized, the manuscript would be returned to the theater with a seal of approval, subject to the required deletions.[19] The censors — only some of whom had a literary background — worked under the direct supervision of Count Josef Sedlnitzky, who led the Polizei- und Zensurhofstelle from 1815 to 1848. In cases of uncertainty regarding the censorship of matters related to religion, Sedlnitzky would frequently consult the Archbishop of Vienna; and doubts concerning the portrayal of affairs of state were referred to the Hof- und Staatskanzlei, over which Metternich presided. Until the death of Emperor Francis II in 1835, a further layer of supervision was provided by the active interest he took in censorship issues.[20]

This level of scrutiny reflects the seriousness with which theater censorship was regarded by all layers of government. For, while theater was considered a necessary distraction from less desirable leisure activities (notably engagement in political affairs),[21] its subversive potential was also clear to the authorities. Like other forms of public discourse in Austria, Viennese theatrical performances were subject to a regime of censorship reputed to be the harshest of all the states in the German Confederation; and this system has widely been characterized as arbitrary and unpredictable, both during its period of operation and since. Just like elsewhere in Germany, the complaints of liberals about the inconsistency of censorship decisions gained momentum in the decades before 1848. In 1845, a *Denkschrift über die gegenwärtigen Zustände der Zensur in Österreich* was published and signed by ninety-nine prominent writers, including Grillparzer. However, the modesty of the writers' demands gives an indication of how firmly established state control of utterance in Austria was. For, instead of calling for an end to censorship, this memorandum merely demanded the correct implementation of the existing codes in order to counter arbitrary practices.[22]

Sources and Hägelin's *Denkschrift*

Unfortunately, our knowledge of the workings of Viennese theater censorship during the Restoration is limited by the destruction of most of the Zensurhofstelle files in the Justizpalast fire of 1927. Sections and summaries of many of these files were, however, published by Karl Glossy between 1915 and 1930 within the context of a series entitled "Geschichte der Theater Wiens."[23] Although incompletely referenced, Glossy's material is carefully dated and persuasively thorough; and it represents an important, if less than ideal, source of information about Austrian theater censorship in the first half of the nineteenth century. Much of the "Geschichte der Theater Wiens" consists of reproductions of censors' reports and procedural instructions; yet, sadly, the volumes contain very few directives regarding the details of policy toward the content of works, although Glossy implies in his introduction that he has seen a substantial number of these.[24]

The introduction to "Geschichte der Theater Wiens" also contains the intriguing assertion that, despite some innovations, Austrian theater censorship until 1848 was based on precepts contained in a 1795 *Denkschrift* prepared by the experienced Viennese censor, Hägelin, to provide guidance for Hungarian censors.[25] This memorandum provides a uniquely detailed account of censorship practices in the late eighteenth century; and, given the reactionary mood of the Austrian establishment between 1795 and 1848, the notion that censorship policy remained fundamentally unchanged between these dates is certainly plausible. Indeed, Glossy's judgment has been accepted by many more recent scholars, who have repeated his claims that Hägelin's memorandum is an important source of information about Viennese censorship practice in the decades prior to 1848.[26]

Given these pronouncements, it is important to stress that there is no evidence that Viennese censors in the early nineteenth century actually used Hägelin's *Denkschrift* as a source of guidance. On the contrary, several of the censors' reports published by Glossy either express uncertainty about or argue in favor of plays that violate Hägelin's instructions.[27] Indeed, the primary sources contained within "Die Geschichte der Theater Wiens" suggest that Austrian censors did not receive detailed instructions at all,[28] which would have made them vulnerable to complaints from their superiors and from influential members of the public. However, it is also clear that most of the precepts laid out in the *Denkschrift* corresponded to the censors' practice until at least 1840;[29] and due to the amount of detail it contains, Hägelin's memorandum provides a useful framework with which to examine censorship practices during the Restoration period.

Early Productions of *König Ottokar*

As already mentioned, the first performance of *König Ottokar* took place at the Burgtheater on 19 February 1825. Having been officially designated the home of German drama in 1810, the Austrian court theater was rapidly establishing itself as the premier theater of German-speaking Europe by the 1820s. This success owed much to the excellent actors from throughout the German lands who performed on the Burgtheater stage, as well as the efforts of Schreyvogel to expand the company's range of German classical and foreign dramas (the latter in translation). The "old" Burgtheater building — which was eventually closed in 1888 — was relatively small and cramped, but it had an intimate atmosphere and superb acoustics, which allowed the actors to speak in a normal conversational tone. The emperor's box was very close to the stage on the first floor, and performances were considered a fashionable leisure activity for both aristocrats and the wealthy bourgeoisie.[30]

In April of the same year, another early production of *König Ottokar* began its run at a very different type of theater. This, the Theater an der Wien, was one of three commercially run *Volkstheater* in Vienna, all of which largely drew their audiences from their local districts. Although members of the aristocracy are known to have watched Volkstheater performances, these were attended principally by members of the petty bourgeoisie, artisans, shopkeepers, minor officials, and more prosperous workers. The commercial theaters of Vienna are closely associated with the various genres of traditional local dialect comedy that flourished during the Restoration period under the influence of such illustrious talents as Johann Nestroy and Ferdinand Raimund.[31] However, before the late 1820s, the Theater an der Wien program was dominated by other genres such as opera, *Spektakelstücke,* serious drama, and — prior to their prohibition in the early 1820s — biblical musicals and children's ballet. By 1825, the Theater an der Wien was experiencing a severe financial crisis caused by the difficulty of filling its enormous auditorium and the large sums of money spent by the owner, Count Ferdinand Pálffy von Erdöd, on generating the spectacular scenic effects so beloved of Viennese audiences. The theater's production of *König Ottokar,* which ran from 4 April till 31 May 1825, represented a last-ditch — and ultimately unsuccessful — attempt by Pálffy to rescue it from financial ruin.[32]

Little information exists about the comparability of the censorship standards that were applied to court and commercial theaters. The reports of a few contemporaries remark upon the crude tone of Volkstheater productions during the 1820s,[33] but there is no evidence that such observations reflect an official policy of allowing such productions more freedom than those of the court theaters.[34] Indeed, even if such a policy had existed, greater latitude regarding obscenities would not reveal anything about the censorship of political topics within Volkstheater productions. In fact, given the social composition of the commercial theaters' audience and their greater corruptibility in the eyes of the ruling class, one would expect the censors for such theaters to be stricter in their treatment of political content. As this is not known, however, the first two productions of Grillparzer's *König Ottokar* offer a valuable opportunity to compare the censorship of a dramatic performance at a court theater with that of the same play at a commercial theater.

Primary Sources

In the *Sämtliche Werke,* or *SW,* we are told that the *Censurbuch* for the Theater an der Wien production is missing.[35] The information provided by the "Lesarten" section about the Theater an der Wien *Ottokar* is therefore based on an 1898 article by Jakob Ziedler, entitled, "Ein Censurexemplar von Grillparzer's *König Ottokars Glück und Ende.*"[36] Ziedler's article was written following first-hand inspection of the Censurbuch and thus provides a detailed physical description of it. The article also informs us that the script handed in for censorship by the Theater an der Wien management was a version of *König Ottokar* that was published by J. B. Wallishausser, the main Viennese theater publishers at the time, and had gone on sale on 19 February 1825. This script had, of course, been passed as suitable for a printed publication. However, due to the more powerful effect of live performance and the wider social range present at theater performances, censorship standards for theater were — as already noted

— considerably stricter.[37] As a result, published scripts had to be censored again for each production.

It is unfortunate that we have to rely on a nineteenth-century article for information about the censorship of *König Ottokar* at the Theater an der Wien. However, Ziedler's article is persuasively thorough and contains a complete list of the deletions and alterations made to the original manuscript. Some of these are in pencil and some in pen. The author attributes the pencil markings to the theater direction, a conclusion which is consistent with the fact that they consist principally of either the alteration or removal of minor characters, the modification of stage directions for music or crowd scenes, or the removal of entire scenes. He ascribes alterations in ink to censorship, a convincing judgment given the censor's verdict and signature — in this case that of Alois Zettler — that appear on the *Censurbuch*, the nature of these changes, and Ziedler's evident familiarity with other censored manuscripts.

Many of the ink markings represent confirmations of markings previously made in pencil,[38] thereby indicating the possibility that the manuscript was scrutinized by two different censors. According to Ziedler, it was common practice for manuscripts to be sent to a practicing writer for initial censorship before the principal censor made the final decision about what could and could not remain in the play. He does not provide a reference for this information, however, and admits that the pencil markings could have been the preliminary work of the main censor. In any case, however, the ink markings clearly represent the final judgment of the censorship authorities.

In addition to listing changes that resulted from the two stages of censorship and the theater direction, Ziedler's article contains some useful information about the reasons for certain alterations and deletions. It tells us, for example, that the Rosenburgs in *König Ottokar* were originally Rosenbergs. Their name was changed because Rosenberg was also the name of a famous family at the time.[39] However, in other respects, his analysis of the play's censorship remains rather incomplete; and crucially, his comments on changes to the drama's political content go no further than the observation that the censors followed their instructions in attempting to protect the state, its offices, and its dignity.

The censorship process undergone by the manuscripts for the Burgtheater production was much more complicated.[40] One version of *König Ottokar*, referred to in the *SW* as "h2," was accepted by the Burgtheater management in the middle of November 1823. It is thought that h2 — which is now missing — was used as the setting copy for Wallishauser's edition of the play,[41] against which the "Lesarten" section of the *SW* compares other manuscripts. During the second half of November 1823, h2 was revised by the Burgtheater management in preparation for censorship, and it is thought that another missing manuscript, "x," was the result of these revisions. The manuscript handed to the censors in late November 1823, "h3," the manuscript intended as a *Spielbuch,* "h4," and "h5," a manuscript prepared by the Burgtheater in December 1824 after they had returned h3 to the authorities for a second round of scrutiny, are all thought to have originated as copies of x. Although the three manuscripts are virtually identical, it is claimed in the *SW* that h4 and h5 are copies of a slightly later version of x than h3. Eventually, on 31 December 1824, h5 was granted verbal approval by the emperor in a private audience with the director of court theaters, Count Moritz von Dietrichstein.[42]

Taken together, h3, h4, and h5 can provide much information about the changes that were made to the Burgtheater production of *König Ottokar* both by, and in anticipation of, the censors. Most reliably, h3, the manuscript initially submitted for censorship, contains many deletions and alterations demanded by the censors before they decided that the play should be banned altogether and gave up their censoring activities. The censors' amendments are still identifiable on the manuscript and were copied on to h4 and h5.

The differences between the original, pre-annotation manuscripts, h3, h4, and h5, and the published version of *König Ottokar,* which, as we have seen, went on sale in early 1825, are a second source of information about the effect of censorship on the Burgtheater production. As already indicated, it is thought that the setting copy for the printed edition was the same as h2, the version (now missing) that was eventually accepted by the Burgtheater. This version was then prepared for submission to the censors for performance; and the result of this preparation was x, of which h3, h4, and h5 are copies.

Although there is no proof that the missing h2 was the setting copy for the printed edition of the play, there are a number of good reasons for believing that this was indeed the case. First, there is no record of Grillparzer or anyone else revising the play accepted by the Burgtheater in preparation for the printed edition. In addition, the printed edition does not contain any deletions or intricate reworkings when compared to h3, h4, and h5. All of the differences between the versions for performance and publication consist of either deletions to the performance manuscripts or the alteration of single words. Such amendments can be overwhelmingly related to the central censorship concerns of religion, politics, and sexual morality, and almost always have the effect of rendering controversial content milder in the performance manuscripts.

This pattern of alterations is consistent with the fact that x was produced at a time when alterations to h2 (of which x was a copy) were unlikely to have been motivated by anything other than censorship pressure. For one thing, Grillparzer had initially submitted his play to the Burgtheater direction in October 1823, before a different version, h2, was accepted in November of the same year. It is therefore probable that any aesthetic changes required by the Burgtheater direction would have been implemented between these two dates. In addition, rehearsals for the play did not begin until *König Ottokar* had been approved for performance in late January 1825 — long after x was produced — so that technically motivated differences between h2 and x also seem unlikely.

Finally, the emperor's correspondence with Sedlnitzky reveals that permission for the performance of h5 was only granted on the condition that changes were made to this manuscript.[43] There is no record of specific alterations demanded by the emperor and the only markings on the manuscript were made by Dietrichstein or Schreyvogel. One therefore imagines either that the required changes were conveyed to the two men by another means, or that they were only given general instructions regarding the type of alterations that had to be made. In any case, these amendments were almost certainly marked on h4 and h5, although they may not have been recorded on h3, which the Burgtheater direction resubmitted to the authorities in late January 1824,[44] and which the emperor only returned to Sedlnitzky on the night before the first performance.[45]

Unfortunately, however, not all changes and deletions marked on h4 and h5 can be attributed to censorship concerns. It is known that, once performances were underway, further sections were cut from the script, both for purely aesthetic reasons and as a response to criticisms from the audience. Although the "Zeugnisse" section of the HKA cites contemporary sources that provide information about some of these cuts, either identifying them specifically or describing at what stage in the play they occurred,[46] it is impossible to be sure in all cases. Nevertheless, a number of other clues provide some indication of the most plausible motivations for the different changes marked on the h4 and h5 manuscripts. For one thing, both manuscripts contain very long sections crossed out in pencil. At such a late stage in the censorship process, it is probably safe to assume that such substantial deletions were due to aesthetic concerns or considerations of audience response. This theory is supported by many contemporary reports that performances of *König Ottokar* became considerably shorter during the course of its run.[47] Among the shorter amendments, on the other hand, are many that are strikingly consistent with well-established censorship concerns, including a substantial number that mirror the changes demanded by the censors for the Theater an der Wien production of *König Ottokar*. Although these deductions are not entirely secure, it is highly probable that such alterations resulted from censorship pressure.

If we look at the way in which the two productions appear to have been altered as a result of censorship, it becomes clear what a devastating impact official control had on performances of *König Ottokar*. The Burgtheater manuscripts — h3, h4, and h5 — together show 120 deviations from the printed edition of the play, which translates into 257 lines out of an original 2988. The situation is even more drastic for the Theater an der Wien production, from which 575 lines were removed. As we will see, these excisions affected a range of thematic areas.

The Institution of Monarchy

In Hägelin's *Denkschrift* of 1795, the first recommendation regarding the protection of the state is as follows:

> Es können in einem monarchischen Staate keine Stücke aufgeführt werden, deren Inhalt auf die Abwürdigung der monarchischen Regierungsform abzielte oder der demokratischen oder einen andern den Vorzug vor der monarchischen einräumte.[48]

The continued relevance of this instruction is demonstrated both by censors' reports from the early nineteenth century[49] and by the explicit prohibition of writings that threaten "das Band zwischen Unterthanen und Fürst locker zu machen" in the Austrian censorship instructions of 1810. At first glance, *König Ottokar* contains nothing that challenges the monarchic principle. None of the characters in Grillparzer's play criticizes the principle, either directly or indirectly. Nor is any suggestion made that the monarchy is inferior to any other form of government. Indeed, no other form of government is mentioned during the course of *König Ottokar*. However, despite this absence of criticism and comparison, early performances of *König Ottokar* still appear to have suffered further deletions in the service of the monarchic principle.

One example of this is the evidence contained within the manuscripts that theater censors were sensitive to utterance that suggested limits to the legitimacy of hereditary succession. Ottokar divorces his Austrian first wife, Margareta, because he wants to marry a younger woman who will bear him children. He attempts to justify his decision on spurious legal grounds, but Margareta sees through him and protests, "Doch was soll Erbrecht, das aus Unrecht stammt?" (v. 214; *SW* I/3:19). This challenge was removed from both performances,[50] although in the Burgtheater manuscript it was part of a longer omitted passage and would not have made made sense had it been left in on its own.[51] It is therefore far from clear that the line in itself was considered intolerable. The situation is far less ambiguous for the Theater an der Wien production, on the other hand, from which line 214 was removed in isolation. The fact that Margareta's other criticisms of the king are allowed to remain in both manuscripts[52] indicates that the censors could tolerate both a woman challenging her husband and a queen criticizing a king. It therefore seems very likely that Margareta's rhetorical question was considered politically dangerous by both sets of censors. Her protest at Ottokar's behavior not only implies a possible conflict between the principles of justice and succession; it also suggests that the former should take precedence over the latter, and thereby places a limit on the claims of hereditary power.

Issues of succession were not always censored more strictly for the Volkstheater production. A few lines later, Margareta implies a similar restriction of the legitimacy of hereditary succession when she declares, "Ein Bettlerkind säß besser auf dem Thron / Als Königssöhne, die das Unrecht zeugte!" (v. 266–67; *SW* I/3:20). Here, the same conflict of ideas is formulated in slightly less direct terms, although it might be thought that the comparison of a "Bettlerkind" with the sons of kings would be considered additionally provocative. However, these lines were only removed from the court theater's manuscripts.[53] It is possible that the censors for the Theater an der Wien production were prepared to tolerate a limited density of challenges to the principle of succession, although given the fact that they deleted the first of Margareta's challenges and allowed the second, it seems safer to attribute this inconsistency to oversight or arbitrariness.

A more pronounced divergence is shown by the attitudes of the two groups of censors toward the casual mention of lands passing from one ruler to another. This issue was not mentioned in Hägelin's memorandum, but clearly represents a potential challenge to the foundations of monarchical authority. Reminders of the frequency and ease with which lands can change rulers pose an implicit threat to a monarch's claim of a sacred and permanent bond with his people. Although the transfer of lands plays a central role in *König Ottokar*, and most references to it are allowed to remain in both productions,[54] there are a number of exceptions in the Theater an der Wien manuscript. In line 1300, for example, Ottokar uses the language of mercantile exchange to explain to the Burggraf how he acquired the Duchy of Carinthia from his uncle, "[d]urch gleicher Erbverträge Wechseltausch" (*SW* I/3:81), a description that was deleted by the Volkstheater censors.[55] The passing of lands between rulers is described in similarly unceremonious terms at the beginning of act five, when one of Ottokar's noblemen, Füllenstein, complains about Ottokar's recent indecisiveness, ending his speech with a description of how his ruler surrendered many of his lands without a fight:

> Da heißts: Zurück! Und Weiden, Weitendorf,
> Und Anger, Stillfried, alle Stellungen
> Am Hasenberg, am Weidenbach, und an der Sulz,
> Läßt er dem Feind, beinahe ohn einen Schwertschlag.
>
> (vv. 2545–48; *SW* I/3:149)

Although Füllenstein's earlier criticisms of his king were allowed to be included in the performance,[56] this quick survey of the many lands surrendered was apparently considered more controversial and was crossed out of the Theater an der Wien manuscript.[57] The same pattern is continued by the deletion of another of Ottokar's speeches toward the end of act four.[58] Here, in a desperate bid to secure the loyalty of his noblemen, he returns to them the lands they had owned before he seized them:

> Den Rosenbergen sei ihr Frauenberg,
> Auch Aussig, Falkenstein. Dir, Neuhaus, Lar;
> Nehmt Laun, Ihr Zierotin; Dub Kruschina!
> Nehmt Eure Güter wieder, und seid fröhlich!
> Wir wollen eins sein, redlich halten aus.
>
> (vv. 2472–76; *SW* I/3:144)

Even worse than the surrender described in the previous example, Ottokar here gives his lands away spontaneously and unceremoniously, an impression that is reinforced by the uneven rhythm of his words. Such an implicit negation of the bond between monarch, lands, and subjects again appears to have been regarded as intolerable by the censors for the Theater an der Wien production.

The censors also appeared sensitive to more general utterances that made clear the potential instability of monarchical rule. Of course, with the fall of King Ottokar constituting the central theme of the play, this uncomfortable fact of life could not be completely removed. However, it is interesting that many superfluous references to Ottokar's decline remain in both postcensorship manuscripts,[59] although the censors do occasionally appear to have been stricter. While this pattern of censorship may indicate a degree of arbitrariness, it it also striking that the authorities were particularly sensitive to mentions of Ottokar's fall that suggest the general transience of earthly power.

For example, when Ottokar meets Margareta's servant, Elisabeth, again shortly before his final battle, he laments his decline as a random act of God:

> Was ich gesammelt ist im Wind zerstoben,
> Der Segen fort, der fruchtend kommt von oben,
> Und einsam steh ich da, von Leid gebeugt,
> Und niemand tröstet mich und hört mich!
>
> (vv. 2662–65; *SW* I/3:158)

While the whole of the above passage was deleted from the Theater an der Wien manuscript, only the first two lines, "Was ich gesammelt ist im Winde zerstoben / Der Segen fort, der fruchtend kommt von oben," were crossed out of the Burgtheater version.[60] These lines may have been considered particularly offensive because they create a potent image of the fragility of monarchical power and privilege, depicting them as powerless in the face of such an unexceptional natural force as the wind. Similar considerations were probably behind an earlier deletion from the Burgtheater production. Following one of Kunigunde's accounts of Ottokar's deteriorating psychological state, Zawisch replies, "Ei gnädige Frau, das Glück ist eben rund!" (v. 2119; SW I/3:126), an assertion that was crossed out of the court theater's manuscript.[61] This piece of folk wisdom represented a serious challenge to an image of royal stability, and it is not hard to see why members of the royal family and aristocracy may not have responded well to such suggestions.

Two further deletions continue this pattern of the Burgtheater audience being protected from reminders of the transience of power, both literal and metaphorical. They both come shortly after Ottokar's death, as Rudolf contemplates his enemy's pitiful corpse. Initially, only two lines were removed by the theater direction from the manuscript they first submitted to the censors:[62]

> Daß als ein Kaiser du begraben werdest,
> Der du gestorben wie ein Bettler bist.
>
> (v. 2964–65; SW I/3:176)

Later on, however, the preceding seven lines were also crossed out of the Burgtheater manuscript.[63] This section may at first have been considered milder than the above quotation because it avoids the provocative word "Bettler" to describe the dead king. Nevertheless, it also paints a poignant picture of the Czech king's fall; and the use of "großer König" to address Ottokar both reminds us of his royal status and emphasizes the fact that kings are not immune to death and decline:

> So liegst du nackt und schmucklos, großer König,
> Das Haupt gelegt in deines Dieners Schoß,
> Und ist von deinem Prunk und Reichtum allen
> Nicht eine arme Decke dir geblieben,
> Als Leichentuch zu hüllen deinen Leib.
> Den Kaisermantel, dem du nachgestrebt,
> Ich nehme ihn und breite ihn über dich [. . .].
>
> (vv. 2957–63; SW I/3:176)

As mentioned at the beginning of this section, the published manuscript of *König Ottokars Glück und Ende* contained nothing that directly challenged the principle of monarchic government protected in both Hägelin's memorandum and Austrian censorship legislation. Yet, as we have seen, those involved in censoring the two plays felt obliged to apply stricter standards than those suggested by the 1795 memorandum in order to protect the foundations of the monarchy from the contents of Grillparzer's play. Despite some inconsistencies, the treatment of this issue broadly reflects the attitudes of the authorities toward the two audiences. While the Volkstheater censors were much less tolerant of casual descriptions of the transfer of lands than their Burgtheater colleagues, the reverse is true for reminders of the impermanence of worldly status. For both productions, however, it is clear that censorship protection of the institution of monarchy resulted in the expurgation of many expressive statements relating to broader political and existential themes, and thus placed considerable limitations on the theatrical representation of such issues.

The Portrayal of Monarchs

Hägelin's memorandum of 1795 also documents the attention paid by censors to the portrayal of royalty in the late eighteenth century. The *Denkschrift* states that no plays could be passed, "worin die Regenten besonders aber die vaterländischen in nachtheiligen oder herabwürdigenden Karackteren geschildert werden."[64] Surviving censorship reports from the 1820s reveal that safeguarding the portrayal of monarchs on stage remained an important concern,[65] which is a logical consequence of the censors' responsibility for protecting monarchical authority in general.

In *König Ottokar,* the characterization of Rudolf certainly contains nothing that would cause the censors to worry about the reputation of "die vaterländischen" rulers. The portrayal of Ottokar, on the other hand, is potentially more problematic. The Czech king is clearly shown to be greedy, vain, and unjust in his treatment of both his first wife Margareta and many of his subjects. Indeed, at several points during the play, the behavior resulting from Ottokar's moral shortcomings is directly criticized by other characters. Margareta makes clear her opinion of Ottokar when she tells Rudolf, "O glaubt nicht, daß den König ich entschuldge! / Fern sei von mir, daß ich je Böses lobe!" (v. 235–36; *SW* I/3:19–20). Similarly, after receiving the news that he has not been chosen as the new German emperor, Ottokar impulsively imprisons a large group of his own nobility due to a fear that they will desert him. Grillparzer does not allow this incident to pass without comment, and the Czech King is calmly told by the Reich's spokesman that "Der Auftritt hier erspart mir die Erklärung, / Warum die Fürsten, Herr, nicht Euch gewählt" (v. 1280–81; *SW* I/3:80). Being a king does not protect Ottokar from criticism.

In addition, many other aspects of the portrayal of Ottokar could be considered "herabwürdigend." The Czech King's darkest moment in the play comes when one of his enemies, Zawisch, cuts the rope of the tent in which he is kneeling down in front of Rudolf, thereby exposing him to general view. This event is clearly perceived as a deep humiliation for Ottokar by all of those around him. We are shown several of his subjects receiving the news with disbelief (v. 2046; *SW* I/3:122), his wife is disgusted by the "Schande" brought upon them by it (v. 2095; *SW* I/3:125), and Ottokar himself suffers a psychological breakdown, which leads him to wander the streets of Prague in disguise (following v. 2022; *SW* I/3:121).

As mentioned in the previous section, many references to Ottokar's humiliation and subsequent psychological breakdown were allowed to remain in both performances. Both a Czech and an enemy of the Habsburgs, King Ottokar was not protected from humiliating representation in the way that one might expect. To be sure, there are some exceptions to this: following Ottokar's exposure kneeling before Rudolf, for example, the Volkstheater censors replaced cries of "Der König kniet" (v. 1961; *SW* I/3:117) from Zawisch and the Czechs with Rudolf's outraged, "Wer that uns dies?";[66] and Kunigunde's scathing reference to her husband's state in lines 2136 to 2137, "Nicht ganz so kläglich als er jetzt dort brütet, / Doch nicht viel besser, weiß der große Gott!" (*SW* I/3:127), was removed from both productions.[67]

Many other reminders of Ottokar's fall are allowed to remain in each of the productions, however. When the despairing king abruptly springs up from his crouched position on the streets of Prague, for example, Kunigunde's sarcastic response serves to reinforce his humiliation:

> O springt nur auf; ich fürchte Euch wahrlich nicht!
> Soll ich die einzge sein von Mann und Frau,
> Die noch vor Ottokar, dem König, zittert.
> (vv. 2188–90; *SW* I/3:129)

Earlier on in the same scene, the queen had shown a similar lack of concern to protect her husband's dignity:

> Sieh hin, da sitzt der Stolze, Übermächtge,
> Dem sonst die Welt zu klein für seine Größe;
> Da sitzt er wie ein Bettler vor der Tür [. . .].
> (vv. 2098–2100; *SW* I/3:126)

Such examples provide an interesting contrast with one of the few passages that were deleted from the Theater an der Wien manuscript in order to protect the Czech king's dignity. This comes shortly before Ottokar's death, when he realizes the error of his ways, and suffers a bout of moral insight as he tries to make sense of his life:

> Geblendet war ich, so hab ich gefehlt,
> Mit Willen hab ich Unrecht nicht getan!

> Doch einmal, ja! — und noch einmal: O Gott,
> Ich hab mit Willen Unrecht auch getan!
>
> (vv. 2863–66; *SW* I/3:168)

Although Ottokar's later declarations of repentance were allowed to remain in both performances,[68] it seems likely that the regret and despair expressed by this particular speech revealed too much of the monarch's vulnerability for the Theater an der Wien audience to be exposed to it.[69] It is also curious, however, that this passage was apparently deemed more humiliating to Ottokar than his wife's scathing commentaries on his decline. It is possible that these were merely considered illustrations of her merciless temperament; but their inclusion nevertheless serves to place further emphasis on Ottokar's decline.

Within the context of the Burgtheater production, the portrayal of Ottokar's faults was evidently regarded as relatively unproblematic. The only modification that occurs in both manuscripts does not relate to dialogue, but to a stage direction. Toward the end of the second act, after he has overheard his chancellor telling Zawisch that Rudolf has been made emperor, Ottokar angrily confronts the chancellor and throws a glove at him. Although a later example of foot stamping was permitted to remain in both performances,[70] the glove-throwing was presumably considered too undignified for a monarch, and was removed from both productions.[71]

The Volkstheater censors, on the other hand, were much less tolerant of Ottokar's moral failings. In his 1898 article on the censuring of the Theater an der Wien production, Jakob Zeidler reports that "[d]as Censurbuch des Theaters an der Wien von 1825 tilgt oder mildert alle Stellen des Textes, welche den Schauspieler veranlassen könnten, den Böhmenkönig recht 'streng,' 'heftig' oder 'hart' darzustellen."[72] Most of these sections appear in the play's final two acts, as the Czech king's downfall and awakening moral sensitivity give rise to violent emotions. Toward the end of the fourth act, for example, after Kunigunde has persuaded Ottokar to take up arms against Rudolf, the Hungarian attempts a reconciliation with her husband. Pained by his wife's earlier ferocity, however, Ottokar brutally rejects her:

> So nicht! So nicht!
> Ich sehe Blut an deinen weißen Fingern,
> Zukünftges Blut! Ich sag: berühr mich nicht.
> Gott hat das Weib aus weichem Ton gemacht
> Und: Milde zugenannt; was bist denn du?
> Wird mein Gedächtnis wach erst und erzählt,
> Wie du den König, da er kam, empfingst,
> Den Gatten, da er rückgekehrt nach Haus [. . .].
>
> (vv. 2411–18; *SW* I/3:141–42)

Only the first two lines of this speech were allowed to remain, so that Ottokar's questioning of Kunigunde's femininity was removed from the production.[73] It may be argued that the exposure of problems in the royal marriage was the real cause for this deletion. However, this seems unlikely given the fact that, only a few lines earlier, Kunigunde's withering warning to her husband, "An eurem Sarge will ich lieber stehn / als mit Euch liegen, zugedeckt von Schande!" (v. 2401–2; *SW* I/3:141), was passed by both groups of censors.

Another example of the efforts of the commercial theaters' censors to tone down Ottokar's character comes earlier on in the fourth act, just as he begins to consider going into battle against Rudolf. Here, Ottokar becomes tormented by the memory of having to kneel down before his enemy, and threatens to kill all those who witnessed it:

> Töten will ich
> Den Letzten, ders mit angesehn!
> Mich selber, wenn ich nicht verlöschen kann
> Das Angedenken jener blutgen Schmach.
> (vv. 2283–86; *SW* I/3:135)

Just as these lines are crossed out of the Theater an der Wien manuscript,[74] so too is a similar example of Ottokar's potentially murderous reaction to the memory of his humiliation in the emperor's tent. When Rudolf's herald demands that he release the hostage Merenberg, Ottokar explains that he does not regard Merenberg as a hostage, but as a traitor. However, after a brief recounting of Merenberg's supposed treachery, Ottokar returns once more to the subject of his exposure when kneeling down before Rudolf, and concludes his speech with a frighteningly irrational justification of his treatment of the man:

> Und dieses Mannes Sohn, er stand dabei
> Und lachte! — Darum mußt du sterben, Mann!
> Die Andern mögen gehn, der eine bleibt!
> (vv. 2334–36; *SW* I/3:137)

Although the entire exchange (lines 2316–37) was crossed out of the manuscript,[75] it seems likely that Ottokar's frantic threats toward Merenberg were sufficient grounds for concern in themselves. A few lines later, Ottokar's proclamation that "wer mir meldet: / Der Merenberg ist tot, der sei willkommen" (v. 2345–46; *SW* I/3:138) is also deleted from the Theater an der Wien manuscript.[76]

One possible explanation for the toning down of the Czech king's character for the Theater an der Wien performance is the desire of the censors there to avoid arousing ethnic tensions. If this were the case, however, we would also expect the Czech King to have been spared more of his humiliating moments. As we have already seen, this did not happen. On the other hand, it is not hard to see why the Volkstheater censors were more sensitive to the portrayal of an excessively harsh monarch than the Burgtheater censors. For, although Ottokar was not a Habsburg, the depiction of his brutal and despotic behavior could endanger the reputation of monarchy in general. Given the broad social range of the Theater an der Wien audience, such negative depictions of absolutist rule doubtlessly appeared unwise.

Interestingly, however, not all of the censors' efforts to create a milder Ottokar for the commercial theater performances flattered the Czech king. There is another group of four or five deletions from the Volkstheater manuscript that also have the effect of rendering Ottokar less "heftig," but, in so doing, remove much more positive images of him from the text. These include many of the Czech king's more energetic speeches, as he vows to resist Rudolf. After giving in to Kunigunde's taunts and deciding to fight against the Habsburg king, Ottokar gives a rousing speech that was deleted by the Volkstheater censors:[77]

> Die Ehre ganz, und auf der Zukunft Tor!
> Was draus erfolgt, wir wollens beide tragen!
> Gott gönn Euch was von dem, was hier erwacht,
> (*Auf seine Brust zeigend.*)
> Und gebe mir die Kraft, die Ihr bewiesen! (vv. 2407–10; *SW* I/3:141)

It is hard to see what is offensive in these words, except perhaps, for the plea to God, which could have been changed or removed without deleting the entire passage. Moreover, the pattern is continued when Ottokar later goes on to address his subjects on the theme of the forthcoming war. Here again, a motivational passage forms the bulk of a speech that was also deleted in its entirety:[78]

> Nun im Begriff zu gehn in einen Krieg
> Für unsers Landes Ruhm und seine Macht,
> Vertrau ich euch, wie ich mir selbst vertraue.
> Wer mißgesinnt ist, wer mein Tun nicht billigt,
> Der schließe sich frei aus von unserm Zug,
> Kein Nachteil soll ihn treffen oder Vorwurf.
> Wer aber gern mir folgt und denkt wie ich,
> Den drück ich an mein Herz und nenn ihn Bruder!
> Den Eid, den ich am Krönungstage schwur
> Bei meines Vaters Sarg, ich wiederhol ihn:
> Treu bis zum Tod! Tut ihr dasselbe!
> Die Welt ist voll von Bösen und von Argen;
> Erneut den Schwur auf eures Königs Schwert.
>   (vv. 2441–54; *SW* I/3:143)

It is possible that this passage was troubling to the censors because it included Ottokar granting his men permission not to fight if they did not follow his cause. However, it does seem that lines 2443 to 2446 could have been modified or deleted without causing the removal of an eleven-line speech. Moreover, these two excised passages represent Ottokar's only inspirational speeches regarding his battle against Rudolf.

This suggests that what Ziedler saw as the "toning down" of Ottokar's character can be perhaps related more to the theme of the excised passages than to the general portrayal of the Czech king. For, although this battle was fought between kings, it nevertheless represented a nationalist challenging of Habsburg authority. Of course, the censors could not remove this rebellion from the script entirely, and it eventually failed anyway. Yet one can nevertheless imagine that the energy behind Ottokar's passionate calls to rebellion was considered a little too rousing to expose to an audience with little guaranteed allegiance to the political establishment.

While both sets of censors were remarkably tolerant of the depiction of Ottokar's downfall, we have seen how the apparent efforts of the Theater an der Wien censors to make the Czech king into a milder character deprived the audience of some of the most effective illustrations of his overwrought mental state, as well as his most passionate and rousing speeches. In contrast, the Burgtheater's relatively lax approach to the portrayal of Ottokar suggests to us that the depiction at the court theater of a king ordering arbitrary arrests and uttering panicked, bloodthirsty wishes was unproblematic. Although those responsible for the portrayal of Ottokar for the court performance were no doubt emboldened by the fact that the Czech king was an enemy of the Habsburgs, their decisions nevertheless demonstrate that tyrannical monarchs could, under some circumstances at least, be tolerated on the Burgtheater stage.

Ethnic Relations

Given its multinational composition, the Habsburg empire had a clear interest in minimizing ethnic tension between its subjects. The implications of this for theater censorship in the late eighteenth century are articulated by Hägelin's *Denkschrift,* which contains the injunction that, "Stoffe oder Karacktere, wodurch ganze Nationen, besonders die freundschaftlichen, gemißhandelt oder als lasterhaft dargestellt werden, können nicht passiert werden."[79] Although no explicit instructions regarding the portrayal of national groups in the early nineteenth century have survived, we have already seen that the prohibitions of *König Ottokar* in 1824 and 1826 were related to considerations of ethnic harmony, which clearly remained an important factor in censorship throughout the 1820s and 1830s.[80]

While the published version of *König Ottokar* contains very few direct attacks on any given nationality, we have seen that conflict between the nations of the Habsburg empire is a central element of its plot. It is therefore interesting that content relating to this theme was treated quite differently by those censoring the two productions. Although neither group of officials was consistently more rigorous than the other in protecting national sensibilities, they do seem to have diverging strategies for the pursuit of this aim.

Only a few passages concerning relations between different nationalities were handled in the same way for both productions. One of these was the following section of the first act, which was removed from both productions,[81] and contains the still powerful Ottokar's description of the fleeing Hungarians after their defeat at Marchegg:

> Und alles floh, was ungrisch fluchen kann,
> Und in die March, daß ihre Zottelbärte
> Wie Schilfgras aus gedämmtem Wasser ragten [. . .].
> (vv. 434–36; *SW* I/3:28)

This deleted passage contains two potentially offensive elements: the crowing reference to the Hungarians' retreat and the mocking of their beards. For the censors of the Burgtheater production, however, laughing at foreign haircuts appears to have been an offense in its own right. Although the following passage from the same scene was initially left untouched by the Burgtheater direction, the censors later objected to it. As a result, Ottokar's disdainful opinion of his visiting Tartars' appearance — which also illustrates the Czech king's dynamic functionalism at this stage — was eventually removed:[82]

> Und sonst die Rüstung! Wozu soll der Haarschopf
> Da oben auf dem Scheitel? Für den Feind wohl?
> Der faßt sich seinen Mann, zieht ihn vom Pferde,
> Und würgt ihn wie er mag. Wär ich ihr König,
> In Einer Nacht ließ ich sie alle scheren!
> (vv. 395–400; *SW* I/3:26)

In contrast, these words were allowed to remain in the Theater an der Wien manuscript. It is possible that its censors interpreted Ottokar's words in a milder light, or that they did not consider the distant Tartars to be in as much need of protection as the Hungarians. On the other hand, however, both sets of censors allowed the Czech king's preceding criticisms of the Tartars' swords to remain in the manuscripts. Perhaps because they were free from the sarcasm of his hairstyle analysis, the following comments were considered acceptable:

> Weist her den Säbel!
> (*Er wiegt ihn in der Hand.*) Viel zu krumm gebogen!
> (*Er tut einen Hieb in die Luft.*)
> Das nimmt dem Hieb die Kraft. Das müßt ihr ändern!
> Ein krummes Schwert mag angehn; doch der Kraftpunkt
> Soll mehr nach oben. Einer meiner Reiter
> Jagt eur Zehn mit seinem breiten Schwert.
> (vv. 390–94; *SW* I/3:26)

While those censoring the Burgtheater production were stricter than their colleagues at the commercial theater regarding Ottokar's "Schopf" speech, far more references to the Czech king's early power over nations belonging to the nineteenth-century Habsburg empire were removed from the Theater an der Wien manuscript. Most of these come shortly after Ottokar's victory over the Hungarians and include the deletion of his smug reassurance that "Vor Ungarn mögt ihr künftig ruhig schlafen" (v. 402; *SW* I/3:26),[83] the changing of his later report that "Der Ungar flieht" into "Die Feinde fliehen" (v. 493; *SW* I/3:31),[84] and the removal of the following proud summary of his growing power:[85]

> In Böhmen herrsch ich, bin in Mähren mächtig;
> Zu Östreich hab ich Steier mir erkämpft,
> Mein Oheim siecht, der Kärnten nach mir läßt.
> (*Vertraulich und leiser*)
> Im nahen Ungarn hab ich meine Hand,
> Die Großen sehn auf mich, die Mißvergnügten;
> Es will mir Schlesien wohl, und Polen schwankt,
> Wie sturmgepeitscht ein Schiff, in meinen Hafen.
> (vv. 598–604; *SW* I/3:36)

By contrast, all of these passages remained unchanged in the Burgtheater production. Indeed, the only clear example of Ottokar's early gloating being removed from the court theater performances is this sneering reaction to the Hungarian king's fury following defeat, which was also deleted from the Theater an der Wien manuscript:[86]

> [Er] zog sich feindlich. Ei, dachte ich mir, Herr,
> Spart Euch die Müh, wir können das viel besser.
> (v. 444–45; *SW* I/3:29)

One further issue which was treated very differently for the two productions was another early speech of Ottokar's, in which he addresses his own people, describing them as primitive and backward:

> Ich weiß wohl, was ihr mögt, ihr alten Böhmen:
> Gekauert sitzen in verjährtem Wust,

> Wo kaum das Licht durch blinde Scheiben dringt;
> Verzehren was der vorge Tag gebracht,
> Und ernten, was der nächste soll verzehren,
> Am Sonntag Schmaus, am Kirmeß plumpen Tanz,
> Für alles andre taub und blind [. . .].
>
> (vv. 468–74; *SW* I/3:30)

This section of Ottokar's speech was removed from the Theater an der Wien manuscript,[87] but was apparently considered inoffensive by those censoring the Burgtheater manuscript. It is possible that the Burgtheater audience were credited with more ability to evaluate and interpret the lines of the play according to who said them, as well as with more loyalty to the Habsburg dynasty. As the morally dubious enemy of the Habsburgs, Ottokar could not, perhaps, count on much sympathy from most of the audience, who might be expected to regard his statements with skepticism.

In the published version of *König Ottokar,* the Czech king's characterization of his people as primitive is followed by an outlining of his plans to improve them:

> Den Deutschen will ich setzen euch in Pelz,
> Der soll euch kneipen, bis euch Schmerz und Ärger
> Aus eurer Dumpfheit wecken, und ihr ausschlagt
> Wie ein gespornstes Pferd. (vv. 478–81; *SW* I/3:30)

These suggestions go a couple of stages further than Ottokar's earlier insults. In addition to characterizing the Germans as superior to the Czechs, they also evoke images of the former nation inflicting suffering on the latter. They could have been regarded as additionally provocative in view of policies by German monarchs to encourage German immigration into Slav regions. Both sets of censors had them removed from the script,[88] although the Burgtheater direction apparently saw no need to remove them until ordered to. Indeed, the replacement lines inserted by Schreyvogel display a renewed disregard for Czech national pride. While the Theater an der Wien censors were able simply to remove the offensive passage without any loss of continuity, Schreyvogel at the Burgtheater inserted the line "Bis Schmerz und Ärger Euch aus Eurer Dumpfheit weckt." References to the alleged "Dumpfheit" of Czechs in the Middle Ages were evidently considered acceptable at the imperial theater.

Other instances of implied comparisons between different nationalities appear to have been viewed more seriously by the Burgtheater direction, however. During a long speech complaining about her life with Ottokar, for example, Kunigunde turns to consider the attractions of Zawisch, and reflects that "bei uns in Ungarn / Trüg er sein Haupt keck unter Gottes Himmel" (v. 986–87; *SW* I/3:61). This expression of extramarital attraction was removed in its entirety from the Theater an der Wien script.[89] The Burgtheater direction, on the other hand, tolerated Kunigunde's admiration for Zawisch, but changed the words, "bei uns in Ungarn," into "in unserem Lande,"[90] presumably in an effort to denationalize Kunigunde's comparison.

This pattern is continued by alterations to Ottokar's claims, during the fourth act, that none of the Czechs have betrayed him. Ottokar repeats his assertion twice in the space of five lines (vv. 2435–39; *SW* I/3:142–43); each time it is changed from "Kein Böhme hat noch seinen Herrn verraten" to "Von meinem Volk ist keiner ein Verräter" in the Burgtheater production.[91] Ottokar's original words were presumably considered to be somewhat provocative due to contemporary prejudices about the Czechs being untrustworthy. Yet the Theater an der Wien censors allowed Ottokar's first claim to remain, but then entirely removed the second as part of one of his longer rousing speeches.[92] This would suggest that they were less worried about the provocative potential of Ottokar's claims than were those censoring the Burgtheater production.

A similar pattern is evident with regard to the treatment of armed conflict between various nationalities. For the Burgtheater production in particular, efforts were clearly made to denationalize the spectacle of the opposing sides fighting each other. In the original manuscript, for example, as the two armies approach each other during the battle scene at the end of the play, one of the Austrians cries out "Die Böhmen nahn!," to which Rudolf replies, "Die Österreicher sind schon da!" (v. 2789; *SW* I/3:165). The first of these lines was removed from the Theater an der Wien manuscript,[93] while the second was allowed to remain. In the Burgtheater manuscripts, on the other hand, the lines are replaced with cries of "Feinde" and "Wir" respectively.[94] Similarly, when Ottokar begins to fight against Seyfried, the original manuscript instructs him to shout out "Hier Böhmen!," to which Seyfried replies, "Und hier Österreich!" (v. 2930; *SW* I/3:173).[95] In the Burgtheater version, however, Ottokar's original cry is substituted by one of "Hier, für den König!," while Seyfried now responds with "Für den Vater hier!" The Theater an der Wien censors, by contrast, permitted the exchange to remain as it was.

Even at the Burgtheater, however, not all passages involving interethnic relations were treated with equal sensitivity. During the third act of the play, a woman comes to see Rudolf and asks him for help, explaining that her house has been burned down by the "Böhmen." In the Theater an der Wien manuscript, "Böhmen" is changed to "Feinde," so as to obscure the nationality of those responsible for the woman's suffering. In the Burgtheater manuscripts, on the other hand, the woman's complaints are allowed to remain as they are. Either those responsible for screening the Burgtheater production did not notice them, or else they were considered harmless. Possibly the mention of Czechs burning down a house in the course of battle was considered less of a threat to ethnic harmony than the direct confrontation between two national armies.

An equivalent lack of consistency, this time on the part of the Volkstheater censors, is revealed by a similar complaint that was allowed to remain in both productions. During a long speech by Margareta in act one, the queen relates how she came to marry Ottokar and describes the condition of Austria before their marriage:

> Denn Brand und Raub verwüstete unser Land;
> Der Ungar hier, der Bayer dort, der Böhme,
> Sie hausten mit dem Schwert in Österreich,
> Verderbend meiner Väter schönes Erbe.
> (vv. 295–98; *SW* I/3:21–22)

Here, Margareta's description of the harm done to Austria by other nations is more powerful than in the previous example, as she makes clear the devastating impact of other nations' soldiers on her country as a whole. Had they wished to, the censors could have removed Margareta's references to specific nationalities, as they had done at other points, and her speech would still have made sense. It is possible that the behavior she describes was considered an acceptable part of war. Structural factors may also have played a role. As a short section in a lengthy speech on an apparently unrelated topic (the history of a marriage), by a woman, it was either overlooked by the censors or considered harmless.

One further issue relevant to the question of national sensitivities is the portrayal of characters that might offend the dignity of a particular ethnic group. We have already seen that many parts of the play that highlight the Czech king's humiliating downfall were allowed to remain in both productions. The depiction of the villainous Czech nobleman, the Iago-like Zawisch, was also largely unaffected by censorship pressures.[96] Another interesting character in this regard is Ottokar's Hungarian second wife, Kunigunde. In many ways, Kunigunde can be seen as the embodiment of contemporary prejudices about Hungarians as being wild, uncivilized, and stupid. When Ottokar's second wife first enters his court, she is dressed as a man and greets the king with a request to join his "Krieger" (vv. 717–19; *SW* I/3:44). As time wears on and she becomes dissatisfied with her new life, she makes no attempt to hide her discontent. Instead, she complains at length about the restrictive conditions at the Czech court (vv. 984–94; *SW* I/3:61), makes thinly-veiled references to Ottokar's failing sexual stamina (vv. 975–77; *SW* I/3:38), and eventually becomes involved in an adulterous affair with Zawisch. She is also unable to understand simple lines in the love poetry sent to her by the Czech nobleman (v. 941; *SW* I/3:58) and delivers mercilessly scornful speeches to Ottokar during his psychological crisis (vv. 2183–87; *SW* I/3:129).

With the censorship of the portrayal of Kunigunde, it is impossible to tell whether alterations that improve her image were made in order to protect her as a Hungarian or to protect her as a queen. Many of her speeches are deleted or substantially shortened in a way that serves to tone down her peculiarities: most of these are her more open sexual references[97] and some of her vicious attacks on the king that were mentioned in earlier sections. In the Burgtheater version, a stage direction that describes the queen stamping her foot is replaced by the instruction "die Königin macht eine ungeduldige Bewegung" (following v. 946; *SW* I/3:59).[98] Yet even after these alterations, Kunigunde still appears as an outspoken, strong-willed, somewhat unintelligent woman with little interest in codes of civilized behavior. Her entrance into the Czech court dressed as a man, for example, remained in both manuscripts; and her desertion of her husband for Zawisch becomes clear when Ottokar is told that they are staying in a tower together (vv. 2612–14; *SW* I/3:152). Both sets of censors also allowed a line to remain in which the queen appears unable to understand the meaning of "weiß wie Schnee" in Zawisch's love poetry (v. 941; *SW* I/3:59), an omission that suggests a certain toleration of such stereotypes.

In predicting the attitudes of the two censors to issues of nationality, we might expect the two sets of censors to have different priorities. We might imagine that the Volkstheater censors were more concerned to prevent the arousing of resentment and hatred between the different nationalities, and that the Burgtheater censors were more anxious to avoid offending their audience. This does appear to have been true to a certain extent. As we have seen, the Theater an der Wien censors were more sensitive to both Ottokar's declarations of power over other nations and the mention of wartime Czech house-burning. However, a serious effort on the part of the Burgtheater censors to avoid offending any members of their audiences appears questionable given their toleration of Ottokar's disparaging comments about the Czechs.

Indeed, in general, both sets of censors display a considerable degree of inconsistency in their treatment of national issues. The most extreme example of this is the Volkstheater censors' pattern of deleting one reference to the Czechs' loyalty and allowing the next one to remain. Yet the same is true of several of the Burgtheater censors' decisions: while they allowed Ottokar's explicitly negative characterization of his people, for example, they showed remarkable sensitivity in their alteration of his claims that no Czech had yet betrayed him. Although the protection of nationalities was clearly an important censorship concern, the consequences of this for dramatic works were remarkably erratic.

Revolution and Betrayal

It appears that, following the French Revolution, a fear of uprisings in Habsburg territory led to a complete ban on the depiction of revolt on the Austrian stage. Certainly, Hägelin's *Denkschrift* is categorical on this matter:

> Hiebey ist noch zu mercken, daß Stücke, welche Aufruhre, Empörungen, Conspirationen wider die Regenten oder andere rechtmässige Regierungen enthalten, diese Laster mögen am Ende gestraft werden oder nicht, derzeit nicht aufs Theater zu bringen seyn.[99]

Censors' reports from the first twenty years of the nineteenth century, on the other hand, suggest that the inclusion of an uprising did not automatically lead to the prohibition of a play, suggesting that the rigid policy of 1795 was relaxed slightly in subsequent decades.[100]

König Ottokar does not contain any revolution in the normal sense of the word. However, Ottokar's final defeat in battle can be substantially attributed to the large number of his subjects who dislike him. Many of his Austrian subjects desert him as a result of his divorce from Margareta; their courage and enthusiasm as they fight against him contrasts sharply with the jaded performance of the Czechs, as Ottokar himself observes:

> Die Böhmen fechten matt, wie man wohl ficht
> Für einen Ungeliebten, notgedrungen.
> Die Östreichsmänner und die Steirer aber,
> Die sonst nur träg mir ihren Dienst erwiesen,
> In Todesengel scheinen sie verwandelt [. . .].
> (vv. 2818–22; *SW* I/3:167)

It is true that the issue of Ottokar's relationship with his people never becomes a central concern of the play. Even so, we are reminded at several points of the steady stream of deserters who abandon their king, and thereby indirectly fulfil Margareta's prophecy that "wie ich scheide, / Schwingt wieder Aufruhr zischend seine Fackel" (v. 626–27; *SW* I/3:37). Although not a revolution in the normal understanding, these events nevertheless illustrate the power of popular discontent.

When we look at the manuscripts handed in to the censors by the two theaters, it becomes apparent that most references to this indirect revolution were regarded as inoffensive.[101] A number of factors probably contributed toward this leniency. The fact that it involved the return of Austrian subjects to the Habsburgs no doubt helped. Secondly, the mass desertion of troops was not a danger facing Habsburg rulers at the time. In addition, however, the abandonment of Ottokar is provoked primarily by his behavior within the personal sphere, rather than the mistreatment or exploitation of his subjects. This circumstance is reinforced by the fact that all references to the desertion are formulated in apolitical terms.

Nevertheless, the play's patriotic sentiment was not enough to remove the censors' sensitivity to all mention of revolution or popular rebellion. Perhaps as a result of prior experience, even the published manuscript only contained three such references anyway. One of these, lines 1550 to 1554, in which the chancellor warns Ottokar of the possible consequences of going to war against Rudolf, was deleted from both manuscripts:[102]

> Die Lande sind nun einmal mißvergnügt,
> Bereit zu Aufstand und Meuterei,
> Sie rufen euch die Deutschen, eh ihrs denkt.
> Und stirbt auch Rudolf, fällt auch er in der Schlacht;
> Ein andrer Kaiser fordert euch dasselbe [. . .].
> (vv. 1550–54; *SW* I/3:96)

Here, the rebellion potentially faced by Ottokar was a response to social conditions and, as such, much closer to the threats facing contemporary Habsburgs than the desertion of troops in response to an unjustified divorce. Moreover, the use of such explicitly political terms as "Aufstand" and "Meuterei" will certainly have rung alarm bells for contemporary censors.

The importance of word usage is further suggested by the deletion of lines 175, 176, and 177 in the censors' manuscript for the Theater an der Wien production.[103] Here, members of the Rosenberg family, who have been campaigning for Berta Rosenberg to be chosen as Ottokar's second wife, are reeling from the shock of seeing their plan fail. In their anger, Milota and Benesch Rosenberg insist that revenge, presumably in the form of action against the king, is necessary in order to restore their family's honor. Zawisch, on the other hand, warns them against such action:

> Die ihr auf offner Straße Racheplane
> Zu tauben Wänden schreit und — offnen Ohren!
> Verschwört euch auf dem Markt und treibt im Zimmer Aufruhr!
> (vv. 175–77; *SW* I/3:17)

The Rosenbergs' vague calls for "Rache" hardly promise the level of organized political action implied by such words as "Verschwört" and "Aufruhr," and Zawisch quickly goes on to dismiss his relatives' plans as a result of "der Rausch des Zorns" (v. 179; *SW* I/3:17). Indeed, although the Rosenbergs appear intent on action against the king, their own calls for revenge are allowed to remain in both manuscripts. It is only Zawisch's rather sneering interpretation of these intentions, which uses the political words "Verschwört" and "Aufruhr," that were removed by the censors for the Volkstheater production.

There is one point at which the language of political revolution is tolerated in both productions. As already mentioned, toward the end of the first act, as Margareta takes her leave from Ottokar, she warns him of the consequences of their divorce, suggesting that it will cost him the loyalty of his Austrian subjects:

> Doch wie ich scheide,
> Schwingt wieder Aufruhr zischend seine Fackel,
> Und gegen Euch [. . .]. (vv. 626–28; *SW* I/3:37)

Despite the use of the inflammatory word "Aufruhr" to refer to a potential political rebellion, Margareta's warning is allowed to remain in both versions. It is possible that her words were simply overlooked by the censors, although this seems unlikely given the degree of scrutiny to which both productions were subjected. Perhaps, like the mass desertions predicted by them, Margareta's "Aufruhr" was tolerated because it referred to an action of loyalty toward the Habsburg dynasty. The fact that she was a woman may also have made her words appear less threatening.

In addition to popular revolt, another potential threat to monarchical power is conspiracy. The instruction quoted by Hägelin at the beginning of this section suggests a close link between the issues of rebellion and conspiracy, and Viennese censors' reports from the early nineteenth century reveal that theatrical representations of the latter continued to be problematic until at least the late 1830s.[104] Moreover, both manuscripts for the 1825 productions of *König Ottokar* suggest that contemporary censors could also object to the depiction of the deceit and treachery associated with conspiracy. For, while references to the Austrians' quiet rebellion against Ottokar were safe from the censors, the same was not necessarily true of even minor acts of deception or betrayal committed by his other subjects. While hiding Kunigunde's "Busenschleife" from a suspicious Ottokar during the second act, Zawisch declares, "Herr, es gibt Dinge, / Die man mit Recht dem König selbst verbirgt!" (v. 1105–6; *SW* I/3:69). Although, as we have seen, both sets of censors appear in general to have been rather relaxed about protecting Ottokar's dignity, Zawisch's declaration of the right of subjects to conceal matters from their kings was removed from both manuscripts.[105] It is true that even the postcensorship manuscripts contained a couple of examples of Ottokar being deceived by Zawisch: his efforts to persuade the Czech king to act against his own best interests, as well as his cutting of the tent rope as Ottokar kneels before Rudolf. However, in the first case, Zawisch's campaigning involved a sustained effort that could not have been removed without the restructuring of several scenes. And similarly, the cutting of the tent rope supplies a central element of the drama's story. The deletion of the deceptive principle contained within Zawisch's protest, on the other hand, was echoed by a number of other changes made to both manuscripts.

In a long speech toward the beginning of the first act, for example, Margareta describes how she has seen through the Rosenbergs' plot to make Berta into Ottokar's queen. The Theater an der Wien censors initially crossed out lines 201 to 213, but then changed their minds and allowed them to remain. The Burgtheater directors, on the other hand, did not allow lines 210 to 214 into the manuscripts they submitted to the censors at all.[106] In both cases, however, the censors did not try to hide the Rosenbergs' desires and efforts to see Ottokar divorced and Berta made queen.[107] The controversial element of their plan seems to be that of acting behind Ottokar's back, which gives the Rosenbergs' actions the character of a conspiracy. This becomes clear when we read closely the lines excised from the Burgtheater manuscript:

> Ich hörte, wie sie seinen Wunsch nach Erben,
> Nach angebornen Folgern seines Throns,
> Mit heuchlerischem Mitleid listig nährten. —
> Ein Wunsch, gar wohl verzeihlich einem König!
> Doch was soll Erbrecht, das aus Unrecht stammt?
> (vv. 210–14; DHA I/3:19)

It may be objected that the final line, with its assault on the values of dynasty, was the sole cause for this deletion. However, this seems unlikely, as the passage makes perfect sense if this line alone is deleted, as was the case for the Theater an der Wien version. Much more plausible is that line 212 was a further source of unease, as the references to "heuchlerischem Mitleid" it contains make clear the deception involved in the Rosenbergs' endeavors. The passage initially crossed out of the Theater an der Wien manuscripts also contains the less striking description of how the Rosenbergs "verstohlen reißen / An den nur allzuschwachen Banden, die / Kaum Ottokarn noch fesselten an mich" (vv. 207–9; SW I/3:19), but little else that was likely to have upset the censors.[108]

One other passage deleted from the Volkstheater manuscript supports the idea that its censors were particularly sensitive to the portrayal of a monarch being deceived. Shortly before the final battle, the Czech king asks Zawisch whether he, as one of the "Ersten [. . .] meines Reiches" (SW I/3:144), will follow his king into battle. Rosenberg promises that he will, although Ottokar does not believe him, and turns to Milota, proclaiming:

> Du Milota, du bist mein Mann.
> Ich glaube wohl, daß du auch hassen kannst,
> Betrügen nicht. (vv. 2486–88; SW I/3:145)

Later on, however, when he ignores Ottokar's pleas for help from his killers, Milota is revealed to be an untrustworthy subject too (v. 2917; SW I/3:172). The above passage, which was removed from the Theater an der Wien manuscript,[109] therefore contains cases of a subject flagrantly lying to his king, and of a king mistakenly deciding to trust one of his subjects. In the absence of any other obvious source of offense, the removal of this passage can be seen as providing further tentative evidence that the censors at the Volkstheater, at least, were anxious to avoid anything that might encourage subjects to act behind their ruler's back.

If the Theater an der Wien censors appear to have been slightly more concerned not to allow their audience to observe a monarch being deceived, this effect is all the more pronounced when it comes to the issue of betrayal. Although the vast majority of Ottokar's complaints about what he sees as the treachery of his Austrian subjects were allowed to remain in both manuscripts,[110] the same is not true for less justified betrayals by those close to him. While Milota explains his eventual abandonment of the king with a reference to the impact on his brother Benesch of Ottokar's rejection of Berta, "Er ist gestorben als ein Sinnberaubter" (v. 2918; *SW* I/3:172), Kunigunde and Zawisch go over to Rudolf largely out of hatred. In the Burgtheater manuscript, this scene is left largely intact: only Habsburg's speech, which condemns Zawisch's disloyalty, is removed from one of the manuscripts.[111] In the Theater an der Wien manuscript, on the other hand, the whole scene is deleted, so that these two highly significant betrayals no longer figure in the play at all.[112]

The more pronounced sensitivity of the Theater and der Wien censors to the representation of a monarch being deceived or betrayed can be related to the revolutionary potential of its socially-mixed audience. Indeed, an intense concern about influencing audience behavior is also reflected by the attitudes of the commercial theater's censors to more trivial attacks on King Ottokar. Although both sets of officials tolerated the pitiful and undignified state of the Czech king during his psychological crisis, references to far less threatening assaults on his power were removed by the Volkstheater censors. As we have already seen, the anger of Benesch and Milota Rosenberg at seeing Berta passed over as Ottokar's second wife causes them to desire revenge against their king. Zawisch's first reaction to their intentions is scornful:

BENESCH: Wenn du — wenn du dich unsrer Sach entziehst,
           Bist du kein Rosenberg; ein Schurk! Nicht wahr?

MILOTA: So ists!

ZAWISCH: Ei ja! Wie führen wirs denn aus?
           Beim nächsten Kirchgang drück dich an den König,
           Und tritt ihm auf den Fuß, das schmerzt verzweifelt,
           Und so bist du gerächt.

BENESCH: Er spottet unser?
           Mein Kopf! Mein Kopf! — Er ist kein Rosenberg!
                              (vv. 165–71; *SW* I/3:16–17)

The above exchange was deleted in its entirety from the Theater an der Wien manuscript.[113] It is unlikely that the family disharmony also represented in this section was the main reason for this, because the two lines that followed this deletion are Milota telling Benesch, "Komm Bruder, laß uns gehen! Wer lachen kann / Bei seines Hauses Schmach, verdient [. . .]" (v. 172–73; *SW* I/3:17). Rather, Zawisch's essentially harmless mock plan of revenge was apparently considered to be a grave assault on the king's dignity. Later on, in act four, we find another Rosenberg suggesting a similarly trivial act of rebellion against Ottokar. As the Czech king sits huddled in a Prague doorway, Benesch urges Berta to throw a clump of earth at him (vv. 2077–90; *SW* I/3:124–25). His words of encouragement are also removed from the Theater an der Wien manuscript,[114] but were allowed, at least at first, to remain in the Burgtheater production. In fact, Benesch's words were eventually cut out as part of a much longer section,[115] which means that it is unlikely that they were the principal cause for the excision.

These two deletions suggest an anxiety about depicting attacks on the king that went far beyond the efforts of the censors to protect his dignity in other parts of the play. As we have seen, the censors for the Volkstheater production also appear very concerned about attempts to deceive the monarch. Both of these concerns can be related to official disapproval of the portrayal of revolution or conspiracy. For, just as harmless attacks on Ottokar could be seen to show the miniscule building blocks of revolution, acts of deception are a central element of conspiracy.

Such anxiety stands in stark contrast to the way in which the abandonment of Ottokar by his Austrian subjects was treated by both groups of censors. The considerations likely to have influenced this decision have already been mentioned. However, although there is evidence that the censors were especially sensitive toward political language, it is also clear that other factors were taken into account, and that words such as "Aufruhr" and "Aufstand" could be tolerated under certain circumstances.

Enlightened Rule

Several of the most puzzling deletions from the Theater an der Wien manuscript involve sections that depict the Habsburg emperor in a particularly positive light. One example of this is the story of how Rudolf donated his horse to a traveling priest who had lost his own, and later led the Archbishop of Mainz to safety "durch Krieg und Brand und Tod" (*SW* I/3 47). In the Burgtheater production, only the ecclesiastical titles were altered; by contrast, the entire episode was crossed out from the Theater an der Wien manuscript.[116]

An equivalent desire to diminish Rudolf's virtues is suggested by later excisions from the commercial theater's *König Ottokar*. One such cut comes in act three, as the Habsburg ruler emerges from his tent, and two of his subjects enthusiastically reveal both the practical nature and popularity of their monarch:[117]

ERSTER BÜRGER:	(*im Vorgrunde*) Gevatter Grobschmied, saht Ihr wohl? Der Kaiser. Den Hammer in der Hand! Vivat Rudolphus!
ZWEITER BÜRGER:	Sei still, sei still! Er tritt schon auf uns zu!

(vv. 1614–16; *SW* I/3:100)

Shortly afterwards, following Rudolf's encounter with the poet Ottokar von Horneck, another exchange is removed which again suggests Rudolf's modesty and close relationship with his people:[118]

RUDOLF:	Ein wackrer Mann!
ERSTER BÜRGER:	Ja Herr, und ein Gelehrter! Er schreibt 'ne Reimchronik, und Ihr, Herr Kaiser, Kommt auch drin vor!
RUDOLF:	In Gutem, will ich hoffen!

(vv. 1704–6; *SW* 1/3:104)

It is important to stress that other demonstrations of Rudolf's popularity with his subjects were permitted to remain in the scripts.[119] The above examples appear significant, however, because they serve to strengthen Rudolf's characterization as an enlightened monarch.[120] In the first exchange, the Habsburg ruler is holding a hammer, which leads him to appear as a practical, working monarch, an embodiment of the Enlightenment ideal of the monarch as the servant of the state. The way in which he talks to his subjects on equal terms in the second example may have supported this image further. Although there is no surviving documentation of official censorship policy toward the Enlightenment in the nineteenth century, Hägelin's memorandum clearly articulates state hostility toward Enlightenment ideals in the years that immediately followed the French Revolution. In a section entitled "Bemerkungen für die jetzigen Zeitumstände," the experienced censor also reveals how closely the authorities associated the Enlightenment with democratic ideals:

> Von dem Worte "Aufklärung" ist auf dem Theater eben so wenig Erwähnung zu machen als von der Freiheit und Gleichheit; denn die neue Philosophie ist im Stande wider dasjenige, was obige Wörter bedeuten, sogar zu deklamiren, weil ihr nur daran ligt, die Ohren des Publikums mit demselben zu familiarisiren.[121]

By showing how the despotic Ottokar is defeated by a Habsburg who embodies Enlightenment ideals, Grillparzer's published manuscript can be seen to advance the superiority of those values. Moreover, in depicting an enlightened Rudolf as the ideal Habsburg monarch, the play also sets up standards of which contemporary Habsburg rulers could, potentially, fall far short.

Another passage deleted from both manuscripts provides further evidence that the censorship authorities were alert to the implications of this opposition. During a long speech of Rudolf's in the third act, the contrast in styles of rule between the Habsburg and Czech monarchs becomes explicit. In his efforts to persuade Ottokar to return Austria and Steiermark to the Reich, Rudolf gives an account of his own principles of rule. He recalls how he, like Ottokar, used to be concerned only with his own ambitions. Later on, however, his perspective changed dramatically and he forsook his earlier vanity to recognize the value of others:

> So fiels wie Schuppen ab von meinen Augen
> Und all mein Ehrgeiz war mit eins geheilt.
> Die Welt ist da, damit wir alle leben,
> Und groß ist nur der ein alleinge Gott!
>
> (vv. 1910–13; *SW* I/3:114)

Although Rudolf does not go on to elucidate the political consequences of this change in focus, there is a clear suggestion that his subjects have benefited from it:

> Wir stehn am Eingang einer neuen Zeit.
> Der Bauer folgt in Frieden seinem Pflug,
> Es rührt sich in der Stadt der fleißge Bürger,
> Gewerb und Innung hebt das Haupt empor [. . .].
>
> (vv. 1920–23; *SW* I/3:114)

Despite the positive propaganda granted to the Habsburg dynasty by Rudolf's speech, it was not included in either 1825 production of *König Ottokar:* lines 1888 to 1929 were removed from the Theater an der Wien manuscript, and lines 1888 to 1911 and 1921 to 1926 were crossed out of the Burgtheater version.[122]

Enlightenment principles were not the only values to elicit a nervous response from those censoring *König Ottokar*. A series of further deletions from both manuscripts suggests that officials could also object to the suggestion of even vague moral criteria against which monarchs could potentially be judged. In the published version of *König Ottokar*, for example, Rudolf's final speech contains a warning to his elder son, in which the latter is told to bear in mind the fate of Ottokar should he ever be tempted to stray from God's laws:

> Du steh in allem deinem Bruder bei!
> Doch solltet ihr je übermütig werden,

> Mit Stolz erheben euren Herrscherblick,
> So denkt an den Gewaltigen zurück
> Der jetzt nur fiel in Gottes strenge Hände,
> An Ottokar, sein Glück und an sein Ende!
> (vv. 2978–82; *SW* I/3:177)

The section is free from any suggestions about Ottokar's treatment of his subjects, which probably explains why it was allowed to remain in the Theater an der Wien production. However, its references to God's punishment for "übermütig" rulers seems to have been considered offensive enough for the Burgtheater direction to have it removed from even their original censorship manuscript,[123] a decision that may well have been influenced by the regular presence of Emperor Francis at the court theater's performances. It does not seem implausible that he was expected to react badly to the prospect of being judged against such standards.

Similar criteria appear to have guided the censorship of the Theater an der Wien production of *König Ottokar*. Just as the Burgtheater direction evidently became nervous about the idea that a king should not be "übermutig," alarm bells rang for the Volkstheater censors at the suggestion that greed was an unsuitable vice for a monarch. As Rudolf tries to persuade Ottokar to return Austria and Steiermark to the Reich, he appeals to the Czech king's vanity, reminding him how he had once been great, "Eh die Gelegenheit des Mehrbesitzes / In Euch entzündet auch den Wunsch dazu" (v. 1882–83; *SW* I/3:113). This hint that greed could be dangerous for a monarch was crossed out of the Theater an der Wien manuscript.[124]

The deletion of such explicit suggestions of a moral code for rulers can be seen as a logical extension of the excision of direct comparisons between the rule of the enlightened Rudolf and that of the often despotic Ottokar. The greater sensitivity of the Theatre an der Wien censors to this issue is suggested by their removal of scenes in which Rudolf's enlightened characteristics were most obviously in evidence: presumably they feared these might arouse dangerous hopes in their audience. Yet despite such efforts, an implicit polarity between the two rulers remains in both productions. Even in the postcensorship Theater an der Wien manuscript, the positive impression we have of Rudolf owes a good deal to his characterization as a competent, morally upstanding ruler who is concerned about the welfare of his subjects. In the middle of the third act, for example, we are allowed to see Rudolf listening attentively to the grievances of his subjects and offering to help them where possible. And in addition, both sets of censors allow Rudolf to slip this rather brief and vague account of the principles of his rule into a longer admonishment of Ottokar:

> Ich habs geschworen,
> Geschworen meinem großen, gnädgen Gott,
> Daß Recht soll herrschen und Gerechtigkeit
> Im deutschen Land; und so soll es sein und bleiben!
> (vv. 1749–52; *SW* I/3:107)

Such examples of Rudolf's rectitude are particularly suggestive due to their juxtaposition with Ottokar's despotic lust for power.[125] Although we are shown the Czech king making plans to advance the economic situation of his people, for most of the play he appears in stark contrast to Rudolf. After being told that many of his Austrian subjects have deserted him, for example, Ottokar's response is anything but constructive:

> All dies weite Land,
> Zur menschenleeren Wüste will ichs machen,
> Daß drin die Füchse hausen und die Wölfe,
> Und nach Jahrhunderten der müßge Wandrer
> Sich streiten soll, wo Neuburg stand und Wien.
> (vv. 1440–44; *SW* I/3:90)

Similarly, Ottokar's fondness for arbitrary arrests stands in stark contrast to Rudolf's insistence on "Gerechtigkeit."[126] In the first section we saw how the Reich's spokesman, upon observing such arrests, tells Ottokar that such behavior made him unsuitable for the position of emperor. In addition, the dissatisfaction of Ottokar's subjects is demonstrated briefly, yet convincingly, in act four when the emperor's herald comes to Prague. He orders all those who have grievances against the Czech crown to follow him to the town hall, along with all those who have "Lehn zu nehmen." The subsequent stage direction reads, "Das Volk tumultuarisch ihm nach. Nur der Kanzler bleibt" (following vv. 2259; *SW* I/3:134). Despite the censors' disapproval of lines that explicitly advance moral standards for rulers, Grillparzer's use of less direct means to present the polarity between the two monarchs' principles of rule means that it is not completely obscured.

Militarism

Several sections of Hägelin's 1795 *Denkschrift* emphasize the protection of military values. In addition to instructions forbidding the negative portrayal of high-ranking officers,[127] the memorandum contains the rule that, "[i]n Ansehung der regierenden Häupter sind jene Ausfälle zu verhüten, wodurch sie durchgehends des Mißbrauches der Gewalt in Absicht auf [. . .] die Verheerungen durch Kriege, Eroberungen beschuldiget werden."[128] Unfortunately, no direct documentation of such policies in the early nineteenth century has survived. However, censors' reports from the period reveal that upholding the reputation of the military continued to be one of their priorities.[129]

The censorship of *König Ottokars Glück und Ende* provides an interesting picture of how the protection of militarism could place restrictions on theatrical performances. The first example of this is a one-line deletion from a scene completely unconcerned with military affairs. During the second act, Kunigunde is forced to present Zawisch, who is aggressively pursuing her, with a sash as a prize in a tournament. After hesitating, Kunigunde gives him the prize, and, in his triumph, Zawisch feigns appreciation of the honor:

> Mit diesem teuren Pfand
> Statt Harnisch angetan, statt aller Waffen,
> Will fahrend ich die weite Welt durchziehen [. . .].
>
> (vv. 1049–51; *SW* I/3:65)

Although Zawisch's devotion to Kunigunde is implied by both the first and third lines of this excerpt, only the second line was deleted. While the Theater an der Wien censors were prepared to tolerate Zawisch's admiration for Ottokar's wife, the words "Statt Harnisch angetan, statt aller Waffen" were removed.[130] The rejection of weapons in favor of a token of love was apparently considered unacceptable.

On a more concrete level, a concern for military values is also indicated by a section removed by the Volkstheater censors from Ottokar's long monologue of repentance. After noticing how his men are fighting without real enthusiasm, the Czech king attributes this to his unpopularity and turns to reflect upon the way in which he has ruled. It is at this point that the deleted section begins (v. 2830; *SW* I/3:167). Turning to address God, Ottokar expresses regret, "daß ich mich unterwand, / Den Herrn der Welten frevelnd nachzuspielen" (v. 2831–32; *SW* I/3:167). He goes on to admire the physical construction of human beings ("kein Königsschloß / Mag sich vergleichen mit dem Menschenleib!" (v. 2844–45; *SW* I/3:168), before regretting his treatment of them:

> Ich aber hab sie hin zu Tausenden geworfen,
> Um einer Torheit, eines Einfalls willen,
> Wie man Kehricht schüttet vor die Tür.
>
> (vv. 2846–48; *SW* I/3:168)

The remainder of the excised passage contrasts Ottokar's disregard for human life with the concern shown by parents toward their children.[131] The Czech king's speech is strikingly apolitical in its language: addressed to God, it does not use the word "Krieg" once, although that is clearly its topic. This may have been a deliberate strategy by Grillparzer to avoid attracting the censors' attention; but if so, it did not work. And indeed, it is easy to see how a monologue in which a king expresses repentance for the deaths of his subjects in war poses a potential threat to military values. Although it could be argued that this passage is merely another instance of the Volkstheater censors' dislike for the suggestion of moral standards for kings, further examples indicate that issues of war and peace were a particular concern.

One pair of lines deleted from the Volkstheater manuscript, for instance, appears within a section that only advances implicitly the responsibility of a monarch for the suffering caused by war. During the third act, Ottokar discusses with Zawisch and the chancellor the possibility of going to war against Rudolf. Eager to see Ottokar embark upon a dangerous military campaign, Zawisch encourages his king to take up arms against the Habsburg. The chancellor, however, is far more cautious, and warns Ottokar of the consequences of this decision for his people:

> [. . .] Und rechnet Ihr für nichts
> Das Unheil und die Greuel in dem Land?
> Die Saat zerstampft, die Wohnungen verbrannt,
> Die Menschen hingeschlachtet wie — daß Gott!
> (vv. 1556–59; SW I/3:96)

Although the first two lines of this quotation were allowed to remain in the Theater an der Wien manuscript, the third and fourth lines were removed.[132] It appears that, although the abstract warning of the "Unheil and Greuel" brought to Ottokar's subjects by war was acceptable, more graphic reminders of what this actually meant were considered intolerable.

The independence of the Volkstheater censors' concern for militarism from wider issues of monarchical morality is indicated even more persuasively by a passage deleted from act four of the drama. As Ottokar sits huddled in a Prague doorway following his humiliation in the Austrian camp, his wife reminisces about the power of her husband before his fall. Although she makes no suggestion at all that a king should be considered responsible for the deaths of his subjects in battle, the following large segment of her speech was removed from both manuscripts:[133]

> Das Leben Tausender in seiner Hand,
> Es hinsetzt, wie zum fröhlich leichten Brettspiel
> Auf das von Blut und Staub geteilte Feld,
> Und ausrief: Schach! Als wenn es Steine wären,
> Vom Künstler plump geformt aus totem Stoff,
> Und Roß und Ritter zubenannt zum Scherz.
> (vv. 2105–10; SW I/3:126)

It is unlikely that these lines were excised because of their connection with Ottokar's humiliating fall from power. Both sets of censors allowed Kunigunde's previous comments to remain, which describe how her husband "sitzt [...] wie ein Bettler vor der Tür" (v. 2100; *SW* I/3:126). Instead, it is probable that the queen's words were considered problematic because they employed imagery that strongly hinted at the indifference of rulers to the fate of their soldiers in battle. Although we have seen that other, more vivid depictions of Ottokar's callous attitude toward his subjects were allowed to remain in both manuscripts, it seems that this particular example was considered intolerable. And certainly, one can imagine how the notion of a king considering battle to be a game and viewing his soldiers as "Steine [...] / Vom Künstler plump geformt aus totem Stoff" could be seen to present a challenge to official accounts of relations between monarch and soldiers within a nation at war.

Military values were offered further protection by the deletion of reminders about the less glorious sides of war. During the final battle scene, for instance, Margareta's chambermaid, Elisabeth, rushes on stage in a state of panic:

FRAU ELISABETH:	(*hinter der Szene*) Gewalt, Gewalt!
RUDOLF:	Wer ruft?
ELISABETH:	(*kommt und wirft sich dem Kaiser zu Füßen*) Ach, gnädger Kaiser! Sie plündern drin im Haus, sie zünden an, Und gönnen selbst den Toten nicht die Ruh! Ach schützt uns Herr!
RUDOLF:	Man soll zu Hilfe sehn! Wer bist du?
ELISABETH:	Ach, der Königin Margrete Von Österreich getreue Kämmerin, Und die dort tragen meiner Frauen Leiche.

(vv. 2941–47; *SW* I/3:174–75)

This illustration of the terror that accompanies armed conflict was also deleted from the Volkstheater manuscript.[134] It could be argued that line 2943, with its reference to the maltreatment of corpses, was the sole cause for this excision. However, this line could have been removed on its own without disrupting the continuity of the scene. It could also be objected that, as we have seen in the section on nationalities, both sets of censors allowed references to the devastation caused by war to remain elsewhere in the play. Nevertheless, the reporting of such events does not threaten to make such a powerful impression on an audience as the appearance of one of its distraught victims.

The deletions made by the Theater an der Wien censors to passages related to militarism therefore indicate an anxiety about the issue that barely existed for those censoring the Burgtheater production. The middle and lower classes' perception of both war and broader military matters were clearly a source of considerable concern. As a result of this, both the depiction and the discussion of war on commercial stages were evidently subject to considerable restrictions.

Sexual Morality

In the introduction to Hägelin's 1795 memorandum, the experienced censor wrote that the theater should be a "Schule der guten Sitten."[135] The most detailed source regarding the implementation of this ideal in the early nineteenth century is the morality section of the 1803 instructions for *Theaterkommissäre*.[136] This paragraph begins with the injunction that all breaches of decency are to be taken very seriously, and, among other things, orders the removal from dramatic performances of both obliquely suggestive passages and "die wärmeren Schilderungen der Liebe, wenn sie den materiellen Teil derselben auf eine schlüpfrige Weise berühren und die Sinnlichkeit wecken."[137] Even before being prepared for performance, the script of *König Ottokar* reflected official anxiety about the morals of its future audience: the play contained neither graphic language nor direct depictions of erotic physical contact. Yet the drama still includes numerous manifestations of sensuality, and these met with varying responses from the authorities.

Much sexual reference was handled in the same way for both productions. This is true, for example, of Margareta's matter-of-fact remarks about the lack of physical attraction in her marriage to Ottokar: probably due to their non-erotic tone, statements such as "War Lust ein Fremdling dieser öden Brust" (v. 253; *SW* I/3:20) and "Hat Gram der Züge Reiz mir ausgelöscht" (v. 240; *SW* I/3:20) were allowed to remain in both sets of performances. At the other end of the spectrum was a speech made by Ottokar's second wife that employs fire imagery to represent physical desire: Kunigunde's report of how, before marrying the Czech king, she had expected him to "dürste nach der feurigen Genossin, / Nach gleichem Mut in gleichgeschwellter Brust" (v. 976–77; *SW* I/3:60) was removed from both manuscripts.[138] It is certainly not hard to see how the potency of the new queen's language ("der feurigen Genossin," "gleichgeschwellter Brust") threatened to awaken the sensuality of theater audiences. More successful, from Grillparzer's point of view, was a speech from act two, in which Kunigunde describes Zawisch's attentions toward her. An avoidance of sensual vocabulary and a disapproving tone may have made it appear innocuous. Yet the Czech queen's words effectively convey the fervor of Zawisch's pursuit, and the frenzied rhythm of her sentences mirrors the sexual agitation of Rosenberg:

KÖNIGIN: [...] Bei meiner Ankunft schriet Ihr gellend auf —
Ihr warts! Ich stand drei Schritte fern und weiß es!
Seitdem verfolgt Ihr rastlos mich mit Blicken,
Mit Blicken, die ich näher nicht bezeichne,
Doch regt sich mir der Ingrimm, denk ich dran.

(vv. 875–79; *SW* I/3:54)

While these examples suggest perceptual similarities between those screening the two performances, others indicate that stricter standards were applied to the erotic content of the Theater an der Wien production — presumably due to greater official anxiety about the corruptibility of its audience. One relevant case is Margareta's account of the vow of celibacy she made following the death of her first husband, Heinrich. Her description, which is only moderately sensual, was permitted to be included in the Burgtheater performances, but not in those at the commercial theater:[139]

Nicht Manneshände sollten je berühren
Den kleinsten Finger mir, des Kleides Saum,
Und selbst ein Weib nicht meine Lippen küssen,
Die einst an Heinrichs teurem Mund geruht.

(vv. 353–56; *SW* I/3:23)

This pattern is repeated by the response of censors to Kunigunde's rejection of Ottokar following his humiliating submission to Rudolf. Following her husband's plea for "Ein Tröpflein Milde," the queen retorts mercilessly:

Solange Ihr Euch nicht von der Schmach gereinigt,
Betretet nicht als Gatte mein Gemach.

(v. 2404–5; *SW* I/3:141)

These words were left entirely unchanged in the court theater manuscript; in the commercial theater performance, however, the second line was replaced with "Ist Kunigunde nicht Euer Weib."[140] As both versions involve an equally brutal rebuff of the king, it seems that the censors for the commercial theater's production considered the image of Ottokar entering his wife's chamber too suggestive for the fragile morals of its audience.

Another interesting issue is the portrayal of the adulterous affair between Kunigunde and Zawisch. One of Hägelin's most adamant instructions regarding the protection against immorality was that neither adultery nor adulteresses could play a role in theatrical performances.[141] And, while there is no conclusive evidence that marital infidelity remained a theatrical taboo, surviving censors' reports from the following decades consistently express disapproval of plays that include adultery.[142] The printed version of *König Ottokar* certainly reflects this official disapprobation: the relationship between Zawisch and the queen is never mentioned explicitly, and we never witness any physical or manifestly romantic contact between the two. However, the published drama also contains numerous reminders of the relationship, including — as we have seen — Zawisch's determined pursuit of Kunigunde, a scene in which the couple seek the protection of Rudolf together, and Ottokar's enraged reaction to news that the "Königin von Böhmen" and her entourage are occupying a clock tower which he comes across:

>OTTOKAR: (*ihn anfassend*) Der Königin von Böhmen? — Das Gefolg?
>Wohl auch sie selbst? — Ha Schurk! — und Zawisch auch?
>Es soll mir wohl tun meinen Zorn zu fühlen!
>(vv. 2612–14; *SW* I/3:154)

As well as stressing Zawisch's proximity to the queen, Ottokar's speech also calls attention to the fact that he has good reason to be angry with the two of them.

Although the affair could have been removed from the play entirely without disrupting the central plot, such oblique references were allowed to remain in both sets of performances. Due to a lack of documentation, it is impossible to know whether this toleration reflected general censoring practice, or — as the section on nationalities might lead us to suspect — whether Kunigunde was granted additional leeway because of her Hungarian origins and her marriage to an enemy of the Habsburgs. Nevertheless, it is clear that those censoring both productions of *König Ottokar* were keen to render the presentation of the Czech queen's adultery as abstract as possible. Several overwrought speeches that accompany Zawisch's courtship of Kunigunde were either toned down or shortened for the two sets of performances.[143] Also removed from both productions was the following unerotic but sentimental scene, in which Kunigunde signals her acceptance of Zawisch's attentions:[144]

>KUNIGUNDE: (*kommt*) Was ist? Wer spielt?
>
>KAMMERFRÄULEIN: (*an der Balustrade*) Ich weiß nicht,
>gnädige Frau.
>Horch! Worte? "Hand wie Schnee, und doch so heiß!"
>Es ist Herr Zawisch Rosenberg. Er singt.
>Soll ich ihn gehen heißen?
>
>KÖNIGIN: (*hat sich gesetzt*) Laß ihn nur,
>Es hört sich gut zu, in der Abendkühle.
>(*Sie stützt ihr Haupt gedankenvoll in die Hand.*)
>(vv. 1343–47; *SW* I/3:83)

Although references to Kunigunde's adultery could be tolerated, it was not permitted for them to be dwelt upon or to appear in a potentially attractive light.

The censorship of erotic content within *König Ottokar* indicates that reminders of sexuality and even adultery could reach the stage, but only if formulated in an oblique manner or sober tone. Standards were particularly strict for the commercial theater, where it seems that even hints of sensual interaction between married couples could be considered unsuitable.

Conclusion

There are a number of difficulties in attempting to detect censorship norms in a play such as *König Ottokar*. First, the small number of examples for each theme makes it hard to be sure of the precise reason for each deletion. This problem is compounded when there are exceptions to what appears to be a general rule and it becomes necessary to speculate about the reasons for such anomalies. In addition, for a play with such a complex and protracted censorship history as *König Ottokar*, it is possible that censorship practices may have been influenced by the controversy itself.

Yet, despite such difficulties, the censorship manuscripts for the two early productions of *König Ottokar* provide much interesting information. Perhaps most importantly, they reveal an asymmetry in the censorship practices for the two productions that reflects the contrasting attitudes of the authorities toward the two audiences. On the one hand, censorship of the Burgtheater production (both by the theater management and by the official censors) appears to have been motivated largely by a desire to avoid offending the members of its establishment audience. Alterations made to the Theater an der Wien production, on the other hand, frequently indicate a deep-seated anxiety about the revolutionary potential and the sensual corruptibility of its audience. As a result, considerably stricter standards were applied to those parts of the Theater an der Wien production that threatened either to encourage political dissent or to awaken sexual urges. Among the most prominent examples of this trend are the removal from the Theater an der Wien manuscript of acts of deceit and petty attacks against Ottokar, the deletion of passages that most explicitly characterize Rudolf as an enlightened king, and the efforts to excise utterance that calls into question the permanence and sacred character of the bond between land and ruler.

Despite these differences, however, the censorship of both productions confirms the importance of presentation to writing under censorship suggested by earlier chapters. In Austria too, provocative content could sometimes pass the censors when crafted in a relatively discreet manner. This is true, for example, of indirect revelations of Kunigunde und Zawisch's adulterous affair, which — unlike more prominent examples of their illicit interactions — were allowed to be included in both productions of the play. And, while explicit discussion of the differences between the principles of rule adhered to by Rudolf and Ottokar were removed from both performance manuscripts, indirect reminders of this polarity were permitted to remain. Finally, although the appearance of a distraught victim of wartime terror was removed from the Theater an der Wien manuscript, other, more distanced and generalized reports of wartime destruction and trauma were evidently regarded as tolerable.

Another noteworthy aspect of the censorship of *König Ottokar* is the incomplete protection granted to non-German minorities. One dimension of this is the insulting passage about Czechs that was allowed to remain in the Burgtheater manuscripts. More significant, however, is the portrayal of royal characters belonging to non-German ethnic groups. Despite her royal status, for example, Kunigunde was allowed to appear as an uncivilized, intellectually deficient adulteress in both productions of the play. Similarly, the toleration of scenes that highlight the Czech king's downfall and abandonment by his subjects form a stark contrast with the censors' diligent efforts to protect the institution of monarchy elsewhere. While doubtlessly compounded by Ottokar's identity as a Habsburg foe, such censorship patterns nevertheless indicate that patriotic sentiment could take precedence over the protection of ethnic groups.

Indeed, the treatment of Ottokar and Kunigunde is all the more striking because it represents the only cases in which the censors of *König Ottokar* did not uphold the standards recommended by Hägelin in 1795. As we have seen, many expurgated sections of the play did not breach any of the 1795 guidelines, and thereby indicate that censorship controls had — in some respects at least — become stricter since the end of the eighteenth century. Of course, it may be suggested that those censoring the productions compensated for the various controversial components of the play by being unusually strict in their treatment of other elements of the play's content. Yet this seems unlikely given their lack of interest in toning down one of the most prominent of these contentious elements: Ottokar's downfall. Another possible objection is that Hägelin's *Denkschrift* only represented a set of guidelines and did not claim to be comprehensive. Nevertheless, the censorship of the Theater an der Wien manuscript in particular indicates the emergence of major censorship concerns — such as the portrayal of enlightened rulers or the depiction of war — that are not even mentioned in the 1795 document. Such developments can be attributed to both an increased fear of the political opposition and the authorities' growing awareness of the ways in which art could use indirect means to deliver a subversive message. As we have seen, the limitations that such practices placed on the literary examination of political, psychological, and ethical themes were considerable.

While it is likely that this increase in the scope of theater censorship was the result of official policies, the preparation for performance of the

König Ottokar manuscripts also suggests the difficulties caused by the absence of a comprehensive set of guidelines for Vienna theater censors. For, despite the undeniable logic behind most deletions, the manuscripts were at various junctures censored inconsistently. Although structural factors contributed at some points, cases where very similar utterances are deleted in one instance and permitted in others suggest an uncertainty on the part of both censors and theater officials regarding what exactly could be allowed. Indeed, further evidence for this incertitude is provided by the fact that many of the differences between the censorship of the two productions of *König Ottokar* cannot be explained by the social composition of their respective audiences. As we have seen, only the Volkstheater censors objected to the suggestion that a monarch must not be greedy, whereas only the Burgtheater direction removed Rudolf's warning to his elder son not to be an "übermütig" ruler once he grew up. The diverging manner in which the issue of nationality was handled for the two performances is another example of such inconsistency.

The difficulties created by this erratic element of Austrian state censorship for both writers and theater management are self-evident.[145] We have already seen how the Burgtheater direction failed to get their specially prepared manuscript of *König Ottokar* authorized for performance first time around. For writers too, it created a fundamental insecurity regarding the kind of utterance that would reach their audience. As a result, they faced a choice between avoiding the enormous group of topics that could possibly be considered controversial or, like Grillparzer, running the risk of seeing their works mutilated by the censors.

Notes

[1] Franz Grillparzer, *Sämtliche Werke: Historisch-kritische Gesamtausgabe,* ed. August Sauer and Reinhold Backmann (Vienna: Anton Schroll, 1909–48), section I, vol. 3, 1931, 1–177 (edition subsequently cited as *SW*).

[2] *SW* section I, vol. 16, 1925, 170.

[3] *SW* I/16:180. For documents relating to the play's prohibition in 1824, see Karl Glossy, "Geschichte der Theater Wiens II (1820–1830)," *Jahrbuch der Grillparzer-Gesellschaft* 26 (1920): 1–155; here 46–51 and 54–55.

[4] See *SW* section I, vol. 18, 1939, 14–46.

[5] See *SW* section I, vol. 17, 1931, 26–27.

[6] Josef Schreyvogel, *Josef Schreyvogels Tagebücher, 1810–1823,* ed. Karl Glossy, 2 vols. (Berlin: Gesellschaft für Theatergeschichte, 1903), 2:337. Schreyvogel had initially been responsible for censoring the poem, and was later reprimanded for authorizing it.

[7] See Schreyvogel, *Josef Schreyvogels Tagebücher,* 2:277.

[8] Several critics have remarked upon the idealized portrayal of Rudolf. See, for example, Heinz Politzer, *Franz Grillparzer: Oder das abgründige Biedermeier* (Vienna: Fritz Molden, 1972), 168–69.

[9] Grillparzer's interest in Ottokar's psychology is reflected in the fact that the latter, rather than Rudolf, is the central character of the play. See also W. E. Yates, *Grillparzer: A Critical Introduction* (Cambridge: Cambridge UP, 1972), 98. The psychological extremes of unreflective dynamism and moral scrupulousness that hinders action are explored in a number of Grillparzer's others dramas, notably *Ein Bruderzwist in Habsburg* and *Des Meeres und der Liebe Wellen*.

[10] See Oskar Teuber and Alexander von Weilen, *Das K. K. Hofburgtheater seit seiner Begründung* (Vienna: Gesellschaft für Vervielfältigende Kunst, 1906), 51. Indeed, W. E. Yates has identified specific parallels between the portrayal of Ottokar's decline and that of King Lear in Shakespeare's play. See Yates, *Grillparzer*, 102.

[11] See Glossy, "Zur Geschichte der Theater Wiens II," 46–51 and 54–55.

[12] See *SW* I/18:46.

[13] See Glossy, "Zur Geschichte der Wiener Theatercensur," *Jahrbuch der Grillparzer-Gesellschaft* 7 (1879): 238–340; here 256–71.

[14] See Glossy, Zur Geschichte der Wiener Theatercensur," 294–97.

[15] The full text of these instructions can be found in Marx, *Die österreichische Zensur*, 68–73.

[16] See W. E. Yates, *Theatre in Vienna*, 26–30.

[17] For the full text of these instructions, see Marx, *Die österreichische Zensur*, 73–76.

[18] See Marx, *Die österreichische Zensur*, 15.

[19] See Yates, *Theatre in Vienna*, 29–30.

[20] For examples of this interaction during the 1820s, see the reproductions of official documents in Karl Glossy, "Zur Geschichte der Theater Wiens II," 49, 51, and 112.

[21] For more on official attitudes toward the theater, see Johann Hüttner, "Theatre Censorship in Metternich's Vienna," *Theatre Quarterly* 37 (1980): 61–69; here 61–62.

[22] See Yates, *Theatre in Vienna*, 37.

[23] Karl Glossy, "Zur Geschichte der Theater Wiens I (1801–1820), [. . .] II (1821–1830) and [. . .] III (1831–1840)," *Jahrbuch der Grillparzer-Gesellschaft* 25 (1915): 1–271; 26 (1920): 1–155; and 30 (1931): 1–152.

[24] At one point, for instance, Glossy refers to the "Wust von Einzelvorschriften" that grew continually. See "Einleitung" to "Geschichte der Theater Wiens I," xxi.

[25] See Glossy, "Geschichte der Theater Wiens I," xxi. The memorandum is quoted in full in Glossy, "Zur Geschichte der Wiener Theatercensur," 298–340.

[26] See, for example, Yates, *Theatre in Vienna*, 28, and Hüttner, "Theatre Censorship in Metternich's Vienna," 64.

[27] A report by Hägelin himself from 1802, for instance, is inconclusive in its verdict on Schiller's *Wallenstein*, although the play involves a revolution. Another from the following year argues in favor of allowing *Macbeth* to be performed, although the

murder of a monarch forms an integral part of its plot. See Glossy, "Zur Geschichte der Wiener Theatercensur I," 9 and 37.

[28] In 1810, Emperor Francis requested information about the guidelines for theater censorship. He was informed that it was very difficult to provide precise instructions, and that the censors were simply told to remove anything offensive to state, religion, or morality (Glossy, "Geschichte der Wiener Theater I," 123–24). The enduring absence of detailed instructions in the following decades is indicated by the reponse of the censor Vogel to complaints made by the emperor about the performance of Nestroy's *Lumpacivagabundus* at the *Theater an der Wien* in 1834. Defending his censorship of the play, Vogel refers to duty of the censor to protect the state, morality, and religion, and then explains how "der bei dem Zensor vorausgesetzte Takt, nämlich sein eigenes Gefühl von Recht und Schicklichkeit ihm als Leitfaden dienen muß" (Glossy, "Geschichte der Wiener Theater III," 95).

[29] The principle that virtue must be rewarded and vice always punished, for instance, can be found both in Hägelin's memorandum (Glossy, "Zur Geschichte der Wiener Theatercensur," 303) and a censor's report from 1827 (Glossy, "Geschichte der Wiener Theater II," 95). For further parallels, see references to Hägelin later on in the chapter.

[30] See especially Yates, *Theatre in Vienna*, 49–62; Verena Keil-Budischowsky, *Die Theater Wiens* (Vienna: Zsolney, 1983), 102–24; and Franz Hadamowsky, *Wien: Theatergeschichte. Von den Anfängen bis zum Ende des ersten Weltkriegs* (Vienna: Jugend und Volk, 1988), 323–42.

[31] For a summary of the development of these genres during the *Vormärz*, see Jürgen Hein, *Das Wiener Volkstheater: Raimund und Nestroy* (Darmstadt: Wissenschaftliche Buchgesellschaft, 1978), 86–97.

[32] See Yates, *Theatre in Vienna*, 87 and 96–98, Keil-Budischowsky, *Die Theater Wiens*, 185–95, and Hadamowsky, *Wien: Theatergeschichte*, 507–16.

[33] See Yates, *Theatre in Vienna*, 30.

[34] Documents reproduced by Glossy reveal that commercial theaters frequently added uncensored material to plays after the first performance. The alarmed responses of the authorities to these violations suggest that the persistance of vulgarities in Volkstheater performances was not the result of official forbearance. See Glossy, "Zur Geschichte Wiener Theater II," 22.

[35] See *SW* I/18:81–82. The fact that the manuscript is not mentioned at all in the relevant section of the *Deutscher Klassiker Verlag* edition of Grillparzer's collected works indicates that it was still missing in 1986, when that edition was published.

[36] Jakob Ziedler, "Ein Censurexemplar von Grillparzer's *König Ottokars Glück und Ende*," in *Ein Wiener Stammbuch: Dem Director der Bibliothek und des historischen Museums der Stadt Wien Dr. Carl Glossy zum 50. Geburtstage, 7. März 1898, gewidmet von Freunden und Landsleuten* (Vienna: Verlag von Carl Konegen, 1898), 287–311. In fact, only the changes attributed by Ziedler to the censors are recorded in the HKA "Lesarten"; these are for the most part accurately copied, although in a couple of cases, changes recorded by Ziedler are either absent from the "Lesarten," or are copied inaccurately. All of the changes used in this chapter have been checked against Ziedler's article.

[37] See Glossy, "Zur Geschichte der Theater Wiens II," 54.

[38] Presumably in order to distinguish between changes initiated by the two censors, the *SW* records changes made by the first censor as "in pencil," although they were confirmed in ink.

[39] Ziedler, "Ein Censurexemplar von Grillparzer's *König Ottokars Glück und Ende*," 308.

[40] For the full details of the manuscripts involved, see *SW* I/18:13–30.

[41] Neither the *SW* nor the *Deutscher Klassiker Verlag* edition of Grillparzer's works contain any information about the censorship of this edition. However, a note from the Staatskanzlei to Sedlnitzky written in June 1824 indicates that no changes to the manuscript were required prior to its publication. The note is reprinted in *Grillparzers Gespräche und die Charakteristiken seiner Persönlichkeit durch die Zeitgenossen*, ed. August Sauer, 6 vols. (Vienna: Verlag des literarischen Vereins, 1904–16), 2:246–47.

[42] Graf Dietrichstein made a note of this approval on the manuscript. See *SW* I/18:78–79.

[43] The relevant piece of correspondence is reprinted in *Grillparzers Gespräche*, 2:246–47.

[44] *Grillparzers Gespräche*, 2:222.

[45] *Grillparzers Gespräche*, 2:247.

[46] Zeugnis no. 244 (*SW* I/18:30) refers to changes made to the end of the third act, for example, while Zeugnis no. 256 (*SW* I/18:32) tells us that by the third performance on 25 of February, Füllenstein's final appearance, in which we see him fight against Rudolf in battle, had been removed.

[47] See Zeugnis no. 256, *SW* I/18:32.

[48] Glossy, "Zur Geschichte der Wiener Theatercensur," 310.

[49] See, for example, Glossy, "Zur Geschichte der Theater Wiens II," 145.

[50] Lines 210–14 absent, h3 h4 h5; line 214 is crossed out in ink, E1w. *SW* I/18:199. "E1w" is the abbreviation used in the *Sämtliche Werke* to refer to the censored script for the Theater an der Wien production of *König Ottokar*.

[51] Lines 208–14 show the impossibility of including line 214 without lines 210–13: "An der nur allzuschwachen Banden, die / Kaum Ottokarn noch fesselten an mich. / Ich hörte, wie sie seinen Wunsch nach Erben, / Nach angebornen Folgern seines Throns, / Mit heuchlerischem Mitleid listig nährten, — / Ein Wunsch gar wohl verzeihlich einem König! / Doch was soll Erbrecht, das aus Unrecht stammt?" *SW* I/3:19.

[52] See, for example, lines 235–37: "Margareta: O glaubt nicht, daß den König ich entschuldge! / Fern sei von mir, daß ich je Böses lobe! / Er handelt unrecht, unerlaubt an mir." *SW* I/3:19–20.

[53] Lines 265–67 absent, h3 h4 h5. *SW* I/18:200.

[54] See, for example, Kanzler to Margareta, lines 581–83: "Euch angewiesen wird, als Leibgeding, / Die Stadt von Krems, das Polan rings um Horn / Und Grevenberg

von unsers Herren Gnade" (*SW* I/3:35); also Ottokar in line 645: "Ich habe eu'r Land den Ungarn abgestritten" (*SW* I/3:39).

⁵⁵ Line 1300 crossed out in ink, E1w. *SW* I/18:248.

⁵⁶ "Das ewge Zaudern, ewige Bedenken! / Und immer rückwärts! Ei, verdamm es Gott! / Der König hat sein Wesen ausgezogen" (*SW* I/3:149).

⁵⁷ Lines 2545–48 crossed out in ink, E1w. *SW* I/18:294–95.

⁵⁸ Lines 2472–76 crossed out in ink, E1w. *SW* I/18:290.

⁵⁹ See, for example Ottokar's second wife, Kunigunde: "Er hat geherrscht; fürwahr er hat geherrscht! / Wie eine Seifenblase ists zerronnen!" (*SW* I/3:127), which immediately precedes a long section crossed out in pencil in h3 h4 h5 (*SW* I/18:279).

⁶⁰ Lines 2662–69 crossed out in ink, E1w. Lines 2662–63 crossed out in pencil, h3 h4; crossed out in red pen, h5. *SW* I/18:299.

⁶¹ Line 2119 crossed out in pencil, h3 h4 h5. *SW* I/18:279.

⁶² Lines 2964–65 absent, h3 h4 h5. *SW* I/18:312.

⁶³ Lines 2958–70 crossed out, h3 h4 h5. *SW* I/18:312.

⁶⁴ Glossy, "Zur Geschichte der Wiener Theatercensur," 311.

⁶⁵ See, for example, Glossy, "Zur Geschichte der Wiener Theater II," 29.

⁶⁶ Line 1961 "Zawisch — Der König kniet!" amended in pencil to "Rudolf (*rasch*) — Wer that uns dies? Ottokar. Ha, Schmach!," E1w. *SW* I/18:274.

⁶⁷ Lines 2135–37 absent, h3 h4 h5; lines 2136–37 crossed out in pencil, E1w. *SW* I/18:279.

⁶⁸ For example lines 2825–28: "Ich habe nicht gut in deiner Welt gehaust, / Du großer Gott! Wie Sturm und Ungewitter / Bin ich gezogen über deine Fluren. / Du aber bists allein der stürmen kann" (*SW* I/3:167).

⁶⁹ Lines 2863–66 crossed out in ink, E1w. *SW* I/18:307.

⁷⁰ In the middle of line 1975, the stage direction, "mit dem Fuße stampfend" is given.

⁷¹ The stage direction "Wirft ihm den Handschuh ins Gesicht; dann" in line 1234 is replaced by "Nach einer Pause," h3 h4 h5; crossed out in pencil, E1w. *SW* I/18:247.

⁷² Ziedler, "Ein Censurexemplar von Grillparzer's *König Ottokars Glück und Ende*," 290.

⁷³ "Ich" in line 2413, to line 2418, crossed out in ink, E1w. *SW* I/18:288.

⁷⁴ "Töten will ich" in line 2283 crossed out in pencil, E1w. Lines 2284–86 crossed out in pencil, E1w. *SW* I/18:283.

⁷⁵ Line 2316 to "Gott!" in line 2337, crossed out in ink, E1w. *SW* I/18:286.

⁷⁶ Lines 2345–46 crossed out in pencil, E1w. *SW* I/18:286.

⁷⁷ Lines 2407–10 crossed out in ink, E1w. *SW* I/18:288.

⁷⁸ Lines 2439–57 crossed out in ink, E1w. *SW* I/18:289.

⁷⁹ Glossy, "Zur Geschichte der Wiener Theatercensur," 313.

[80] See also Glossy, "Zur Geschichte der Wiener Theater III," 83.

[81] "[W]as ungarisch fluchen kann" in line 434 replaced by "hinstürzend in die March," h3 h4 h5; crossed out in pencil, E1w. Lines 435–36, absent h3 h4 h5; crossed out in pencil, E1w. *SW* I/18:204.

[82] Lines 395–99: next to the first verse a cross in pencil and red pen. As a result, all verses removed by Schreyvogel, h3, absent, h4 h5. *SW* I/18:203.

[83] Line 402 crossed out in pencil, E1w. *SW* I/18:203.

[84] "Der Hunger flieht" in line 493 amended in pencil to "Die Feinde fliehen," E1w. *SW* I/18:205.

[85] Lines 598–604 crossed out in pencil, E1w. *SW* I/18:213.

[86] Lines 444–45 absent, h3 h4 h5. *SW* I/18:204.

[87] Line 468 to "Gott" in line 484, crossed out in pencil, E1w. *SW* I/18:205.

[88] Line 478 to "Pferd" in line 481, bracketed out in pencil by the censor, later removed by Schreyvogel, and replaced by: "Bis Schmerz und Ärger Euch aus Eurer Dumpfheit weckt," h3; absent and replaced by "Bis Schmerz und Ärger euch Aus Eurer Dumpfheit wecken," h4; absent and replaced by "Bis Schmerz und Ärger Euch aus Eurer Dumpfheit wecken," h5. Lines 468 to "Gott" in line 484 crossed out in pencil, E1w. *SW* I/18:205.

[89] "[B]ei uns" in line 986 to line 994, crossed out in pencil, E1w. *SW* I/18:239.

[90] "[B]ei uns in Ungarn" in line 986 replaced with "in unserem Lande," h3 h4 h5. *SW* I/18:240.

[91] Line 2435 amended in pencil by an unknown hand to "Von meinem Volk ist keiner ein Verräter!," h3 h5; amended by Schreyvogel first to "Der Meinen hat noch keiner mich verrathen," and then to "Von meinem Volk ist keiner ein Verräther!," h4. Line 2439 crossed out by an unknown hand; replaced in ink by an unknown hand to "Von meinem Volk ist keiner ein Verräther," h3 h5; changed in the same way in pencil, h4. *SW* I/18:289.

[92] Lines 2439–57 crossed out in ink, E1w. *SW* I/18:289.

[93] "Die Böhmen nahn" in line 2789 crossed out in ink, E1w. *SW* I/18:305.

[94] "Böhmen" in line 2789 crossed out in pencil and changed to "Feinde," h3 h4 h5. "Die Österreicher" in line 2789 crossed out in pencil and changed to "Wir," h3 h4 h5. *SW* I/18:305.

[95] "Hier Böhmen!" in line 2930 crossed out in pencil by an unknown hand and changed to "Hier, für den König!," h3; changed in the same way in ink by Schreyvogel, h4 h5. "Und hier Österreich!" in line 2930 crossed out in pencil by an unknown hand and changed to "Für den Vater hier!" h3; changed in the same way in ink by Schreyvogel, h4 h5. *SW* I/18:310.

[96] Bruce Thompson describes Zawisch as "the only true villain" in all of Grillparzer's plays. See Bruce Thompson, *Franz Grillparzer* (Boston: Twayne, 1981), 53.

[97] See, for example, her description of how, back in Hungary, "was nur Mann hieß in dem weiten Reich. / Und Leben war und Feuer, Glut und Mut!" (*SW* I/3:60) had been at her service (lines 971–72, crossed out in ink, E1W; line 971 absent, h3 h4 h5). *SW* I/18:239.

[98] After line 946 the stage direction "stampft mit dem Fuße" is replaced by "macht eine ungeduldige Bewegung," h3 h4 h5. *SW* I/18:239.

[99] Glossy, "Zur Geschichte der Wiener Theatercensur," 329.

[100] See note 28 and Glossy, "Zur Geschichte der Wiener Theater I," 179 and 199.

[101] See, for example, Zawisch in lines 793–94, "Die Österreicher reißen tüchtig aus, / Seit Margareta fort, die Königin" (*SW* I/3:49), and later on, Milota in lines 1013–15, "Alle Österreicher, / Seitdem die Königin Margrete fern, / Sind übeln Sinns und schleichen fort vom Hof" (*SW* I/3:62).

[102] Lines 1550–54, crossed out in pencil, h3 h4; the same in pencil and red pen, h5; crossed out in ink, E1w. *SW* I/18:254.

[103] Lines 175–76 crossed out in ink, E1w. Line 177 crossed out in pencil, E1w. *SW* I/18:197.

[104] See Glossy, "Zur Geschichte der Wiener Theater III," 135.

[105] "Zawisch" in line 1105 to line 1107, absent, h3 h4 h5; first the last line crossed out in pencil, then everything crossed out in ink, E1w. *SW* I/18:244.

[106] Lines 210–14 absent, h3 h4 h5. *SW* I/18:199.

[107] See, for example, Zawisch talking to Milota and Benesch: "Ihr wolltet selbst des Königs Ehe getrennt, / Habt jahrelang euch weidlich drum" (*SW* I/3:15).

[108] The full passage was: "Der starre Milota, der Geifrer Benesch, / Und Zawisch, jener Schlimmste wohl von allen, / Mit Reichtum, Macht und Hoffnung auf den Thron — / Ja, so weit ging der Übermütgen Stolz — / Verlockten sie das leichtbetörte Kind. / Seit lange sah ich sie, die bösen Engel / Des Königs, meines Herren, verstohlen reißen / An den nur allzuschwachen Banden, die / Kaum Ottokarn noch fesselten an mich. / Ich hörte, wie sie seinen Wunsch nach Erben, / Nach angebornen Folgern seines Throns, / Mit heuchlerischem Mitleid listig nährten. — / Ein Wunsch, gar wohl verzeihlich einem König!" (*SW* I/3:18).

[109] Lines 2479–89 crossed out in ink, E1w. *SW* I/18:279.

[110] For example, to the Viennese mayor, following the fall of Vienna to imperial troops: "Ha, schändlicher Verräter! / So gabst du meine Burg?" (*SW* I/3:111).

[111] Lines 2770–76 crossed out in pencil and ink, h5. *SW* I/18:305.

[112] Lines 2755–76 crossed out in ink, E1w. *SW* I/18:304.

[113] Lines 165–71 crossed out in ink, E1w. *SW* I/18:196.

[114] Lines 2077–90 crossed out in ink, E1w. *SW* I/18:277.

[115] Lines 2040–90 crossed out in pencil, h3 h4 h5. *SW.* I/18:277.

[116] Line 746 to "Ihr" in line 759, crossed out in pencil, E1w. *SW* I/18:230.

[117] Scene 13, lines 1614–16 crossed out in ink, E1w. *SW* I/18:263.

[118] "Erster Bürger" in line 1704, to line 1706, crossed out in ink, E1w. *SW* I/18:268.

[119] See, for example, the following exchange between two Habsburg citzens among the throng who have come to see their ruler: "Erster Bürger (*der sich mit seinem Nachbar durch die Menge in den Vordergrund gearbeitet hat*): hier ist ein guter Platz,

hier laßt uns bleiben! / Zweiter Bürger: Wenn er nur vorkommt, daß wir ihn auch sehn" (*SW* I/3:99).

[120] Cf. Thompson, *Franz Grillparzer*, 46.

[121] Glossy, "Zur Geschichte der Wiener Theatercensur," 333.

[122] Lines 1888–1911 crossed out in pencil, h3 h4; crossed out in red pen, h5. Lines 1893–1911 also crossed out in pencil, h5. "Euch bleibt'" in line 1888 to line 1929, first crossed out in ink, then reinstated, then crossed out again, E1w. Lines 1921–26 crossed out in pencil, h3 h5. *SW* I/18:272.

[123] Lines 2977–82 absent, h3 h4 h5. *SW* I/18:313.

[124] Lines 1882–83 crossed out in ink, E1w. *SW* I/18:272.

[125] Another perspective on the two rulers can be found in Dagmar Lorenz, *Grillparzer, Dichter des sozialen Konflikts* (Vienna: Böhlau, 1986), 115–30. Lorenz argues that Rudolf is as tyrannical as Ottokar, and that the play aims to criticize the system of monarchy as a whole. Although Lorenz makes some interesting points about the characterization of Rudolf, her argument is ultimately unconvincing.

[126] Cf. Yates, *Grillparzer*, 100–101.

[127] Glossy, "Zur Geschichte der Wiener Theatercensur," 314.

[128] Glossy, "Zur Geschichte der Wiener Theatercensur," 326.

[129] Glossy, "Zur Geschichte der Theater Wiens II," 24.

[130] Line 1050 crossed out in ink, E1w. *SW* I/18:241.

[131] Line 2830 to "Leib" in line 2860, crossed out in ink, E1w. *SW* I/18:307.

[132] Lines 1558–59 crossed out in ink, E1w. *SW* I/18:254.

[133] Lines 2105–10 crossed out in ink, E1w; lines 2105–9 crossed out in pencil, h3 h4 h5. *SW* I/18:278.

[134] Lines 2941–47 crossed out in ink, E1w. *SW* I/18:311.

[135] Glossy, "Zur Geschichte der Wiener Theatercensur," 299.

[136] These instructions are reproduced in Karl Glossy, "Zur Geschichte der Theater Wiens I," 59–64.

[137] See Glossy, "Zur Geschichte der Theater Wiens I," 62.

[138] Lines 976–77 crossed out in pencil, E1w; in place of lines 975–77, the words, "In seiner Jahre Kraft und seines Ruhms," h3 h4 h5. *SW* I/18:239.

[139] Lines 353–56 crossed out in ink, E1w. *SW* I/18:202.

[140] Lines 2404–5 changed in pencil to "Ist Kunigunde nicht Euer Weib," E1w. *SW* I/18:288.

[141] Glossy, "Zur Geschichte der Wiener Theatercensur," 317–19.

[142] Glossy, "Zur Geschichte der Theater Wiens I," 22, 30–31, 49, 56, and 67, and "Zur Geschichte der Theater Wiens III," 88–89.

[143] For example, the following agitated complaint by Kunigunde to Zawisch: "Nur erst, beim Tanz, als ich die Hand Euch reichte, / Ja, Frecher, ja! Ihr drücktet mir die Hand!" (*SW* I/3:54.). These lines were crossed out in pencil from E1w and were absent from h3 h4 h5. *SW* I/18:237.

[144] Lines 1342–47 crossed out in pencil, E1w; lines 1342–47 bracketed off in pencil, h3; bracketed off in pencil and ink, h4; bracketed off in ink h5. *SW* I/18:249.

[145] See, for example, the complaints of the Burgtheater actor Carl Ludwig Costenoble about the unpredictability of censorship decisions in his diaries: Carl Ludwig Costenoble, *Aus dem Burgtheater 1818–1837: Tagebuchblätter*, 2 vols. (Vienna: Konegen, 1889), 2:195 and 265–66.

6: The Artist Fights Back: Franz Grillparzer's *Des Meeres und der Liebe Wellen*

IN THE YEARS THAT FOLLOWED the first performances of *König Ottokar*, Franz Grillparzer's relationship with the Viennese censorship authorities remained troubled. Despite the playwright's essential loyalty to the Habsburg dynasty and popularity with contemporary theatergoers, the restrictions placed by censorship on his writing continued to cause him intense frustration. His resentment is perhaps expressed most powerfully in the following diary extract from April 1826:

> Wer mir die Vernachläßigung meines Talentes zum Vorwurf macht, der sollte vorher bedenken, wie in dem ewigen Kampf mit Dummheit und Schlechtigkeit endlich der Geist ermattet. Wie, um nicht immerfort verletzt zu werden, endlich kein Mittel übrig bleibt, als sich unempfindlich zu machen, wie kein Aufschwung möglich ist, wenn man bei jeder Flügelbewegung an den Plafond der Censur anstößt, und die Arbeit aufhört ein Vergnügen zu seyn, wenn das Hervorgebrachte die Quelle tausendfältiger Unannehmlichkeiten wird [. . .].[1]

This was not an isolated outburst. Another diary entry written in March of the same year describes how Grillparzer was finding it difficult to write due to the aftereffects of the *König Ottokar* affair (*SW* II/8:196). A couple of months later, he had fresh cause for irritation after a poem he had written in honor of the emperor's recovery from a serious illness displeased the empress by depicting two women at her husband's bedside, when in reality she had been the only female present (*SW* II/8:205). And in March 1828, Grillparzer was exasperated by the emperor's attempt to buy the exclusive rights for his latest play, *Ein treuer Diener seines Herrn* (*SW* II/8:294–95). Although the drama had been approved by the censors, the emperor evidently felt suspicious of its contents.

Grillparzer's conflicts with the authorities during these years were not restricted to censorship affairs. In February 1826, for example, the writer was summoned to the police in connection with an incident that had occurred during the previous autumn. In November 1825, he had been present when his friend, the painter Moritz Daffinger, had insulted a military police guard. It was alleged that Grillparzer had both applauded his friend's comments and made similar remarks of his own. After an investigation stretching out for several months, the writer was given an official reprimand. Due to his status as a government employee (he worked as a middle-ranking civil servant in the ministry of finance), Grillparzer was also threatened with double the normal punishment should any similar accusations be made against him in the future.[2] Two months later, he was woken by police officers, who ordered him to get up and present all of his writings for their inspection. In the course of his subsequent interrogation and house arrest he discovered that he was being investigated in connection with a raid on the *Ludlamshöhle*, a literary society to which he belonged (*SW* II/8:203). No charges were brought against the playwright, but the police actions nevertheless exposed him to another dimension of the heavy restrictions that the Viennese authorities placed upon public life.

During the same months that bore witness to this intense contact with the Viennese police, Grillparzer devised the storyline for the drama *Des Meeres und der Liebe Wellen*.[3] Eventually completed in 1829 and performed at the Burgtheater in 1831, the play is based on the classical story of Hero and Leander, yet includes a number of elements drawn from the playwright's experiences in Restoration Vienna. The language of the tragedy is characterized by the frequent use of Viennese colloquialisms;[4] and it is generally accepted that the characters of Hero, and of Leander's friend, Naukleros, are based on two of Grillparzer's acquaintances: the former on Marie von Smolenitz, with whom the writer had two affairs, and the latter on Daffinger, who became Marie's husband. In addition, Hero's movements at the end of act three were inspired by Charlotte von Paumgartten, the wife of Grillparzer's cousin, who had on one occasion set a lamp down on the floor before illicitly kissing the playwright.[5]

One further significant parallel between contemporary Vienna and the world of *Des Meeres und der Liebe Wellen* is the play's portrayal of a community firmly in the grip of official surveillance. Despite the drama's classical setting, there is little that escapes the attention of the high priest and his guards on the island of Sestos. Early on in the play, for example, Hero is approached by Leander and Naukleros, the two strangers from Abydos, while she is fetching water, and she warns them that she need only raise her voice and guards will come to her rescue (v. 735–36; *SW* I/4:121). After Leander is almost discovered in the priestess's room that night, she worries that he will be captured on his way back to Abydos (v. 1198; *SW* I/4:146). Although witnessed jumping into the sea by a guard, Leander does reach home, but it appears that, even there, he has not escaped the high priest's impressive security system. For upon arrival back at his hut, Leander is greeted with the news that spies have been sent out from Sestos to search for him (v. 1555–56; *SW* I/4:172).

The levels of manpower and organization required for such security operations appear somewhat unlikely for a religious community ruled by a lone priest without any bureaucratic support. The oppressive surveillance portrayed in Grillparzer's Sestos can therefore be seen as a comment on conditions in Vienna during the late 1820s. Given the playwright's painful brushes with police and censorship authorities in the years when he composed the play,[6] it is certainly likely that he was preoccupied with the issue of government authoritarianism.

In addition to presenting this telling depiction of state surveillance, however, *Des Meeres und der Liebe Wellen* also provides an unusually good basis for an exploration of the interactions between official censorship on the one hand, and both literary writing and theatrical performances on the other. The full details of almost all the drafts leading up to the performance of the play are reproduced in the "Lesarten" section of the *Historisch-kritische Gesamtausgabe*. This not only supplies us with indications of the effects of preemptive self-censorship on the play's composition; it also allows us to see which sections of the play were cut out by the censors. Finally, the inclusion of Grillparzer's responses to the censors' complaints also gives us an idea of the kind of negotiations that were possible for a leading playwright.

Self-Censorship

Both the classical setting and the verse form of *Des Meeres und der Liebe Wellen* serve to distance the play from the reality of Restoration Austria, thereby rendering it less vulnerable to censorship cuts;[7] and Grillparzer's diary and letters do not mention the effects of censorship pressure on the play. Nonetheless, a comparison of the tragedy's early manuscripts indicates that its composition was significantly limited by censorship regulations. Three complete drafts of the tragedy, labeled H1, H2, and H4 in the *SW*, preceded h1, the manuscript that was handed in to the Burgtheater direction in March 1829. Grillparzer started work on H1 in autumn 1826[8] and had written a first draft of the drama's first four acts by 1828. He then started work on a second draft of the play: H2. For the next year, the playwright continued to alter and extend both H1 and H2. Progress made on H1 was always copied into H2, but alterations and extensions to H2 were not always transferred into H1.[9] H2 therefore represents a later stage in the composition process than H1. H4 began as a fair copy of H2, but was substantially altered before being copied into h1.[10] h3, a near identical copy of h1, was submitted to the censors in early 1831 in order to gain permission for the performances of *Des Meeres und der Liebe Wellen* at the Burgtheater,[11] which began on 5 April of the same year.

While these drafts of *Des Meeres und der Liebe Wellen* provide much information about the play's composition, discerning the role of censorship in the process is not entirely straightforward. Grillparzer's diary entries suggest that the vast majority of the changes he made to various drafts of the play were motivated primarily by aesthetic concerns;[12] and the large number of alterations makes it difficult to evaluate thoroughly the possible role of censorship in each individual change. As Grillparzer left no written statements alluding to the influence of censorship on these early drafts, such analysis would in any case remain speculative for the vast majority of alterations.

Nevertheless, two factors do enable us to gain insights into the restrictions placed by censorship on the composition of *Des Meeres und der Liebe Wellen*. First, Grillparzer continued to modify the play long after it had been submitted to and performed at the Burgtheater.[13] These changes were made with the publication of the play in mind, for which less rigorous censorship standards applied than for stage performances.[14] In several cases, Grillparzer's modifications to the manuscript at this stage revert to the versions used in the early drafts. In such instances, only h1 and h3 — the manuscripts prepared for performance at the Burgtheater — deviate from Grillparzer's early drafts. Censorship pressure is therefore most obvious reason for the alterations. Secondly, the earliest manuscripts, H1 and H2, contain several groups of changes that all serve to modify a particular element of the play's content. Where there is no obvious aesthetic reason for these changes, and the alterations reflect known censorship concerns, they too can often be linked to censorship pressure.

Sexual Morality

The duty of Austrian censors to protect "die Sittlichkeit" is mentioned explicitly in paragraph 10 of the Austrian Zensurvorschrift of 1810[15] and had a substantial impact on the composition of *Des Meeres und der Liebe Wellen*. The clearest evidence for this is supplied by the H1 manuscript version of a speech by Naukleros in act two, in which the young man enthusiastically describes the large number of women present at Hero's initiation ceremony as a priestess of Aphrodite. Here, Grillparzer replaced "Busen" first with "Brüsten" and then with "Häuptern" in line 615, "üppigen Hüften" with "runden Hüften" in line 616, and "Brust" with "Wuchs" in line 655 (*SW* I/4:117).[16]

Such examples point toward the more general restraint that Grillparzer had to exercise in his treatment of sensuality. Admittedly, *Des Meeres und der Liebe Wellen* does include some physical contact between Hero and Leander during their illicit meeting in the priestess's tower. At one point, for example, Hero parts her visitor's hair (following v. 1195; *SW* I/4:146), and shortly before his departure she kisses him briskly (v. 1258; *SW* I/4:150). More erotic thoughts and desires, on the other hand, are presented either discreetly or indirectly. One example is the song that Hero sings about Leda and the swan,[17] which does not employ any clearly sexual vocabulary, but nevertheless serves to indicate both her awakening sensuality and the potential for sexual transgression that accompanies it. Similarly, Naukleros's most appreciative references to female anatomy are buried deep within an eighty-one-line monologue (vv. 572–653; *SW* I/4: 155–57). While focusing principally on uncontroversial heads, feet, and shoulders, he also evokes the image of "runden Hüften" in line 616, and, after a safe gap, refers to breasts in coyly familial terms as "die begabtern, reichen Schwestern" of women's shoulders (v. 634; *SW* I/4:116).

Toward the end of act four, Hero's physical longing for Leander is not given direct expression, but translated into a yearning for the wind of the night that comes from Abydos. In the following passage, gesture is used to avoid explicit commentary, as the priestess's position, "*in halbliegender Stellung,*" reveals her sensual frame of mind. Her repeated references to Leander ("von ihm nur, ihm, von ihm") also make it clear that she is preoccupied by the thought of him, but her physical wishes are addressed to the wind, so that her speech contains no manifest indecencies:

> HERO: [. . .] (*sie hat die Füße an sich auf die Ruhebank gezogen und in halbliegender Stellung*)
> Wie süß, wie wohl! — Komm Wind der Nacht
> Und kühle mir das Aug, die heißen Wangen!
> Kommst du doch übers Meer, von ihm.
> Und, o, dein Rauschen und der Blätter Lispeln,
> Wie Worte klingt es mir: von ihm nur, ihm, von ihm.
> Breit aus die Schwingen, hülle sie um mich
> Um Stirn und Haupt, den Hals, die müden Arme,
> Umfaß, umfang! Ich öffne dir die Brust.[18]

Efforts to convey a sense of sexual excitement while avoiding explicit language similarly characterize Grillparzer's ending to act three, in which Leander pays Hero an unexpected and transgressive visit in her tower. After granting her guest permission to return the next day, the priestess finally persuades him to leave her tower before retiring to her room. Leander curses with frustration and then waits at her closed door before exclaiming:

> Und doch! Ihr Fußtritt stockt — Ich höre Schritte
> Leis' auf den Zeh'n — Kehrt sie zurück? Götter!
> (v. 1261–62; *SW* I/4:151; also *SW* I/19:353)

Here, Leander's thrilled cry of "Götter," which comes immediately before the curtain falls, provides a coded anticipation of later excitement.

In addition to employing such evasive strategies, Grillparzer also adjusted non-erotic passages of the h1 and h3 manuscripts, and at several points removed even weak hints of sexual vitality in his characters for the

Burgtheater performances. At one point in act two, for example, Naukleros encourages Leander to regain an interest in life following the death of his mother. In most manuscripts, he urges his friend, "Allein dann kehre zu den Freuden wieder / Die sie dir gönnt, die du ihr länger gönntest" (v. 525–26; *SW* I/4:113). Although the passage contains no hint of sexual activity between mother and son, the words "den Freuden" were replaced by "der Freude" in h1 and h3 (*SW* I/19:306), presumably in order to eliminate any sensual connotations carried by the original expression.

Likewise, in act four, the priest begins to suspect that the man spotted jumping into the sea by the temple guard was one of the youths from Abydos. At first he is unable to believe that anyone could be so bold, but then, in every manuscript apart from h1 and h3, he reconsiders: "Und doch! Ist nicht das Jünglingsalter kühn?" (v. 1356; *SW* I/3:159). In the two Burgtheater manuscripts, however, the author replaced "Jünglingsalter" with "Knabenalter" (*SW* I/19:363), thereby denying his characters' sexual maturity. Grillparzer was clearly keen to remove unnecessary intimations of the youths' virility.

Hero and the High Priest

Another dimension of the censors' concerns about sexual morality is suggested by a series of changes relating to the relationship between Hero and her uncle, who is also the high priest on the island of Sestos. Although *Des Meeres und der Liebe Wellen* contains no indication of an incestuous relationship between these two characters, a number of changes made to the Burgtheater manuscripts, h1 and h3, suggest that their interactions were expected to attract intense scrutiny by the censors. A first indication of this is provided by the list of characters at the beginning of the Burgtheater manuscripts. The identification of the high priest as Hero's uncle — present in all other manuscripts — is crossed out of h1 by Schreyvogel and absent from h3 (*SW* I/19:241). And during Hero's initiation ceremony toward the end of the first act, the familial dimension of their relationship is again obscured in only h1 and h3. While all other manuscripts include the stage direction, "*Hero mit Schleier und Kopfbinde an der Seite des Oheims*," in the two Burgtheater manuscripts, "Oheims" is replaced by "Oberpriesters" (*SW* I/19:301–2). Apparently, the description of Hero standing next to a man named as her uncle and wearing a veil at the head of a procession was too reminiscent of an improper wedding-like scenario.

Further evidence of nervousness about this issue is provided by act two, when the high priest discovers Hero talking to Leander and Naukleros in defiance of temple law. Determined to separate them as quickly as possible, the priest leads his niece off by the hand. As he does so, he initially tells her, in manuscript H1, "Im Tempel harrt noch mancherlei zu tun" (v. 854; *SW* I/4:128). At a later point, however, Grillparzer changed the last two words of this sentence to "Geschäft." This alteration does not change the line's rhythm, but seems primarily designed to make it completely clear that the priest intended Hero to attend to temple business and to exclude any other possible interpretations. The playwright's preference for the original version is suggested by the fact that all of the post-h3 manuscripts revert to "zu tun."[19]

Given this pattern of changes, it is easy to suspect censorship as the motivation for a stylistic peculiarity in act four. Here, the priest surprises Hero as she sings the song about Leda and the swan. It is clear from the priestess's exclamation of "Wer faßt mich an?" (v. 1647; *SW* I/4:163) that he has touched her, but the absence of a stage direction at this point means that we are given no indication of what form this physical contact has taken, leaving a range of possibilities open. This imprecision seems peculiar given the number of times that the play was revised prior to performance, and is untypical of Grillparzer, who, as many critics have noted, paid great attention to the visual impression made by his plays.[20] On the other hand, however, the omission of the stage direction meant that the censors' attention would not be focused unnecessarily on this apparently sensitive action.

Marriage and Family

One of the many directives relating to moral propriety in Hägelin's 1795 memorandum forbids utterance that suggests the equality of births in and out of wedlock. Hägelin's explanation for this is that "Der Staat protegirt rechtmäßige Ehen und Geburten aus guten Gründen,"[21] a sentiment echoed in a censor's report of 1805 that recommends the prohibition of a play because of its lack of respect for "die Würde des Ehestands."[22] Censorship protection of the institution of family went beyond disapproval of adultery, fornication, and illegitimate children, however. Hägelin's memorandum also forbids the theatrical representation of parents mistreating their offspring.[23] And in 1812, Emperor Francis complained about a play that had been approved for performance although it contained a father and son who were unable to recognize one another. In the emperor's opinion, this work was unsuitable for performance because it denigrated one of "die ehrwürdigsten Verhältnisse."[24]

State concern about the portrayal of family relationships is also reflected in the first act of *Des Meeres und der Liebe Wellen*. Grillparzer's changes to early drafts of the play include several that serve to obscure or tone down utterances in which Hero expresses her rejection of contemporary family structures. Two of these lines relate specifically to marriage and are prompted by the complaints of loneliness made by Hero's mother, who wants her daughter to return home and marry. The young priestess responds with a lengthy complaint about the young men of her homeland, describing them as "von gleichem Sinn und störrisch wildem Wesen. [...] Je minder denkend, um so heft'ger wollend" (vv. 308–10; *SW* I/4:98). In the two earliest versions of this scene, Hero openly expresses her horror at the thought that her mother could expect her to marry such a man, exclaiming, "Und unter solchen, sag' es nur, gesteh's nur! / Denkst du dereinst die Tochter zu vermählen?," and "einem Solchem, sag' es nur, gedenkst du / Dereinst wohl gar die Tochter zu vermählen?" (*SW* I/19:272). In later manuscripts, however, this line avoids the ideological keyword "vermählen" and no longer presents the idea of marriage as the main source of Hero's outrage. Instead, she asks her mother, "Und unter solche wünschest du dein Kind? / Vielleicht wohl gar —"; and the meaning of this vague second line is only revealed indirectly by her mother's vehement response, which cleverly uses the rhyming of "verhehlen" and "vermählen" to indicate that the latter word has been replaced by a dash in the priestess's question:

> Was soll ich dirs verhehlen?
> Das Weib ist glücklich nur an Gattenhand.
>
> (vv. 318–20; *SW* I/4:98)

Their conversation continues with Hero referring to the problems of her mother's marriage. The earliest drafts of this speech conclude with an explicit rejection of marriage: in H1 the young priestess initially expresses her outrage with the line, "Und wagst zu reden mir von solchem Glück?," before this was changed to the even more radical "Und willst in gleiche Sklaverei dein Kind?" (*SW* I/19:273). In later manuscripts, however, Hero avoids the inflammatory term "Sklaverei" and refrains from questioning directly the "Glück" insisted upon by her mother. Instead, she expresses her opposition to marriage in a rhetorical question that contains no reference to the state of marriage at all: "Und wagst zu sprechen mir ein solches Wort?" (v. 326; *SW* I/4:98).

A third passage that was toned down for later manuscripts involves Hero's complaints to the high priest about the dysfunctional relations in her parents' home. In the H1 manuscript, this substantial description forms the central focus of reader and audience interest as an explanation of her adamant refusal to return to her parents:[25]

> HERO: Mich? Von hier? Vergebens.
> Ich heim in ihrer Sorgen dunkle Wohnung?
> Aus meiner Göttin lichtem Heiligthum
> Zurück in engen Trachtens niedre Kreise
> Wo Unfried herrscht, und jeder ewig uneins

> Fast mit sich selbst, dann mit den Andern Allen
> Mit jeglichen Tag den Knäuel fester wirrt
> Der seines Geistes freie Übung bindet.
> Wohl stürmisch giengs in meiner Ältern Hause
> Der Vater wollte was kein Andres wollte,
> Und stieß mich an, und zürnte ohne Grund.
> Dem Bruder galt ein Jahr, um das er alter,
> Und daß ich nur ein Weib, für Grund genug
> Als Ziel mich seiner Launen zu begehren.
> Die Mutter duldete und schwieg.
> Ich wieder heim? Die Götter wollens nicht. (*SW* I/19:257)

In all later manuscripts, however, this account is significantly altered. It is not only some seven lines shorter. Hero's description is also moved to a position where it is far less relevant to the conversation in progress and therefore somewhat eclipsed by the central matter in hand, namely the priest's insistence that her parents are missing her:

> PRIESTER: Sie denken dein und sehnen sich nach dir.
> HERO: Ich weiß das anders, doch du glaubst es nicht.
> War ihnen ich doch immer eine Last,
> Und fort und fort ging Sturm in ihrem Hause.
> (vv. 198–201; *SW* I/4:90)

The marginal status of this description is reinforced by other factors. Although it represents a substantial shift in focus, for example, the account is introduced by the casual conjunction "und." And instead of reacting to Hero's words with surprise or concern, the priest merely pursues his previous enquiries about whether or not Hero would like to return home with them. As a result, the oppressive conditions within the new priestess's home appear as an insignificant detail.

Similar structural features within the earliest drafts of *Des Meeres und der Liebe Wellen* serve to obscure other utterances that imply criticism of contemporary family structures. One example of this is an allusion to physical abuse suffered by Hero's mother that is positioned some 200 lines after the main description of life in her family home. It occurs when Hero tries to persuade her to seek refuge in the temple and seeks to reassure her that "hier schlägt man keine Wunden [. . .]" (v. 389; *SW* I/4:102). As the main topic of the speech is the benefits offered by the temple, the full implications of Hero's "Wunde" line are far from obvious. Similarly, the play contains no explicit commentary on the dysfunctional interactions between Hero's parents; and despite the full instructions provided by Grillparzer's stage directions at most other points, we only find out about the weeping of her mother through her husband's brief remark upon it (v. 264; *SW* I/4:95).

One imagines that the playwright's efforts to obscure criticisms of marriage and family life within the text of *Des Meeres und der Liebe Wellen* played an important role in the late discovery of such elements by Grillparzer scholars.[26] However, although the playwright evidently felt under pressure to minimize the direct discussion of such issues, the performance manuscript does allow the audience to witness the disdainful attitude of Hero's father toward his wife. During the visit of the priestess's parents to Sestos, for instance, we see how he attempts to dominate the scene, referring to his wife dismissively as "kränkelnd schon und alt" (v. 243; *SW* I/4:93; also *SW* I/19:259). And when Hero remarks upon the silence of her mother, her father merely complains that his wife normally talks both inappropriately and far too much (v. 253–55; *SW* I/4:94). Even when she starts to cry, her husband is only momentarily distracted, briefly remarking "Nun weint sie gar. Daß doch!" before returning his attention to the high priest (v. 264; *SW* I/4:95). Of course, the presence of the emperor and other members of the establishment at Burgtheater performances may have restricted the actors' interpretation of such scenes. Yet even so, their inclusion in the censorship manuscript reveals that, in the absence of more explicit commentary, such scenic depiction offered one means of portraying the subjugation suffered by many women in marriage.

The Masses

In some ways, both the performed and the published versions of *Des Meeres und der Liebe Wellen* suggest that its composition was relatively unaffected by the censors' concern to prevent challenges to monarchical authority. For instance, although certain accounts of censorship in the Restoration have suggested that the terms "Volk" and "Freiheit" were taboo,[27] Grillparzer apparently felt no compulsion to avoid either the former, which appears ten times in the dialogue and stage directions of the first act alone, or the latter, which occurs five times in the play's dialogue.

Another interesting inclusion in the censorship manuscript (as well as all other drafts) of *Des Meeres und der Liebe Wellen* is a dialogue in which the temple servant Janthe expresses contempt for Hero's elevated social status. Censors' reports from throughout the early nineteenth century repeatedly express disapproval of various challenges to the social hierarchy;[28] and it might therefore be expected that no manifestations of social disharmony were tolerated by Austrian censors.

Yet at the beginning of the first act, an argument breaks out between Hero and Janthe over the issue of some neglected chores and rapidly reveals social tensions. When the servant makes a sarcastic attack on what she sees as Hero's social pretensions, the priestess insists on her superiority:

JANTHE: Verzeih, wir sind gemeines, niedres Volk.
    Du freilich, aus der Priester Stamm entsprossen —

HERO: Du sagst es.

JANTHE: Und zu Höherem bestimmt.

HERO: Mit Stolz entgegn' ich: ja.

JANTHE: Ganze andre Freuden,
    Erhabnere Genüsse sind für dich.

HERO: Du weißt, ich kann nicht spotten; spotte nur!

(vv. 73–78; *SW* I/4:84)

Despite the challenge to the social hierarchy included in this exchange, it was included in the Burgtheater performance. One imagines that it considered less of a threat due to Janthe's sarcasm — which may have been employed deliberately by the author in order to avoid a direct challenge to the social order — and the servant's low social status, which may have meant that her words were not expected to be taken seriously.

Certainly, other alterations to early versions of *Des Meeres und der Liebe Wellen* indicate that Grillparzer did not predict a completely indifferent response by the censors to the behavior of the lower orders. Manuscript changes to the only crowd scene in the drama — Hero's initiation ceremony — involve a toning-down of the actions and utterances of the masses present. For example, the people's original cry of "Glück mit dem Volk" in the H1 version of the ceremony is modified to "Glück mit uns" in all subsequent manuscripts (*SW* I/19:302). Given the democratic overtones of the first version, it is almost certain that the change was motivated by censorship concerns. Coming from the mouths of a crowd of people demanding happiness, the word "Volk" was evidently considered more problematic than in other circumstances.

In addition, another set of changes earlier on in the same scene indicates the censors' sensitivity to the movements of the *Volk*. It has been observed that the people entering the temple for Hero's initiation ceremony initially appear as a formless and chaotic mass.[29] Later stage directions in the same scene, however, suggest that Grillparzer felt under pressure to emphasize the orderliness and controlled nature of the people's movements. Although disorderly crowds may not have prompted a ban or even been deleted by the censors, they could have raised the officials' level of suspicion toward other elements of the scene's content, such as the people's cry of "Glück mit uns." By presenting the censors with a well-behaved crowd, one imagines that Grillparzer hoped to induce a less nervous attitude toward the people's demand for happiness.

The first piece of evidence for this concern with controlled crowd movements is supplied by successive drafts of a stage direction that interrupts line 459 and first appears in the H2 manuscript. In this earliest version, the stage direction reads "*Das Volk hat sich nach und nach, der linken Seite entlang, gezogen, bis dahin wo die beiden Freunde stehen.*" In later manuscripts, however, the more controlled verb "sich ordnen" is used in place of "sich ziehen" (*SW* I/19:300). Immediately after this description, however, we hear Naukleros telling someone to stop pushing him (v. 459; *SW* I/4:106), which confirms that Grillparzer did not intend the crowd to be especially well-behaved. Instead, the substitution of "sich ordnen" for "sich ziehen" within a stage direction that is unseen by the play's audience seems to have been intended as a device to calm the worries of censors for whom a large group of unruly *Volk*, however peaceful, cheerful, and non-political, were a cause for concern.

This pattern is repeated by Grillparzer's changes to another stage direction some thirty lines later. This instruction, which refers initially to the temple guard, appears in H1 as "*Das Volk ordnend, das sich auf der linken Seite aufstellt*" (*SW* I/19:301). In the censorship manuscript, however, the stage direction indicates that the previously amorphous crowd is now standing in rows ("*Das Volk ordnend, das auf der linken Seite sich in Reihen stellt*"). The uncontrolled mass of people who, only minutes before, had forced their past way the guard, have now — without any apparent difficulty — been brought to stand in lines by one person alone. The playwright's desire to emphasize the controllability of the people is reinforced by his alterations to the H2 manuscript at this point. The first version of this stage direction initially read, "*Das Volk ordnend, das sich von der linken Seite des Hintergrundes aus sich an derselben Seite bis nach vorne hin in Ordnung stellt.*" Grillparzer later replaced "in Ordnung" with "in Reihen,"[30] presumably in order to avoid using both "ordnet" and "Ordnung" in the same sentence. Clearly, the "rows" of the later manuscripts originated from a concern to increase the level of order in the scene. Given Naukleros's complaints of pushing and the disorderly connotations of the *Volk* in the rest of the scene,[31] it is highly improbable that Grillparzer wished the spectators at Hero's initiation ceremony to be so exceptionally well-behaved. Instead, this repeated emphasis on order arose from the playwright's desire to elicit a more favorable response to his drama from its censors.

Official Censorship

The censorship manuscript of *Des Meeres und der Liebe Wellen* was submitted to the authorities in early 1831, only months after the July Revolutions of 1830, yet before the conservative reaction had set in. In many German states, popular uprisings and political agitation during this period had increased the influence of liberal groupings, who attempted to persuade rulers that reforms were needed in order to avert revolution. Many accounts of Restoration Vienna assert that the city's political climate was not significantly affected by the events of 1830,[32] and certainly any changes in censorship practices were insufficient to prompt a revision of Grillparzer's tragedy by either the playwright himself or the court theater direction: a comparison of the 1831 manuscript of the play with the version that had been prepared for the planned Burgtheater performance in 1829 reveals the two to be virtually identical (*SW* I/19:241–478).

On 25 March 1831, the h3 manuscript was returned to the Burgtheater direction with the judgment that the play could be performed providing certain changes were made. Altogether, the censors objected to twenty-three sections of the tragedy.[33] In most cases, the offensive content was simply crossed out; most of these deletions were either one or two lines long, although some were as short as three words and others as long as five lines. At certain points, however, the censors proposed alternative versions of the material they had removed. In some instances, these replacement passages were needed so that the play would make grammatical and logical sense. More frequently, however, this was not the case: many substitutions involved changing only one or two words of Grillparzer's text and seem to have been motivated primarily by a desire to minimize disruption to the original.

According to the *SW*, *Des Meeres und der Liebe Wellen* was censored by three different officials: two initial censors working in pencil and a final one working in pen. Accordingly, three different markings on h3 are reported: pencil marks in the margin, pencil marks within the text itself, and ink marks also within the main body of the text. Only about a third of the offensive passages display all three types of marking, however, with the ink markings repeating those made in pencil: the rest are marked either only in pencil or only in ink.

Where the passages are only marked in ink, it seems likely that the censors working in pencil had either not noticed the problematic elements, or else had not considered them harmful enough to be removed. Where changes are made in pencil only, one can imagine that the censor working in ink did not consider the alterations important enough to reinforce himself. These pencil-only alterations were definitely considered valid, however: this is clear from the fact that Grillparzer and Josef Schreyvogel, the Theatersekretär at the Burgtheater, responded to all such complaints, even though they were not repeated in ink.

The first section to be censored was marked by all of the officials. This concerned the last three lines of the following passage, which contain Hero's forceful denunciation of the subjugation suffered by her mother within marriage, and which were simply removed from the play (*SW* I/19:182):

MUTTER:	Was sollt' ich dirs verhehlen?
	Das Weib ist glücklich nur an Gattenhand.
HERO:	Das darfst du sagen, ohne zu erröten?
	Wie? und mußt hüten jenes Mannes Blick,
	Des Herren, deines Gatten? Darfst nicht reden,
	Mußt schweigen, flüstern, ob du gleich im Recht [. . .].

(vv. 319–24; *SW* I/4:98; see also *SW* I/19:272)

This deletion appears to vindicate Grillparzer's toning down of other lines in which Hero expresses horror at the thought of either marrying, or returning home to her unhappy family. Criticisms of marriage were evidently unacceptable to the authorities. However, the success of Grillparzer's fragmented and often oblique presentation of dysfunctional family and married life is shown by the fact that no other passages relating to this theme were altered. Clearly, the authorities either did not see, or else did not fear, the implications of the troubled interactions between Hero's parents, the priestess's fleeting hints of horror at the prospect of marriage, or the passing reference to the physical abuse suffered by her mother. Of course, it could be argued that the scene exposing the abusive relationship between Hero's parents could not have been removed without forcing the censors to rewrite the scene completely. However, this is not the case with the other material mentioned, the survival of which suggests that Grillparzer's efforts to obscure and fragment such elements was successful. This separation of controversial elements to enable the indirect presentation of a subversive message is strongly reminiscent of the techniques employed by Heine in both *Briefe aus Berlin* and *Reise von München nach Genua*; and its implications for the delivery of proscribed thought is the same for both authors. For although Grillparzer's indirect presentation of domestic discontent may not have provided such a forceful critique of family structures as the earliest manuscripts, it nevertheless allowed the play to present a negative image of domestic patriarchy.

The religious building in Sestos, on the other hand, elicited a much more vigilant attitude from the censors. The portrayal of Christian priests, worship, and institutions on stage was strictly forbidden in Restoration Austria;[34] and as a result, all three censors endeavored to remove any traces of similarity between the pagan religion practiced in Sestos and Roman Catholicism. Grillparzer had partially anticipated these concerns by changing the office of Hero's uncle from "Priester" to "Oberpriester" for the censorship manuscript (*SW* I/19:79), so that he did not bear the same title as a priest in the Catholic Church.

This precaution did not go far enough for the censors, however. They all objected to Naukleros referring to a religious building in Sestos as a "Gotteshäuslein" (v. 453; *SW* I/4:106). The second censor working in pencil suggested "Tempel" as a replacement, while the censor working in ink preferred "Tempelein" (*SW* I/19:183). Shortly afterwards, when the two men from Abydos observe Hero's initiation ceremony, all three censors again disapproved of Naukleros's telling Leander that he should move closer in order to see "Wie sie die Weihen üben" (v. 490; *SW* I/4:109). Since consecrations are also a central element of Christian worship, the second censor writing in pencil replaced the words "Weihen üben" with the exclusively pagan "Opfer bringen," a substitution that was then repeated in ink (*SW* I/19:183). The final censor was even concerned that Hero's initiation ceremony might contain visual reminders of Christian customs. Although the text at this point contained no transgressions of censorship law, he anticipated the illicit potential of this scene, and wrote by the side of its initial stage direction (following v. 481; *SW* I/4:108), "Diese religiöse Handlung, die Kleider der Priester [. . .] darf nicht an christliche Gebräuche [. . .] erinnern" (*SW* I/19:183).

The ability of the censors to look beyond the obvious is also demonstrated by their reactions to the play's political content. To be sure, they were surprisingly tolerant in some respects. Perhaps influenced partly by its apolitical phrasing and the people's orderly movements at that particular point, for example, none of the three officials sensed anything revolutionary in the cries of "Glück mit uns" (vv. 486, 493 and 497; *SW* I/4:109–10). Nor did any of them object to the Janthe's challenge to social hierarchy mentioned in the previous section.

Yet, despite their acceptance of these elements, all three officials complained about the third line in the following speech of Hero's (*SW* I/19: 182–83), in which she urges a servant to release some doves found nesting on the temple grounds:

> Da gilt es denn zu reden, kleines Ding!
> (*Das Körbchen dem Diener gebend*)
> Du nimms und trag es hin, und gib ihm die Freiheit,
> Die Freiheit wie das Tier sie kennt und wünscht.
> (vv. 379–82; *SW* I/4:102)

Here, the censors allowed the first "Freiheit" to remain in the manuscript, thereby revealing that the word in itself was not sufficient to justify a deletion.[35] More probable as a motivation for the cut is the context within which the term is used. For, while the passage does not contain an explicitly subversive message, the idea of the lower orders both desiring and being granted freedom has clear political implications. This is also true, however, of Janthe's statement "eine Dienerin begehrt der Freiheit" (v. 2134; *SW* I/4:211) at the end of the play, which did not arouse objections from any of the censors. It is therefore likely that the use of "Freiheit" twice in two consecutive lines caused the censors to respond more strictly to the implications of Hero's speech.

Like the authorities' initial reaction to King Ottokar's second marriage some seven years earlier, other passages deleted from the *Meereswellen* manuscript document the continuing sensitivity of Viennese censors to historical parallels. Despite the tragedy's remote setting, the censors were clearly alert to the implications of more general statements that could arouse doubts about the Habsburgs' style of rule. In act two, as we have seen, the high priest interrupts an illegal meeting between Leander, Naukleros, and Hero, whom he leads away from the foreign visitors. Annoyed at this interference, Naukleros questions the priest's motives:

> Selbstsücht'ger, Eigenmächt'ger, Strenger, Herber!
> So schließest du die holde Schönheit ein,
> Entziehst der Welt das Glück der warmen Strahlen
> Und schmückst mit heil'gem Vorwand deine Tat?
> (vv. 860–63; *SW* I/4:128)

Although the first three lines of this criticism were allowed to remain in the manuscript, all three censors complained about line 863 (*SW* I/19: 183). In view of the efforts of many German rulers of the period, including the Habsburgs, to use Christian principles to legitimize the traditional social order, one can see why this description of religious arguments being used hypocritically, to mask less honorable intentions, was considered problematic.

Another example of this kind of sensitivity is provided by the crossing out of a line spoken by the priest in act five. After Leander's drowned body has been discovered on the shores of Sestos, the priest asks a guard impatiently why it was brought to the temple. The guard replies that this is dictated by temple custom, an explanation that the high priest immediately accepts:

> PRIESTER: Wills so der Brauch, wohlan!
> Die Bräuche muß man halten, sie sind gut.
> (v. 1997–98; *SW* I/4:201)

Although these lines may at first glance appear innocuous, both the second censor working in pencil and the censor working in ink crossed out the second line (*SW* I/19:184). The first pencil censor may not have detected any sarcasm in the priest's words, but both of his colleagues were skeptical about the sincerity of this clumsy and unconditional endorsement of tradition. Given the value placed on tradition by the Habsburg monarchy, potentially sarcastic remarks that might ridicule the keeping of customs for their own sake were clearly unwelcome.

It was the play's sexual content, however, that provoked the largest number of censorship complaints. While Hero's playing with Leander's hair and the couple's brief kiss were accepted by the censors, other manifestations of sensuality contained within the h3 manuscript of *Des Meeres und der Liebe Wellen* exceeded the limits of their toleration. The most obvious transgressions were noticed by all three censors. In two cases this involved the use of manifestly sexual vocabulary, as in line 357, when the priest uses the phrase "was sich paart" to explain why the nesting doves had to be removed from the temple grounds. Similarly, it is likely that Naukleros's mention of women's "weißen Schultern" and "runden Hüften" in lines 615 and 616 (*SW* I/4:116) alerted all three censors to the eroticism of the passage. Both of these phrases were crossed out of the manuscript (*SW* I/19:183–84).

Despite Grillparzer's efforts to diminish the sensual flavor of *Des Meeres und der Liebe Wellen,* many less explicit passages were also noticed by all of the censors. The coded intimation of a sexual encounter between Hero and Leander at the end of act three, for instance, was clearly unacceptable to them. The officials' replacement for this scene removed any suggestion of a second stage to the encounter. Following Hero's final plea to Leander to leave the tower immediately (v. 1258; *SW* I/4:150), the officials closed the scene with the newly initiated priestess hurrying away through the door (*SW* I/19:183).

An even more striking indicator of the censors' sensitivity to sensual allusion is supplied by the reaction of all of the play's censors to the song, "Leda und der Schwan." Although the lines sung by Hero only relate relatively innocuous scenes of Leda stroking the swan (vv. 726–27 and 1043–44; *SW* I/4:121 and 137) and being called to return to the gods (vv. 708–11; *SW* I/4:119), the censors removed all specific mention of Leda from the script (*SW* I/19:183:84). The sensitivity of all three censors to the naming of Leda is clearly demonstrated by lines 726 to 729 (*SW* I/4:121). The first two lines of this passage, "Sie aber streichelt / Den weichen Flaum," were left untouched, whereas Hero's subsequent statement, "Mein Oheim meint ich soll das Lied nicht singen / Von Leda und dem Schwan," was a source of complaint for all of the censors. It seems that, due to the transgressive sexuality contained within the story of Leda, even references to its innocuous scenes were considered potentially indecent.

Other attempts to disguise sensual utterance came closer to success. Embedded within an extremely long speech, Naukleros's euphemistic description of breasts as the gifted and rich sisters of shoulders was missed by both censors working in pencil, as was his less oblique, but equally poetic reference to "all den Schätzen so beglückten Leibes" (*SW* I/19: 183). However, only one example of erotic expression was overlooked by all three censors: the passage in which Hero links her longing for Leander with the sensual motion of the wind ("Breit aus die Schwingen, hülle sie um mich," v. 1812; *SW* I/4:188). Perhaps due to the metaphorical and associative nature of this speech — which employs similar strategies to Kunigunde's overwrought description of Zawisch's determined pursuit of her in *König Ottokar* — it too passed unscathed into the performance manuscript.

On the whole, it can be said that official censorship had a substantial impact on *Des Meeres und der Liebe Wellen*. Admittedly, these effects were in some ways less devastating than might have been expected. The censors' acceptance of the portrayal of familial dysfunction, the people's shout of "Glück mit uns," and Hero's erotic "Breit' aus die Schwingen" speech, for example, indicates that visual depiction and the avoidance of ideological keywords could allow challenging material to be performed. In addition, the officials' practice of finding substitutes for offensive words, rather than cutting out entire lines, shows a desire to leave works of literature as unimpaired as possible.

Even so, in most areas, the use of three censors to check the contents of the *Meereswellen* manuscript led to the enforcement of strict censorship standards. Although certain evasive strategies — such as the placing of forbidden material within long speeches, the omission of revealing stage directions, and the use of sarcasm, metaphor, and allusion, — could be successful in hiding controversial content from one or even two of the censors, as far as the topics of religion, sex, and politics were concerned, there was little that could escape the attention of all three. Moreover, while some of the alterations demanded by the censoring officials, for instance, the renaming of temple buildings and practices, were essentially cosmetic, this was by no means the case for all of them. The numerous objections to the play's sensual content, in particular, represent a serious obstacle to the presentation of one of its central themes.[36] The removal of the Leda myth used to represent Hero's sensual yearning, for example, constitutes a severe disruption of the play's poetic structure. And similarly, the change to the end of the scene in Hero's tower not only ruins what had been a dramatic climax ("Ich höre Schritte / Leis' auf den Zeh'n / Kehrt sie zurück? — Götter!"), but also effectively amounts to a rewriting of the play's intended plot.

Grillparzer's Corrections

Although the censors' alterations to *Des Meeres und der Liebe Wellen* left the play making both grammatical and logical sense, they were not final.[37] According to the *SW*, Grillparzer and Schreyvogel worked together on responses to the censors' objections up until the end of act three. From this point onwards, however, Schreyvogel addressed the officials' complaints on his own. The result of these two phases was two very different styles of correction. While the director of the Burgtheater was content to confirm the censors' alterations, and only modified one change himself, Grillparzer was far less compliant. The only corrections he implemented were the superficial alterations required to disassociate the pagan religion at Sestos from the Roman Catholic Church. In all other cases, the playwright was evidently the driving force behind numerous attempts to reclaim ground from the censors and move the text back toward its original version.

In some instances, Grillparzer's efforts involved making some genuine concessions to the censors. At certain points, for example, he reinstated a deleted passage with the most offensive words altered. This is the case with his reaction to the rejection by all three censors of Naukleros's enthusiastic description of the women at Hero's initiation ceremony:

> Ein wallend Meer, mit Häuptern, weißen Schultern
> Und runden Hüften an der Wellen Statt. (v. 615–16; *SW* I/4:116)

Grillparzer's replacement for these undeniably erotic lines avoided the provocative formulation "runden Hüften," but retained the sensuous rocking motion ("ein wallend Meer," "an der Wellen Statt") of the original:

> Ein wallend Meer, mit Häuptern, reichen Locken
> Und weißen Schultern an der Wellen Statt. (*SW* I/19:183)

The playwright proposed a similar compromise solution to another pair of lines from the same speech that had also been deleted by the censor working in ink. At this point, Naukleros is attempting to convince Leander of the joys offered by the female body, and the lines include the description of breasts as the sisters of women's shoulders, discussed earlier:

> Den Schultern, die beschämt nach rückwärts sinkend,
> Platz räumen den begabtern, reichen Schwestern [. . .].
> (v. 633–34; *SW* I/4:116)

Clearly identifying "den begabtern, reichen Schwestern" as the main source of disapproval, Grillparzer replaced the second line with "Den Kampplatz räumend, wo sie hold besiegt" (*SW* I/19:183). Here again, however, an element of eroticism is retained through verbs of motion ("beschämt nach rückwärts sinkend"), so that the spirit, if not the letter, of the original is preserved.

In other cases, however, Grillparzer conceded far less ground. Later on in the same speech by Naukleros, the censors deleted the line "Und all den Schätzen so beglückten Leibes?" The playwright's response was to substitute "Reichtum" for "Schätzen," but to leave the rest of the line as it had been before (*SW* I/19:183). The use of the more general term "Reichtum" may have avoided the specific anatomical references implied by "Schätzen," but allows the line to remain as an unmistakable celebration of sensual pleasures. Although the second version may have been slightly less offensive than the first, the retention of the phrase "so beglückten Leibes" means that the line preserves a distinctly erotic flavor.

A similarly incomplete "correction" comes in response to the censors' deletion of the charge of hypocrisy made toward the high priest by Naukleros. We have already seen how line 863, "Und schmückst mit heil'gem Vorwand deine Tat?" (*SW* I/4:128) was deleted from the censorship manuscript, presumably because it exposed the use of religious pretexts for selfish acts. The playwright's replacement — "Und schmückst mit hohlem Vorwand deine Tat?" (*SW* I/19:183) — certainly denied Naukleros's accusation an explicitly religious element, but nevertheless conserved the idea of an authority figure using a pretext to disguise a base motivation, and therefore retained its unwelcome implications for contemporary political leaders. Moreover, although the second version of line 863 no longer mentions religion directly, the high priest's reference to temple law in his justification for separating Hero from the foreigners remains in the text, so that even the second version of the line implies a connection between religion and hypocritical rule. Indeed, had the word "heiligen" been the only offensive element, it seems likely that the censors would have proposed a substitute, as they did at numerous other points,[38] instead of demanding the removal of the entire line.

In other instances, Grillparzer's efforts to conserve his original text led him to feign misunderstanding of the censors' objections. As already mentioned, the very first lines to be deleted from *Des Meeres und der Liebe Wellen* involve Hero's condemnation of the oppression experienced by her mother within marriage:

> Wie? und mußt hüten jenes Mannes Blick,
> Des Herren, deines Gatten? Darfst nicht reden,
> Mußt schweigen, flüstern, ob du gleich im Recht [. . .].
> (vv. 322–24; *SW* I/4:98)

We have already seen Grillparzer's efforts to tone down his criticism of marriage in the early versions of *Des Meeres und der Liebe Wellen*, which indicate his awareness of the censors' sensitivity to this issue. However, his reaction to this deletion was to pretend ignorance, and to respond as though he believed the entire passage had been deleted due to a misunderstanding about one word. By replacing "Des Herren, deines Gatten" with "Des Gatten, der dein Meister," the playwright attempted to suggest that all three lines had been removed because Hero had used the word "Herren," which might also mean God, to refer to her father. He reinforced this step with a note in the margin that read "muß so bleiben und ist offenbar nur durch ein Mißverständnis ausgestrichen" (*SW* I/19:182). Despite this confident tone, it is hard to imagine that Grillparzer believed this one word was the cause of a three-line deletion. As we have seen, in cases where only a single word in a passage was problematic, the play's censors tended to find a more suitable replacement for that word rather than removing several lines. And if they had been unable to think of such a substitution, they could have simply removed "Des Herren" from the beginning of line 323, and the passage would have continued to make sense.[39]

Grillparzer's response to another deletion, this time in act three, was similar. In line 1047, Hero is alone in her tower and has just found herself again singing the song about Leda and the swan. Reflecting upon the loneliness of her situation, she laments, "Kein Schwan, kein Adler bringt Verlaßnen Trost" (*SW* I/4:137). This line was presumably deleted as a result of its reference to the forbidden sensuality of the Leda myth: no other references to the swan had been allowed to remain by the censors. Despite this, Grillparzer reinstated the line with the swan reference intact. Instead, he replaced "Adler" with "Flügelbothe" (*SW* I/19:183), implying that he believed that the censors only objected to the mention of the Habsburg birds of prey. Not only does the word "Adler" pass unscathed in line 626, but the replacement of the original eagle with another bird would also have been an easy substitution for the censors themselves to make. As in the above example, however, Grillparzer used the alteration of an insignificant detail as a means to allow more problematic material — the forbidden eroticism of the Leda myth — to be included in the manuscript.

At other points, the author of *Des Meeres und der Liebe Wellen* abandoned all pretense of acting to appease the authorities. He refused, for example, to accept the censors' new ending to act three, which concludes with Hero telling Leander to leave and then exiting the room herself. Although Grillparzer did not dare to return to the original, in which Hero initiates a second stage to the encounter, he did write a conclusion which left such a possibility open. In this second version, Hero tells Leander to go, but he protests. She then leaves the room, but the curtain falls with Leander pleading with her ("Wenn ich dir flehe! Hero!), so that a question mark remains over her final response (*SW* I/19:183).

Most brazen of all, however, was Grillparzer's reaction to the censors' removal of the last five lines of the amorous plea addressed to Hero by Leander toward the end of act three:

> Nicht mindestens die Hand? —
> Und dann! — Sie legen Lipp an Lippe,
> Ich sah es wohl, und flüstern so sich zu,

> Was zu geheim ist für die geschwätz'ge Luft
> Mein Mund sei Mund, der deine sei dein Ohr!
> Leih' mir dein Ohr für meine stumme Sprache!
>
> (vv. 1240–45; *SW* I/4:149)

Although the last three lines of this passage were marked by all three censors, Grillparzer simply did not accept their objection and, without any further explanation, wrote "bleibt" in the margin (*SW* I/19:183).

Despite this assertiveness on the part of Grillparzer, Schreyvogel's compliant response to the censors' complaints suggests that negotiation and protest were far from common practice. Instead, it seems significant that Grillparzer had been repeatedly exasperated by censorship problems during the late 1820s, and that the composition of *Des Meeres und der Liebe Wellen* was significantly affected by the need to appease its censors. One therefore imagines that, after the tragedy suffered such disruptive cuts despite his precautions, he felt compelled to attempt a more defiant stance, although its outcome was uncertain. Unfortunately, Grillparzer's letters and diary entries contain no information about why the playwright abandoned work on the "corrections" after act three. Yet, given Schreyvogel's more cautious approach to the task, it is possible that a dispute between the two men led to the director continuing alone.

For Grillparzer himself, however, recent experiences may have provided him with reason to be optimistic about the results of his combative approach to the censors' objections. An examination of his letters suggests that his annoyance at censorship restrictions alternated with a strong intimation of his value to the Habsburg Empire as an essentially loyal and successful playwright. The existence of a thriving theatrical scene in Vienna was not simply a matter of pride to the monarchy: numerous official documents from the period make it clear that theater was considered a vital instrument in distracting all classes of Viennese from being led astray, both morally and politically.[40] From the early 1820s onwards, therefore, Grillparzer had used his poetic achievements both as an argument for promotion and pay raises, and as an excuse for extending his official leave.[41]

Furthermore, in addition to the frustration they caused Grillparzer, the censorship conflicts surrounding *König Ottokar* and *Ein treuer Diener seines Herrn* in the 1820s may have indicated to the playwright that oppressive measures were not always in the authorities' best interest. In the case of *König Ottokar*, the curiosity generated by the drama's prohibition was such that, when a production was eventually permitted, its early performances attracted enormous audiences.[42] One imagines that a desire to avoid this kind of adverse publicity led emperor Francis to try to buy the exclusive rights to *Ein treuer Diener seines Herren* in the spring of 1828 rather than banning it outright. Moreover, despite the playwright's initial despondency at the emperor's offer (II/8:194–95), his protests to police chief Sedlnitzky eventually resulted in Francis' withdrawing the proposals. This favorable outcome may well have persuaded Grillparzer that it could be worthwhile to challenge the authorities' decisions on *Des Meeres und der Liebe Wellen* only three years later. Indeed, the following extract from one of Sedlnitzky's reports to the emperor on *Ein Treuer Diener seines Herren* reveals that, despite its iron-fisted image, Metternich's state was prepared to make compromises in the service of serious art:

> Allergnädigster Herr! Schon in der älteren Zeit haben die Dichter nicht selten das Spiel wilder Leidenschaften zum Gegenstande ihrer dramatischen Arbeiten gemacht; weit häufiger thun diese die Dichter neuerer Zeit, und die Erfahrung lehrt, daß die neueren Dichter sich in der Darstellung wilder Leidenschaften und revolutionärer Scenen bey ihren dramatischen Arbeiten vorzugsweise gefallen, und daß nur mit wenigen Ausnahmen Theaterstücke ernsterer Art vorkommen, welche von der Censur, rücksichtlich der grellen Behandlung des Gegenstandes, nicht zu beanständigen wären. Wenn derley dramatische Producte mit voller Strenge von der Darstellung auf der Bühne hintangehalten werden wollten: so würde in der neuesten Zeit, wo der Mangel guter dramatischer Dichter von den Theaterdirectionen allgemein gefühlet wird, es bald dahinkommen, daß beynahe kein Theaterstück ernsterer Gattung zur Aufführung zugelassen werden könnte. (*SW* III/2:340–41)

Unfortunately the censorship files on *Des Meeres und der Liebe Wellen* are no longer present in the police archives of the Allgemeines Verwaltungsarchiv in Vienna.[43] However, there are good reasons to suspect that similar considerations paid a significant role in the authorities' response to the concessions that were demanded by its author. In the same year that Grillparzer's classical tragedy underwent censorship, a shortage of high-quality dramas was again mentioned in an Austrian state document as an argument in favor of relaxing censorship standards for a production at the Burgtheater. In correspondence relating to Ernst Raupach's play *König Enzio*, Metternich conceded that it was unsuitable to be staged in a Catholic country, but concluded that, due to scarcity of suitable repertoire for the court theater, its performance should nevertheless be authorized.[44] And following the corrections made by Grillparzer and Schreyvogel to the h3 manuscript of *Des Meeres und der Liebe Wellen*, it was presented to the censors once again. They must have approved the new amendments, for these were all copied on to the h1 manuscript that was used for the 1831 Burgtheater performances (*SW* I/19:182). Given the thorough censorship to which *Des Meeres und der Liebe Wellen* was initially subjected, it is unlikely that the acceptance of Grillparzer's changes was the result of an oversight. Instead, a concern for the condition of the court theater — not to mention the fear of a scandal and the risk of prompting the exile of one of Vienna's finest playwrights — seems to have led the authorities to accept a compromise.

Conclusion

This examination of the effects of censorship on *Des Meeres und der Liebe Wellen* has revealed a complex relationship between the censoring authorities and the play's author. While censorship undeniably placed considerable constraints on both the initial composition and performance of the drama, the analysis has also indicated that some possibilities did exist for writers — especially those who were both successful and largely loyal — to fight back.

Grillparzer's preemptive alterations to early versions of the tragedy provide a reflection of the official concerns and reveal how censorship pressure affected the composition of the play. The treatment by both Grillparzer and Schreyvogel of interactions between Hero and the high priest, for example, suggest a high level of vigilance regarding covert hints of incest. More generally, there is strong evidence that anxiety about the censors' responses to representations of sexuality and dysfunctional family life led the playwright to tone down several sections of the play, either presenting such material in an oblique manner or removing it altogether.

In addition, some of the playwright's other changes to the early *Meereswellen* manuscripts seem to represent more than an attempt to preempt official censorship. There are indications that, by reducing the amount of controversial material contained within his play, Grillparzer hoped to make the censors more favorably disposed toward those problematic elements he was determined to conserve. Evidence for such prioritizing is provided by the writer's alterations to the movements of the people watching Hero's initiation ceremony. Even in their original form, the stage directions at this point seem far less threatening than the masses' democratically tinged cry of "Glück mit uns." The fact that the people's proclamation was permitted by the censors to be repeated three times may well owe something to the playwright's earlier careful attention to the presentation of their movements.

We have also seen how Grillparzer attempted to avoid censorship cuts to *Des Meeres und der Liebe Wellen* by using subtle evasive techniques such as irony, fragmented presentation, omitted stage directions, visual depiction, metaphor, symbolic allusion, and the avoidance of ideological keywords. Such strategies were most successful for the negative portrayal of married and family life, perhaps because the censors were unaccustomed to such themes being presented indirectly. By contrast, the officials were able to detect much more hidden material in the spheres of religion, politics, and sex: few examples of *Zensurstil* in these areas were missed by all of the censors. Nevertheless, the fact that several cases of evasive presentation were overlooked by at least two of the censors demonstrates that such strategies did offer some hope of success. As a result, the employment of three officials for the censorship of one play appears to have been a wise precaution on the part of the authorities, and demonstrates the extent to which evasive strategies posed a genuine threat to the effectiveness of the censorship system.

In the end, however, Grillparzer's most successful resistance to state censorship was an act of open defiance. Motivated, it seems, by a combination of desperation and creeping awareness of his value to the Habsburg regime, the concessions demanded by and granted to the playwright cast new light on the relationship between censoring state and censored writer. It is true that, in his apparent uncertainty about the outcome of his challenge, Grillparzer made some attempts to disguise the nature of his demands by removing offensive keywords and pretending to misunderstand the censors' complaints. Nevertheless, the thorough scrutiny to which his first draft was subjected, along with the playwright's more open demands at other points, means that the authorities cannot have been unaware of his ploy. Instead, their reluctance to enter into conflict with one of Austria's most successful and relatively loyal writers over an essentially nonpolitical play led them to accept his demands. For while censorship pressure had a substantial effect on the initial composition of *Des Meeres und der Liebe Wellen*, the censors did not have the final word on the version staged at the Burgtheater in 1831. Against all expectations, it seems that the social and political value of theater to the oppressive police state that his own tragedy obliquely depicted enabled Grillparzer to force that state into compromise.

Notes

[1] Franz Grillparzer, *Sämtliche Werke: Historisch-kritische Gesamtausgabe*, ed. August Sauer and Reinhold Backmann (Vienna: Anton Schroll, 1909–1948), section II, vol. 8, 1916, 204 (edition subsequently cited as *SW*). A revised version of this chapter appeared in the 2007 number of the Immermann-Jahrbuch.

[2] *SW* section III, vol. 1, 1913, 435.

[3] *SW* section I, vol. 4, 1925, 77–211.

[4] See E. E. Papst, *Grillparzer: "Des Meeres und der Liebe Wellen"* (London: Edward Arnold, 1967), 21.

[5] See *SW* section I, vol. 19, 1939, 196.

[6] The first complete drafts of the play were composed between 1826 and 1829.

[7] See Christian Grawe, "Grillparzers Dramatik als Problem der zeitgenössischen österreichischen Theaterzensur," in *"Was nützt der Glaube ohne Werke . . .": Studien*

zu Franz Grillparzer anläßlich seines 200. Geburtstages, ed. August Obermayer, Otago German Studies 7 (Dunedin: University of Otago, 1992), 162–90; here 184. The use of historically and geographically remote settings as a means of evading censorship restrictions is well-documented within other censorship contexts too. See, for example, Lev Loseff's discussion of this strategy within Russian literature written under Tsarist and Communist censorship: Loseff, *On the Beneficence of Censorship: Aesopian Language in Modern German Literature,* trans. Jane Bobko (Munich: Otto Sagner, 1984).

[8] See *SW* I/19:148.

[9] See *SW* I/19:153–69.

[10] See *SW* I/19:170.

[11] Another manuscript, h2, was submitted to the censors in 1829. Although it was approved, the play's performance was postponed for two years on account of the illness and eventual death of Sophie Müller, who was supposed to play Hero. Due to the time that had elapsed since the first round of censorship, a new manuscript (h3) had to be submitted to the censors in 1831. Unfortunately, h2 went missing prior to the compilation of the *SW*.

[12] See, for example, his diary entries for 20 March 1826 (*SW* II/8:196), 18 February 1829 (*SW* II/8:331), and 21 February 1829 (*SW* II/8:335).

[13] See *SW* I/19:170–78 and 184–85.

[14] See Grawe, "Grillparzers Dramatik," 164.

[15] The full text of this law can be found in the appendix of Marx, *Die österreichische Zensur,* 73–76.

[16] See *SW* I/19:309–10. ("Lesarten" for all cited examples).

[17] In the myth to which this song refers, Leda is seduced (or, in some versions, raped) by a swan, who is Zeus in disguise.

[18] The version of this passage quoted here is the same as that found in the Burgtheater manuscripts, but its phrasing and punctuation is slightly different from that which appears in the *SW Des Meeres und der Liebe Wellen* text. For the version of the speech printed in the *SW*, see vv. 1807–14; *SW* I/4:188. *SW* I/19:432 (part of the "Lesarten" section for the play) gives details of the deviations. In future cases where a passage quoted is different from that printed in the *SW*, page references to both the main *SW* text and the relevant "Lesarten" details will be given.

[19] See *SW* I/19:320 ("Lesarten" for all examples cited in this paragraph).

[20] See, for example, Thompson, *Franz Grillparzer,* 67.

[21] The memorandum is reprinted in Glossy, "Zur Geschichte der Wiener Theatercensur," 298–340. The passage referred to here is on 332.

[22] Glossy, "Zur Geschichte der Theater Wiens I," 82.

[23] Glossy, "Zur Geschichte der Wiener Theatercensur," 316.

[24] Glossy, "Zur Geschichte der Wiener Theater I," 145.

[25] The role of Hero's experience of family life in motivating her decision to become a priestess, and therefore in contributing to the tragedy, has been noted by several commentators. See, for example, Politzer, *Franz Grillparzer,* 213.

[26] See W. E Yates, "Grillparzer and the Fair Sex," in *Grillparzer und die europäische Tradition*, ed. F. Wagner (Vienna: Hora, 1987), 71–83; here 79–80.

[27] See, for example, H. H. Houben, *Der gefesselte Biedermeier*, 230.

[28] One report from 1834, for example, cites as one of the main reasons for prohibiting a play "die versuchte Rechtfertigung seiner Mißheirat durch eine erlauchte Person" contained within it. The report is reproduced in Glossy, "Geschichte der Theater Wiens III (1830–1840)," 88.

[29] Michael Perraudin, *Literature, the "Volk" and the Revolution in Mid-Nineteenth Century Germany* (Oxford and New York: Berghahn, 2000), 161.

[30] See *SW* I/19:301 ("Lesarten" for this and the previous example cited).

[31] See Perraudin, *Literature, the "Volk" and the Revolution*, 61.

[32] See, for example, Brose, *German History 1789–1871*, 155–57.

[33] Full details of all of the censors' complaints can be found in *SW* I/19:181–84.

[34] This principle is elucidated in Hägelin's memorandum (see Glossy, "Geschichte der Wiener Theatercensur," 305–9, 313, and 320–35), and confirmed by countless censors' reports of the subsequent decades (see, for example, Glossy, "Zur Geschichte der Theater Wiens I," 241 and 243).

[35] The word was also tolerated at lines 381, 573, and 832. See *SW* I/4:102, 115, and 127; and *SW* I/19:181–84.

[36] As several critics have noted, the attraction between Leander and Hero is primarily sensual in nature. See, for example, Dagmar C. G. Lorenz, *Grillparzer, Dichter des sozialen Konflikts* (Vienna: Böhlau, 1986), 51–57.

[37] A full account of the reactions of the two men to the censors' complaints can be found in *SW* I/19:181–84.

[38] See, for example, the censors' reactions to references to religious buildings, as discussed in the previous section; also, their treatment of line 2053, in which they replaced the word "Gürtel" with "Schleier," in order to remove a suggestion that Hero had lost her virginity to Leander (*SW* I/19:181–84).

[39] The willingness of the censors simply to delete words from a line, regardless of the disruption of rhythmic structure that this could cause, is shown by their removal of the words "sich paart" from line 357: "Alles, was sich paart, bleibt ferne diesem Hause" (*SW* I/19:182).

[40] For examples, see Glossy, "Zur Geschichte der Theater Wiens II (1820–1830)," 26, 83, and 135. For more details of official attitudes toward the theater see Hüttner, "Theatre Censorship in Metternich's Vienna," 61–62.

[41] See, for example, *SW* section 3, vol. 2, 1924, 399.

[42] See contemporary accounts in *SW* I/18:24.

[43] It is almost certain that the files were destroyed in the 1927 Justizpalast fire. They were not among those published by Glossy.

[44] See Glossy, "Zur Geschichte der Theater Wiens III," 65.

Conclusion

IN HER ANALYSIS of the relationship between literature and censorship during the Restoration period, Edda Ziegler discusses the difficulty of determining precisely the effect of press controls on contemporary texts. Drawing attention to the importance of *Selbstzensur* in writing practices during the period, Ziegler points out that this process starts with the "gedankliche [. . .] Konzeption eines Textes" and therefore can never be reconstructed in its entirety.[1] It is impossible to know how much material was suppressed due to censorship pressure and never written down.

Ziegler's reminder of the indeterminable reach of censorship controls is important and calls to mind the image of censorship as a "Schere im Kopf" that prevents not only the recording, but also the development of subversive thoughts within the consciousness of writers. Indeed, one can go a stage further and speculate about the broader influence of tightly controlled public discourse upon contemporary imaginations. At the end of *Briefe aus Berlin,* for instance, Heine describes how the literary tastes of contemporary German writers were shaped by the conditions under which they operated. Censorship is not mentioned explicitly among the restrictive factors, but, given the references to censorship measures that permeate the text, one imagines that Heine counted state press controls among the major causes of a turning away from social reality:

> der arme Deutsche verschließt sich in seine einsame Dachstube, faselt eine Welt zusammen, und in einer aus ihm selbst wunderlich hervorgegangenen Sprache schreibt er Romane, worin Gestalten und Dinge leben, die herrlich, göttlich, höchstpoetisch sind, aber nirgends existiren.[2]

It certainly seems inevitable that state censorship molded the collective and individual realities from which art emerged during the Restoration period; and that its total effects on public discourse and private imaginations were simultaneously both far-reaching and ultimately unknowable.

Despite this final caveat, it has been possible to gain insights into the relationship between literature and state censorship in Restoration Germany. Even during the conservative 1820s, state repression clearly did not succeed in eliminating all dissent from the minds of German subjects, and we have seen how literary writers attempted to communicate various forms of unorthodox thought through their work. As one would expect, many of these deviations from official political, religious, social, and moral ideology were suppressed prior to publication or performance. Others, however, were able to reach the public sphere and therefore provide an impression of what was possible for contemporary authors, as well as of the types of literary expression that were encouraged by censorship pressures. In addition, comparison of tolerated and repressed utterance has enabled us to identify some of the factors that determined the boundaries between permissible and impermissible expression.

Of course, it is well established that censorship standards differed from state to state within Germany, as well as according to the forms taken by literary expression and its expected audience or readership. We have seen that far stricter standards were applied to the theatrical performances of Grillparzer's dramas in Austria than to texts by Grabbe and Heine in Prussia; and that Austrian theater censorship was particularly rigorous for performances attended by members of the middle and lower social classes. Yet censorship practices were not determined by state ideology alone. In comparison with the totalitarian regimes that would emerge in the following century, Restoration governments had far fewer financial resources at their disposal for the employment of officials to enforce censorship laws. Apart from Austria, none of the German states — including Prussia — were able to screen all works published in other, potentially more liberal states: a deficiency that precluded total government control of printed matter. Another source of inconsistency was the interpretation and application of censorship norms by the censors themselves, a process that was doubtlessly rendered less efficient by the time pressure under which many officials fulfilled their duties. Finally, the prohibition of a book or play could both increase interest in the works concerned and draw unwelcome attention to state repression. As was the case in other censorship regimes, government awareness of this danger could result in additional leeway being granted to successful writers, whose works were the focus of particular public interest: both the flexible censorship of Grillparzer's *Des Meeres und der Liebe Wellen* by the severe Austrian authorities and the Prussians' acceptance of overtly revolutionary discourse within *Reise von München nach Genua* can be seen as tacit acknowledgments of the limits of state power.

One might expect such impediments to the efficient implementation of censorship principles to result in arbitrary practices, and to some extent they did. However, despite the differing professional and censorship contexts within which Heine, Grabbe, and Grillparzer wrote, their texts suggest some general patterns that characterized the interaction between censorship and literature during the period. First, we have seen substantial evidence that, on the whole, censorship controls were most effective at suppressing material that posed a direct threat to the ruling classes in the state concerned. Expression that was officially proscribed but less closely linked to these elites, on the other hand, could often be tolerated. Perhaps the clearest example of this is publication of attacks on both the Catholic clergy and mediocre contemporary writers in Grabbe's *Scherz, Satire, Ironie und tiefere Bedeutung*. In theory, both groups were protected by Prussian censorship law, and the fact that Grabbe's attacks were tolerated in Prussia is doubtless a reflection of their irrelevance for the predominantly Protestant Prussian elites. In addition, however, both elements of characterization and other material potentially offensive to Czechs and Hungarians in *König Ottokars Glück und Ende* were tolerated by Austrian censors, whereas even subtle intimations of limits to monarchical authority in the same play were removed. Finally, while the sensitivity of both Prussian and Austrian officials toward potentially erotic content could be seen as an exception to this trend, it also reflects contemporary fear of sensuality as a socially disruptive force.

Beyond such thematic patterns, we have also seen evidence that the differential enforcement of censorship precepts stimulated writers to find modes of literary expression that posed less of an obvious threat to the contemporary political and social order. The best-known example of this is the employment of various forms of esoteric communication that aimed to disguise proscribed content from the censors. Yet in addition, this study has identified several examples of nonconformist and even subversive ideas reaching the public sphere that were clearly accessible on a literal level, but at the same time crafted in a manner that mitigated their appearance as a menace to the establishment of the time.

One dimension of this was the various means by which the writers succeeded in expressing subversive thought in a relatively abstract manner. Such approaches allowed the authors to contradict official ideology without displaying animosity toward Restoration institutions. In both *Briefe aus Berlin* and *Reise von München nach Genua*, for instance, Heine communicates his revolutionary ideals clearly while simultaneously obscuring the implications of these principles for the established order in Germany. An equivalent pattern is revealed by anti-religious utterance in both *Briefe aus Berlin* and Grabbe's early plays. While these works include fundamental contradictions of Christian theology, such messages are largely embedded in phrasing, imagery, and situations not usually associated with religious discussion, and are kept far away from the mention of religious practices or institutions. Devoid of references to contemporary religious and political elites, such passages were not suppressed despite their impermissibility in principle.

Also important were the various means by which the writers and their editors reduced the vigor and intensity of subversive utterance within their literary works. Such endeavors mirror the criterion of an "anständiger Ton" expressed in several contemporary censorship laws;[3] and they also appear as a logical extension of the obsession of the authorities with ideological keywords.[4] More importantly, however, they demonstrate that censorship could restrict not only the communicative dimension of literary expression, but also its emotional tenor. Of the three writers under examination here, the most extensive and intricate techniques for limiting the energy and aggression of openly subversive content were developed by Heine, whose political commitment was accompanied by an unusually inventive response to censorship pressure. In *Briefe aus Berlin* and *Reise von München nach Genua*, the author was able to express obvious opposition to the Restoration while at the same time avoiding negative vocabulary, the verbal cues associated with protest, and the direct expression of critical links, and blurring the focus of his most dangerous thoughts. Variations on this theme can also be seen in Kettembeil's removal of provocative language from disturbing scenes in *Herzog Theodor von Gothland*, and, in Grillparzer's *König Ottokars Glück und Ende*, in the author's deft treatment of the adulterous relationship between Zawisch and Kunigunde, which — even after censorship — was clearly implied, but never commented on explicitly.

Closely related to such efforts is the presentation of dangerous material in a manner that pushes it to the margins of audience and reader perception. Several of the works under examination here include subversive content that was clearly accessible to a moderately attentive reader or theatergoer, but was unlikely to remain a focus of interest for long. One example is the subtle depiction of the mistreatment suffered by Hero's mother at the hands of her husband in *Des Meeres und der Liebe Wellen*, which, unlike the priestess's explicit rejection of marriage, survived the play's first round of censorship. The absence of exclamation marks at the end of provocative sentences in *Scherz, Satire, Ironie und tiefere Bedeutung* results in a similar effect. Finally, Heine's efforts to limit the density of critical utterance led to the intricate construction of passages in which such expression is diluted by ostensibly uncritical sections of text.

Not only provocative material was affected by writers' efforts to adjust the relationship between acceptable and inflammatory content within literary works. One last common feature of the texts under discussion here is the adjustment of less dangerous utterance in the hope of making a favorable impression on the censors and thereby inducing a more lenient or less vigilant attitude toward the same text's nonconformist ingredients. Such endeavors represent an extension of the well-established use of apparently innocuous genres such as travel or historical literature for the packaging of critical opinion, and they could take a variety of forms. By toning down crowd movements in *Des Meeres und der Liebe Wellen*, for example, Grillparzer evidently hoped to remove material that could heighten censors' sensitivity to more dangerous parts of the drama. Another strategy was the inclusion of content designed to compensate for nonconformist utterance, as exemplified by Heine's flanking of critical opinion with gestures of sympathy for the Prussian government in *Briefe aus Berlin* and Grabbe's drawing attention to elements that function in opposition to illicit material within the economy of his dramas. One further form of censorship-induced contextualization was the addresses and letter from Tieck with which Grabbe prefaced the two volumes of his *Dramatische Dichtungen,* in the hope — as we have seen — of altering the censors' perception of his works. Although we do not know which of these strategies succeeded in altering the authorities' responses to the texts concerned, they nevertheless illustrate the wide scope of interaction between censorship and literary texts.

Ziegler may well be correct to identify unrecorded instances of *Selbstzensur* as the most significant effect of censorship on literary writing during the Restoration: clearly this is unverifiable. Certainly, the restraints imposed by censorship pressure upon subversive expression precluded the detailed, sustained, and engaging treatment of a multitude of compelling themes, and thereby decisively narrowed the scope of contemporary literature. On the other hand, however, we have also seen that the interaction between censorship and writing during the 1820s was not confined to the excision, or even the disguising, of material that violated censorship norms. State control of utterance during the period was unquestionably strict, but it was not total. In northern Germany in particular, censorship codes were not always fanatically enforced, and this encouraged nonconformist writers to seek modes of expression that would be tolerated by the authorities. Indeed, for literary imaginations faced with the task of reaching the public across the barriers of censorship, one can see how responses to state control could become an integral part of the creative process. In some cases — most notably that of Heine — this close relationship with censorship could stimulate the development of subtle and inventive forms of literary expression. As writers attempted to depict controversial events and communicate subversive ideas in a manner that would not provoke state sanctions, they were spurred on to greater expressive resourcefulness. The result of this search for oblique, associative, and ostensibly innocuous means of literary representation was frequently the emergence of intricate, sophisticated, and ingenious texts that owe at least some of their richness to the limits imposed by state censorship. We should not, therefore, be surprised that, despite the undeniable frustrations it had caused both him and his colleagues, one reported reaction of Heine to the abolition of state censorship in 1848 includes a genuine acknowledgment of the stylistic impulses it had provided:

> ach! Ich kann nicht mehr schreiben, ich kann nicht, denn wir haben keine Censur! Wie soll ein Mensch ohne Censur schreiben, der immer unter Censur gelebt hat? Aller Styl wird aufhören, die ganze Grammatik, die guten Sitten.[5]

Notes

[1] Ziegler, *Literarische Zensur in Deutschland 1819–1848,* 172.

[2] Heinrich Heine, *Historisch-kritische Gesamtausgabe der Werke,* 6:53.

[3] See, for example, Mannes und Weber, *Zensur im Vormärz (1815–1848),* 147–48, and Breil, *Die Augsburger "Allgemeine Zeitung,"* 134.

[4] See, for example, Klaus Kanzog, "Zensur: literarische," 998–1049.

[5] Werner, *Begegnungen mit Heine,* 2:108.

Bibliography

Aigner, Dietrich. "Die Indizierung 'schädlichen und unerwünschten Schrifttums' im Dritten Reich." *Archiv für Geschichte des Buchwesens* 11 (1971): 933–1034.

Anglade, René. "Die Engländer in der Hofkirche: Zugleich ein kleiner Beitrag zur Poetik Heines." *Euphorion* 78 (1984): 415–34.

Altenhofer, Norbert. *Harzreise in die Zeit: Zum Funktionszusammenhang von Traum, Witz und Zensur in Heines früher Prosa*. Dusseldorf: Heinrich-Heine-Gesellschaft, 1972.

———. *Die verlorene Augensprache: über Heinrich Heine*. Leipzig: Insel, 1993.

Assmann, Aleida, and Jan Assmann. "Kanon und Zensur als kultursoziologische Kategorien." In *Kanon und Zensur: Archäologie der literarischen Kommunikation II*, edited by Aleida Assmann and Jan Assmann, 7–27. Munich: Fink, 1987.

Aufenanger, Jörg. *Das Lachen der Verzweiflung: Grabbe. Ein Leben*. Frankfurt am Main: Fischer, 2001.

Bachmaier, Helmut, ed. *Franz Grillparzer*. Frankfurt am Main: Suhrkamp, 1991.

Betz, Alfred. *Ästhetik und Politik: Heinrich Heines Prosa*. Munich: Hanser, 1971.

Biermann, Armin. "'Gefährliche Literatur': Skizze einer Theorie der literarischen Zensur." *Wolfenbütteler Notizen zur Buchgeschichte* 13.1 (1988): 1–28.

Blackbourn, David. *History of Germany 1780–1918: The Long Nineteenth Century*. 2nd ed. Malden, MA: Blackwell, 2003.

Blumenauer, Elke. *Journalismus zwischen Pressefreiheit und Zensur: Die Augsburger "Allgemeine Zeitung" im Karlsbader System (1818–48)*, Medien in Geschichte und Gegenwart 14. Cologne: Böhlau, 2000.

Böhm, Hans. "Heinrich Heine und die Selbstzensur: Zu *Deutschland: Ein Wintermärchen*." In *Im Vorfeld der Literatur: Vom Wert archivalischer Überlieferung für das Verständnis von Literatur und ihrer Geschichte. Studien*, edited by Karl-Heinz Hahn, 186–97. Weimar: Bohlaus, 1991.

Bourdieu, Pierre. "Censorship and the Imposition of Form." In *Language and Symbolic Power*, edited by John B. Thompson, translated by Gino Raymond and Matthew Adamson, 137–59. Oxford: Polity, 1992.

Brandes, Helga. *Die Zeitschriften des Jungen Deutschland: Eine Untersuchung zur literarisch-publizistischen Öffentlichkeit im 19. Jahrhundert*. Opladen: Westdeutscher Verlag, 1991.

Breil, Michaela. *Die Augsburger "Allgemeine Zeitung" und die Pressepolitik Bayerns: Ein Verlagsunternehmen zwischen 1815 und 1848*. Tübingen: Niemeyer, 1996.

Breuer, Dieter. *Geschichte der literarischen Zensur in Deutschland*. Heidelberg: Quelle und Meyer, 1982.

Breuilly, John, ed. *Nineteenth-Century Germany: Politics, Culture and Society 1780–1918*. London: Arnold, 2001.

Briegleb, Klaus. "Heine und Preußen. Notierungen zur 'Vorrede' vom 18. Oktober 1832." In *Opfer Heine? Versuche über Schriftzüge der Revolution*, 45–70. Frankfurt: Suhrkamp, 1986.

———. "Schriftstellernöte und literarische Produktivität. Zum Exempel H. Heine." In *Neue Ansichten einer künftigen Germanistik*, edited by Jürgen Kolbe, 121–59. Munich: Hanser, 1973.

Brockmeier, Peter, and Gerhard R. Kaiser, eds. *Zensur und Selbstzensur in der Literatur*. Wurzburg: Königshausen & Neumann, 1996.

Brose, Eric Dorn. *German History 1789–1871: From the Holy Roman Empire to the Bismarckian Reich*. Providence: Berghahn, 1997.

Brummack, Jürgen, ed. *Heinrich Heine: Epoche — Werk — Wirkung*. Munich: Beck, 1980.

Burt, Richard, ed. *The Administration of Aesthetics: Censorship, Political Criticism, and the Public Sphere*. Cultural Politics 7. Minneapolis: University of Minnesota Press, 1994.

Buschmann, Silke. *Literarische Zensur in der BRD nach 1945*. Frankfurt: Lang, 1997.

Carr, William. *A History of Germany 1815–1990*. 4th ed. London: Arnold, 1991.

Castelli, Ignaz Franz. *Memoiren meines Lebens*. 2 vols. Vienna: Kober & Markgraf, 1861; reprinted Munich: Winkler, 1969.

Cortesi, Antonio. *Die Logik von Zerstörung und Größenphantasie in den Dramen Christian Dietrich Grabbes*. Bern: Lang, 1986.

Costenoble, Carl Ludwig. *Aus dem Burgtheater 1818–1837: Tagebuchblätter*. 2 vols. Vienna: Konegan, 1889.

Cowan, Roy C. *Christian Dietrich Grabbe*. New York: Twayne, 1972.

Denkler, Horst, and Karl Prümm, eds. *Die deutsche Literatur im Dritten Reich: Themen — Traditionen — Wirkungen*. Stuttgart: Reclam, 1976.

Deuchert, Norbert. *Vom Hambacher Fest zur badischen Revolution: Politische Presse und Anfänge der Demokratie 1832–1848/9*. Stuttgart: Thiess, 1983.

Ehrlich, Lothar. *Christian Dietrich Grabbe: Leben, Werk, Wirkung*. Berlin: Akademie, 1983.

Eisenhardt, Ulrich. "Die Garantie der Pressefreiheit in der Bundesakte von 1815." *Der Staat* 10 (1971): 339–56.

———. "Wandlungen von Zweck und Methoden der Zensur im 18. und 19. Jahrhundert." In *"Unmoralisch an sich . . ." Zensur im 18. und 19. Jahrhundert*, edited by Herbert G. Göpfert and Erdmann Weyrauch, 1–35. Wolfenbütteler Schriften zur Geschichte des Buchwesens 13. Wiesbaden: Harrassowitz, 1988.

Emerson, Donald E. *Metternich and the Political Police: Security and Subversion in the Habsburg Monarchy*. The Hague: Martinus Nijhoff, 1969.

Espagne, Michel. "Die tote Maria. Ein Gespenst in Heines Handschriften." *Deutsche Vierteljahrsschrift für Literaturwissenschaft und Geistesgeschichte* 57 (1983): 298–320.

Freud, Sigmund, *Die Traumdeutung*, 11th ed. Fischer: Frankfurt am Main, 2001.

Freund, Winfried, ed. *Grabbes Gegenentwürfe: Neue Deutungen seiner Dramen*. Munich: Fink, 1986.

Frühwald, Wolfgang. "Der Regierungsrat Joseph von Eichendorff." *Internationales Archiv für Sozialgeschichte der deutschen Literatur* 4 (1979): 37–67.

Fuchs, Karlheinz. *Bürgerliches Räsonnement und Staatsräson: Zensur als Instrument des Despotismus dargestellt am Beispiel des rheinbündischen Württemberg (1806–1813)*. Göppingen: Kümmerle, 1975.

Fülleborn, Ulrich. *Das dramatische Geschehen im Werk Franz Grillparzers: Ein Beitrag zur Epochenbestimmung der deutschen Dichtung im 19. Jahrhundert*. Munich: Fink, 1966.

Galley, Eberhard, and Alfred Estermann, eds. *Heinrich Heines Werk im Urteil seiner Zeitgenossen*. 6 vols. Hamburg: Hoffmann und Campe, 1985.

Galley, Eberhard. "Politische Aspekte in Heines italienischen Reisebildern." In *Internationaler Heine-Kongreß Düsseldorf 1972*, edited by Manfred Windfuhr, 386–98. Hamburg: Hoffmann und Campe, 1973.

Gebhardt, Armin. *Franz Grillparzer und sein dramatisches Werk*. Marburg: Tectum, 2002.

Glossy, Karl, ed. *Literarische Geheimberichte aus dem Vormärz*. Vienna: Konegen, 1912.

———. "Zur Geschichte der Theater Wiens I (1801–1820)." *Jahrbuch der Grillparzer-Gesellschaft* 25 (1915): 1–271.

———. "Zur Geschichte der Theater Wiens II (1820–1830)." *Jahrbuch der Grillparzer-Gesellschaft* 26 (1920): 1–155.

———. "Zur Geschichte der Theater Wiens III (1831–1840)." *Jahrbuch der Grillparzer-Gesellschaft* 30 (1931): 1–152.

———. "Zur Geschichte der Wiener Theatercensur." *Jahrbuch der Grillparzer-Gesellschaft* 7 (1879): 238–340.

Goldstein, Robert Justin, ed. *The War for the Public Mind: Political Censorship in Nineteeth-Century Europe.* Westport, CT: Praeger, 2000.

Göpfert, Herbert G., and Erdmann Weyrauch, eds. *"Unmoralisch an sich . . .": Zensur im 18. und 19. Jahrhundert,* 309–25. Wolfenbütteler Schriften zur Geschichte des Buchwesens 13. Wiesbaden: Harrassowitz, 1988.

Grabbe, Christian Dietrich. *Werke und Briefe: Historisch-kritische Gesamtausgabe in sechs Bänden.* 6 vols. Ed. Akademie der Wissenschaften in Göttingen. Emsdetten: Lechte, 1960–73.

Grawe, Christian. "Grillparzers Dramatik als Problem der zeitgenössischen österreichischen Theaterzensur." In *"Was nützt der Glaube ohne Werke . . .": Studien zu Franz Grillparzer anläßlich seines 200. Geburtstages,* edited by August Obermayer, 162–90. Otago German Studies 7. Dunedin: Department of German, University of Otago, 1992.

Green, Jonathon. *The Encyclopedia of Censorship.* New York: Facts on File, 1990.

Grillparzer, Franz. *Sämtliche Werke: Historisch-kritische Gesamtausgabe.* 42 vols. Ed. August Sauer and Reinhold Backmann. Vienna: Schroll, 1909–48.

Grözinger, Elvira. "Die 'doppelte Buchhaltung.' Einige Bemerkungen zu Heines Verstellungsstrategien in den *Florentinischen Nächten.*" *Heine-Jahrbuch* 18 (1979): 65–83.

Grubačić, Slobodan. *Heines Erzählprosa: Versuch einer Analyse.* Stuttgart: Kohlhammer, 1975.

Grübel, Rainer, "Wert, Kanon und Zensur." In *Grundzüge der Literaturwissenschaft,* edited by Heinz Ludwig Arnold and Heinrich Detering, 601–22. Munich: DTV, 1997.

Habermas, Jürgen. *Strukturwandel der Öffentlichkeit: Untersuchung zu einer Kategorie der bürgerlichen Gesellschaft,* 17th ed. Frankfurt am Main: Suhrkamp, 1990.

Hadamowsky, Franz. *Wien: Theatergeschichte: Von den Anfängen bis zum Ende des ersten Weltkriegs.* Vienna: Jugend und Volk, 1988.

Harrison, Nicholas. *Circles of Censorship: Censorship and its Metaphors in French History, Literature and Theory.* Oxford: Clarendon, 1995.

Hauschild, Jan-Christoph, and Heidemarie Vahl, eds. *Verboten! Das Junge Deutschland 1835: Literatur und Zensur im Vormärz.* Dusseldorf: Droste, 1985.

Hegele, Wolfgang. *Grabbes Dramenformen.* Munich: Fink, 1970.

Hein, Jürgen. *Das Wiener Volkstheater: Raimund und Nestroy.* Darmstadt: Wissenschaftliche Buchgesellschaft, 1978.

Heine, Heinrich. *Historisch-kritische Gesamtausgabe der Werke.* Düsseldorfer Ausgabe, ed. Manfred Windfuhr and others, 16 vols. Hamburg: Hoffmann und Campe, 1973–97.

———. *Werke, Briefwechsel, Lebenszeugnisse: Säkularausgabe,* ed. Nationale Forschungs- und Gedenkstätten der klassischen deutschen Literatur in Weimar und Centre National de la Recherche Scientifique in Paris, 27 vols. to date. Berlin and Paris: Akademie Verlag and Editions du CNRS, 1970–.

Heinemann, Gerd. *Die Beziehungen des jungen Heine zu Zeitschriften im Rheinland und in Westfalen: Untersuchungen zum literarischen Leben der Restaurationszeit.* Geschichtliche Arbeiten zur Meinungsbildung und Kommunikationsmitteln in Westfalen 1. Münster: Aschendorff, 1974.

Hermand, Jost. *Der frühe Heine: ein Kommentar zu den "Reisebildern."* Munich: Winkler, 1976.

Hoefer, Frank Thomas. *Pressepolitik und Polizeistaat Metternichs: die Überwachung von Presse und politischer Öffentlichkeit in Deutschland und den Nachbarstaaten durch das Mainzer Informationsbüro (1833–1848).* Dortmunder Beiträge zur Zeitungsforschung 37. Munich: Saur, 1983.

Höhn, Gerhard. *Heine-Handbuch: Zeit, Person, Werk.* Stuttgart: Metzler, 1987.

Holquist, Michael. "Corrupt Originals: The Parodox of Censorship." *PMLA* 109.1 (1994): 14–25.

Hömberg, Walter. "Verhinderte Liberalisierung zwischen Juli und Märzrevolution (1830–1840)." In *Deutsche Kommunikationskontrolle des 15. bis 20. Jahrhunderts,* edited by Heinz-Dietrich Fischer, 97–113. Munich: Saur, 1982.

Hömberg, Walter. *Zeitgeist und Ideenschmuggel: die Kommunikationsstrategie des Jungen Deutschland.* Stuttgart: Metzler, 1975.

Houben, Heinrich Hubert. *Der ewige Zensor: Längs- und Querschnitte durch die Geschichte der Buch- und Theaterzensur.* Kronberg/Ts: Athenäum-Verlag, 1978; first published as: *Polizei und Zensur.* Berlin: Gersbach, 1926.

———. *Der gefesselte Biedermeier: Literatur, Kultur, Zensur in der guten, alten Zeit.* Leipzig: Haessel, 1924; reprinted Hildesheim: Gerstenberg, 1973.

———. *Hier Zensur — wer dort?: Antworten von gestern auf Fragen von heute.* 2nd ed. Leipzig: Hassel, 1924; reprinted Hildesheim: Gerstenberg, 1975.

———. *Verbotene Literatur von der klassischen Zeit bis zur Gegenwart: Ein kritisch-historisches Lexikon über verbotene Bücher, Zeitschriften und Theaterstücke, Schriftsteller und Verleger.* 2 vols. Berlin: E. Rowohlt, 1924–28.

Huber, Ernst Rudolf. *Dokumente zur deutschen Verfassungsgeschichte.* 2 vols. Stuttgart: Kohlhammer, 1961.

Hüttner, Johann. "Das Burgtheaterpublikum in der ersten Hälfte des 19. Jahrhunderts." In *Das Burgtheater und sein Publikum,* edited by Margret Dietrich, 2 vols. Vienna: Verlag der österreichischen Akademie der Wissenschaften, 1976–89.

———. "Grillparzers Theaterbild im Vergleich zu seinen Werken in der Aufführungspraxis." In *Grillparzer und die europäische Tradition: Londoner Symposium 1986,* edited by Robert Pichl and others, 57–70. Vienna: Hora, 1987.

———. "Theatre Censorship in Metternich's Vienna." *Theatre Quarterly* 37 (1980): 61–69.

———. "Vor- und Selbstzensur bei Johann Nestroy." *Maske und Kothurn* 26 (1980): 234–48.

Ingelhardt, Louis Edward. *Press and Speech Freedoms around the World, from Antiquity until 1998: A Chronology.* Westport, CT: Greenwood Press, 1998.

Jäger, Manfred. "Das Wechselspiel von Selbstzensur und Literaturlenkung in der DDR." In *"Literaturentwicklungsprozesse": Die Zensur der Literatur in der DDR,* edited by Ernest Wichner and Herbert Wiesner, 18–49. Frankfurt am Main: Suhrkamp, 1993.

Jansen, Sue Curry. *Censorship: The Knot that Binds Power and Knowledge.* Oxford: Oxford UP, 1988.

Kaiser, Herbert. "Scherz, Satire, Ironie und tiefere Bedeutungslosigkeit: Zu Grabbe's Lustspiel." In *Grabbes Gegenentwürfe: Neue Deutungen seiner Dramen,* edited by Winfried Freund, 17–31. Munich: Fink, 1986.

Kaiser, Joachim. *Grillparzers dramatischer Stil.* Munich: Hanser, 1961.

Kanowsky, Walter. *Vernunft und Geschichte: Heinrich Heines Studium als Grundlegung seiner Welt- und Kunstanschauung.* Bonn: Bouvier, 1975.

Kanzog, Klaus. "Textkritische Probleme der literarischen Zensur: Zukünftige Aufgaben einer literaturwissenschaftlichen Zensurforschung." In *"Unmoralisch an sich...": Zensur im 18. Und 19. Jahrhundert,* edited by Herbert G. Göpfert and ErdmannWeyrauch, 309–25. Wiesbaden: Harrassowitz, 1988.

———. "Zensur, literarische." In *Reallexikon der deutschen Literaturgeschichte,* edited by Klaus Kanzog, Werner Kohlschmidt, and Wolfgang Mohr, 2nd ed., 5 vols. Berlin: de Gruyter, 1958–88.

Kapp, Friedrich. "Die preußische Preßgesetzgebung unter Friedrich Wilhelm III 1815–1840: nach den Akten im Königlich Preußischen Geheimen Staatsarchiv." *Archiv für die Geschichte des Deutschen Buchhandels* 6 (1881): 185–249.

Keil-Budischowsky, Verena. *Die Theater Wiens.* Vienna: Zsolney, 1983.

Ketelsen, Uwe-K. *Völkisch-nationale und nationalsozialistische Literatur in Deutschland 1890–1945.* Stuttgart: Metzler, 1976.

Klinkenberg, Ralf H. *Die Reisebilder Heinrich Heines: Vermittlung durch literarische Stilmittel.* Frankfurt: Lang, 1981.

Knütter, Hans-Helmuth. "Zur Vorgeschichte der Exilsituation." In *Die deutsche Exilliteratur 1933–1945,* edited by Manfred Durzak, 27–39. Stutgart: Reclam, 1973.

Kogel, Jörg-Dieter, ed. *Schriftsteller vor Gericht: verfolgte Literatur in vier Jahrhunderten.* Frankfurt: Suhrkamp, 1996.

Kopp, Detlev. *Geschichte und Gesellschaft in den Dramen Christian Dietrich Grabbes.* Frankfurt: Lang, 1982.

Kopp, Detlev, and Michael Vogt, eds. *Grabbe und die Dramatiker seiner Zeit: Beiträge zum II. Internationalen Grabbe-Symposium 1989.* Tübingen: Niemeyer, 1990.

Kortländer, Bernd. *Heinrich Heine.* Stuttgart: Reclam, 2003.

Kortländer, Bernd, and Joseph A. Kruse, eds. *Das Junge Deutschland: Kolloquium zum 150. Jahrestag des Verbots vom 10. Dezember 1835: Düsseldorf, 17.- 19. Februar 1986.* Hamburg: Hoffmann und Campe, 1987.

Kramer, Margarete. *Die Zensur in Hamburg 1819–1848: Ein Beitrag zur Frage staatlicher Lenkung der Öffentlichkeit während des deutschen Vormärz.* Hamburg: Buske, 1975.

Kuttenkeuler, W., ed. *Heinrich Heine: Artistik und Engagement.* Stuttgart: Metzler, 1973.

Lechner, Silvester. "Eine Ästhetik des Zensors Johann Ludwig Deinhardstein als Kritik." In *Literatur in der sozialen Bewegung: Aufsätze und Forschungsberichte zum 19. Jahrhundert,* edited by Alberto Martino, 284–326. Tübingen: Niemeyer, 1977.

———. *Gelehrte Kritik und Restauration: Metternichs Wissenschafts- und Pressepolitik und die Wiener "Jahrbücher der Literatur" (1818–1849).* Tubingen: Niemeyer, 1977.

Lenman, Robin. "Germany." In *The War for the Public Mind: Political Censorship in Nineteeth-Century Germany,* edited by Robert Justin Goldstein, 35–80. Westport, CT: Praeger, 2000.

Levine, Michael G. *Writing through Repression: Literature, Censorship, Psychoanalysis.* Baltimore: Johns Hopkins UP, 1994.

Löb, Ladislaus. *Christian Dietrich Grabbe.* Stuttgart: Metzler, 1996.

Lorenz, Dagmar. *Grillparzer, Dichter des sozialen Konflikts.* Vienna: Böhlau, 1986.

Loseff, Lev. *On the Beneficence of Censorship. Aesopian Language in Modern Russian Literature.* Trans. Jane Bobko. Munich: Otto Sagner, 1984.

Mann, Michael. *Heinrich Heines Musikkritiken.* Hamburg: Hoffmann and Campe, 1971.

Mannes, Gast, and Josiane Weber. *Zensur im Vormärz (1815–1848): Literatur und Presse in Luxemburg unter der Vormundschaft des Deutschen Bundes.* Luxembourg: Bibliothèque Nationale, 1998.

Marx, Julius. "Die amtlichen Verbotslisten: Neue Beiträge zur Geschichte der österreichischen Zensur im Vormärz." *Mitteilungen des österreichischen Staatsarchivs* 9 (1956): 150–85.

———. *Die österreichische Zensur im Vormärz.* Vienna: Verlag für Geschichte und Politik, 1959.

Mayr, Josef Karl. *Metternichs geheimer Briefdienst: Postlogen und Postkurse.* Vienna: Adolf Holzhammers Nachfolger, 1935.

Mechtenberg, Theo. "Vom poetischen Gewinn der Zensur." *Deutschland Archiv* 9 (1985): 977–84.

Mende, Fritz. *Heinrich Heine: Chronik seines Lebens und Werkes.* 2nd ed. Stuttgart: Kohlhammer, 1981.

Meyn, Matthias. "Staatliche Repressionsmaßnahmen und 'Karlsbader Beschlüsse' (1819–1832)." In *Deutsche Kommunikationskontrolle des 15. bis 20. Jahrhunderts,* edited by Heinz-Dietrich Fischer, 75–96. Munich: Saur, 1982.

Müller, Beate, ed. *Zensur im modernen deutschen Kulturraum.* Studien und Texte zur Sozialgeschichte der Literatur 94. Tübingen: Niemeyer, 2003.

Müller, Joachim. *Franz Grillparzer.* Stuttgart: Metzler, 1963.

Nipperdey, Thomas. *Deutsche Geschichte 1800–1866: Bürgerwelt und starker Staat.* 2nd ed. Munich: Beck, 1984.

Oesterle, Günter. *Integration und Konflikt: Die Prosa Heinrich Heines im Kontext oppositioneller Literatur der Restaurationsepoche.* Stuttgart: Metzler, 1972.

Ohles, Frederik. *Germany's Rude Awakening: Censorship in the Land of the Brothers Grimm.* Kent, OH: Kent State UP, 1992.

Oswald, Stefan. "Heinrich Heine: *Reise von München nach Genua.* Ironisierung eines Genres." In *Italienbilder: Beiträge zur Wandlung der deutschen Italienfassung 1770–1840,* edited by Stefan Oswald, 136–42. *Germanisch-Romanische Monatsschrift:* Beiheft 6. Heidelberg: Winter, 1985.

Otto, Ulla. *Die literarische Zensur als Problem der Soziologie der Politik.* Bonner Beiträge zur Soziologie 3. Stuttgart: Enke, 1968.

Pabel, Klaus. *Heines "Reisebilder": Ästhetisches Bedürfnis und politisches Interesse am Ende der Kunstperiode.* Munich: Fink, 1977.

Pagenkopf, Martin. *Das preußische OVG und Hauptmanns "Weber": Ein Nachtrag zum 125. Geburtstag von Gerhart Hauptmann.* Cologne: Bundesanzeiger, 1988.

Papst, E. E. *Grillparzer: "Des Meeres und der Liebe Wellen."* London: Edward Arnold, 1967.

Perraudin, Michael. *Literature, the "Volk" and the Revolution in Mid-Nineteenth Century Germany.* Oxford and New York: Berghahn, 2000.

Plachta, Bodo. *Damnatur — Toleratur — Admittitur: Studien und Dokumente zur literarischen Zensur im 18. Jahrhundert.* Tübingen: Niemeyer, 1994.

———. *Zensur.* Stuttgart: Reclam, 2006.

Platen, August von. *Sämtliche Werke: Historisch-kritische Ausgabe mit Einschluß des handschriftlichen Nachlasses.* Ed. Max Koch and Erich Petzet, 12 vols. Hildesheim: Georg Olms, 1969., vol. 10, 89–176.

Post, Robert C., ed. *Censorship and Silencing: Practices of Cultural Regulation.* Los Angeles: The Getty Research Institute, 1998.

Politzer, Heinz. *Franz Grillparzer: Oder das abgründige Biedermeier.* Vienna: Fritz Molden, 1972.

Preisendanz, Wolfgang. "Der Funktionsübergang von Dichtung und Publizistik." In *Heinrich Heine: Werkstrukturen und Epochenbezüge,* edited by Wolfgang Preisendanz, 2nd ed, 21–68. Munich: Fink, 1983.

———. *Heinrich Heine: Werkstrukturen und Epochenbezüge.* 2nd ed. Munich: Fink, 1983.

Preussische Gesetz-Sammlung Berlin: Staatsministerium, 1810–1933.

Radlik, Ute. "Heine in der Zensur der Restaurationsepoche." In *Zur Literatur der Restaurationsepoche 1815–1848: Forschungsreferate und Aufsätze,* edited by Jost Hermand and Manfred Windfuhr, 460–89. Stuttgart: Metzler, 1970.

Raumer, Friedrich von. *Lebenserinnerungen und Briefwechsel.* 2 vols. Leipzig: Brockhaus, 1861.

Reeves, Nigel. *Heinrich Heine: Poetry and Politics.* Oxford: Oxford UP, 1974.

Reisner, Hanns-Peter. *Literatur unter der Zensur: die politische Lyrik des Vormärz.* Literaturwissenschaft-Gesellschaftswissenschaft 14. Stuttgart: Klett, 1979.

Remmel-Gortat, Barbara. *Deutscher Journalismus im Vormärz: Die Pariser Berichterstattung der "Allgemeinen Zeitung" von 1840 bis 1843 und Heinrich Heines "Lutezia."* Diss. Düsseldorf, 1991.

Rieder, Heinz. *Wiener Vormärz: das Theater, das literarische Leben, die Zensur.* Vienna: Bergland, 1959.

Robertson, Ritchie. *Heine.* London: Peter Halborn, 1988.

Rosenfeld, Sophia. "Writing the History of Censorship in the Age of Enlightenment." In *Postmodernism and the Enlightenment,* edited by Daniel Gordon, 117–45. London: Routledge, 2001.

Sammons, Jeffrey L. *Heinrich Heine.* Stuttgart: Metzler, 1991.

———. *Heinrich Heine: A Modern Biography*. Princeton: Princeton UP, 1979.

Sauer, August, ed. *Grillparzers Gespräche und die Charakteristiken seiner Persönlichkeit durch die Zeitgenossen*. 6 vols. Vienna: Verlag des literarischen Vereins in Wien, 1916.

Sauerland, Karol. "Gattungsgeschichtliche Reflexionen zu Heines *Reisebildern*." In *Zu Heinrich Heine*, edited by Luciano Zagari and Paulo Chiarini, 79–88. Stuttgart: Klett, 1981.

Schauer, Friedrich. "The Ontology of Censorship." In *Censorship and Silencing: Practices of Cultural Regulation*, edited by Robert C. Post, 147–68. Los Angeles: Getty Research Institute, 1998.

Schaum, Konrad. *Grillparzer-Studien*. Bern: Lang, 2001.

Schneider, Franz. *Pressefreiheit und politische Öffentlichkeit: Studien zur politischen Geschichte Deutschlands bis 1848*. Berlin: Luchterhand, 1966.

Schneider, Ronald. "Die Muse 'Satyra.' Das Wechselspiel von politischem Engagement und poetischer Reflexion in Heines *Reisebildern*." *Heine-Jahrbuch* 16 (1977): 9–19.

Schoeller, Wilfried F. "Unerwünschte Zeugenschaft: Klaus Mann." In *Schriftsteller vor Gericht: Verfolgte Literatur in vier Jahrhunderten*, edited by Jörg-Dieter Kogel, 266–80. Frankfurt am Main: Suhrkamp, 1996.

Schreyvogel, Josef. *Josef Schreyvogels Tagebücher, 1810–1823*. Ed. Karl Glossy. 2 vols. Berlin: Gesellschaft für Theatergeschichte, 1903.

Schulz, Gerhard. "Naturalismus und Zensur." In *Naturalismus: Bürgerliche Dichtung und soziales Engagement*, edited by Helmut Scheuer, 93–121. Stuttgart: Kohlhammer, 1974.

Seidler, Herbert. *Studien zu Grillparzer und Stifter*. Vienna: Bohlaus Nachfolger, 1970.

Sheehan, James J. *German History 1770–1866*. Oxford: Oxford UP, 1989.

Siemann, Wolfram. "Ideenschmuggel und das Los deutscher Zensoren im 19. Jahrhundert." *Historische Zeitschrift* 245 (1987): 71–106.

———. "Von der offenen zur mittelbaren Kontrolle: Der Wandel in der deutschen Preßgesetzgebung und Zensurpraxis des 19. Jahrhunderts." In "Unmoralisch an sich . . .": Zensur im 18. Und 19. Jahrhundert, edited by Herbert G. Göpfert and Erdmann Weyrauch, 293–308. Wiesbaden: Harrassowitz, 1988.

Škreb, Zdenko. *Grillparzer: Eine Einführung in das dramatische Werk*. Kronberg: Scriptor, 1976.

Snook, Jean M. "A Tale of Two Monuments: Social Criticism in Brentano's *Geschichte vom braven Kasperl und dem schönen Annerl*." *Seminar* 39 (iii) (2003): 187–202.

Spencer, Hanna. *Dichter, Denker, Journalist: Studium zum Werk Heinrich Heines.* Bern: Lang, 1977.

Stein, Peter. "Prototyp einer Denk- und Schreibweise": Heinrich Heines *Reisebilder* als Auftakt zur "Julirevolution der deutschen Literatur." In *Heinrich Heine: Ästhetisch-politische Profile,* edited by Gerhard Höhn, 50–65. Frankfurt: Suhrkamp, 1991.

Taylor, Ronald. *Berlin and its Culture: A Historical Portrait.* New Haven: Yale UP, 1997.

Teuber, Oskar, and Alexander von Weilen. *Das K. K. Hofburgtheater seit seiner Begründung.* Vienna: Gesellschaft für Vervielfältigende Kunst, 1906.

Thompson, Bruce. *Franz Grillparzer.* Boston: Twayne, 1981.

Townsend, Mary Lee. *Forbidden Laughter: Popular Humor and the Limits of Repression in Nineteenth-Century Prussia.* Ann Arbor: U of Michigan P, 1992.

Treml, Manfred. *Bayerns Pressepolitik zwischen Verfassungstreue und Bundespflicht (1815–1837): ein Beitrag zum bayerischen Souveränitätsverständnis und Konstitutionalismus im Vormärz.* Beiträge zu einer historischen Strukturanalyse Bayerns im Industriezeitalter 16. Berlin: Duncker & Humblot, 1977.

Vogt, Michael. *Literaturrezeption und historische Krisenerfahrung: Die Rezeption der Dramen Christian Dietrich Grabbes 1827–1945.* Frankfurt am Main: Lang, 1983.

Walla, Friedrich. "Johann Nestroy und die Zensur: Krokodil am Geistesstrom oder die jungere Schwester der Inquisition." *Nestroyana* 9 (1989–1990): 22–34.

Walther, Joachim. "Der fünfte Zensor — das MfS als letzte Instanz." In *Zensur im modernen deutschen Kulturraum,* edited by Beate Müller, 131–47. Tübingen: Niemeyer, 2003.

Wehler, Hans-Ulrich. *Deutsche Gesellschaftsgeschichte,* 4 vols. Munich: Beck, 1987–2003.

Weidl, Erhard. *Heinrich Heines Arbeitsweise: Kreativität der Veränderung.* Hamburg: Hoffmann und Campe, 1974.

Werner, Hans-Georg. "Komik des Niedrigen: Zu Grabbes *Scherz, Satire, Ironie und tiefere Bedeutung.*" In *Grabbe und die Dramatiker seiner Zeit: Beiträge zum II. Internationalen Grabbe-Symposium 1989,* edited by Detlev Kopp and Michael Vogt, 135–48. Tübingen: Niemeyer, 1990.

Werner, Michael, ed. "Das 'Augsburgische Prokrustesbett': Heines Berichte aus Paris 1840–1847 (*Lutezia*) und die Zensur." *Cahier Heine* 1 (1975): 42–65.

———. *Begegnungen mit Heine: Berichte der Zeitgenossen 1797–1846.* 2 vols. Hamburg: Hoffmann und Campe, 1973.

———. "Heines *Reise von München nach Genua* im Lichte ihrer Quellen." *Heine-Jahrbuch* 14 (1975): 24–46.

———. "Der politische Schriftsteller und die Selbstzensur: Zur Dialektik von Zensur und Selbstzensur in Heines Berichten aus Paris 1840–1844 (*Lutezia*)." *Heine-Jahrbuch* 26 (1987): 29–53.

Wichner, Ernest, and Herbert Wiesner, eds. *"Literaturentwicklungsprozesse": Die Zensur der Literatur in der DDR.* Frankfurt: Suhrkamp, 1993.

Willett, John. *Art and Politics in the Weimar Period: The New Sobriety 1917–1933.* New York: Pantheon, 1978.

Windfuhr, Manfred. *Heinrich Heine: Revolution und Reflexion.* Stuttgart: Metzler, 1969.

———. "Heinrich Heines deutsches Publikum (1820–1860). Vom Lieblingsautor des Adels zum Anreger der bürgerlichen Intelligenz." In *Literatur in der sozialen Bewegung: Aufsätze und Forschungsberichte zum 19. Jahrhundert,* edited by Alberto Martino, 260–83. Tübingen: Niemeyer, 1977.

Wolf, Hubert. *Die Macht der Zensur: Heinrich Heine auf dem Index.* Dusseldorf: Patmos, 1998.

Wulf, Joseph. *Literatur und Dichtung im Dritten Reich: Eine Dokumentation.* Gütersloh: Sigbert Mohn, 1963.

Wülfing, Wulf. *Junges Deutschland: Texte, Kontexte, Abbildungen, Kommentar.* Munich: Hanser, 1978.

———. "Reisebericht im Vormärz. Die Paradigmen Heinrich Heine und Ida Hahn-Hahn." In *Der Reisebericht,* edited by Peter J. Brenner, 333–62. Frankfurt: Suhrkamp, 1989.

———. "Reiseliteratur." In *Deutsche Literatur: Eine Sozialgeschichte,* edited by Horst Albert Glaser, 10 vols. Reinbek: Rowohlt, 1980–97; vol. 6, *Vormärz. Biedermeier, Junges Deutschland, Demokraten. 1815–1848,* edited by Bernd Witte, 180–94. Reinbek: Rowohlt, 1980.

Yates, W. E. *Grillparzer: A Critical Introduction.* Cambridge: Cambridge UP, 1972.

———. "Grillparzer and the Fair Sex." In *Grillparzer und die europäische Tradition,* edited by F. Wagner, 71–82. Vienna: Hora, 1987.

———. *Theatre in Vienna: A Critical History, 1776–1995.* Cambridge: Cambridge UP, 1996.

Ziedler, Jakob. "Ein Censurexemplar von Grillparzer's *König Ottokars Glück und Ende.*" In *Ein Wiener Stammbuch: Dem Director der Bibliothek und des historischen Museums der Stadt Wien Dr. Carl Glossy zum 50. Geburtstage, 7. März 1898, gewidmet von Freunden und Landsleuten,* 287–311. Vienna: Konegen, 1898.

Ziegler, Edda. *Julius Campe: Der Verleger Heinrich Heines.* Hamburg: Hoffmann und Campe, 1976.

———. *Literarische Zensur in Deutschland, 1819–1848: Materialien, Kommentare.* Munich: Hanser, 1983.

———. "Zensurgesetzgebung und Zensurpraxis in Deutschland 1819 bis 1848." In *Buchhandel und Literatur: Festschrift für Herbert G. Göpfert zum 75. Geburtstag am 22. September 1982,* edited by Reinhard Wittmann and Bertold Hack, 185–220. Wiesbaden: Harrassowitz, 1982.

Index

Alexandrine, Princess of Prussia, 84
Altenberg, censorship in, 18
anti-Semitism, 54, 95, 96
Assmann, Aleida, 2
Assmann, Jan, 2
Austria: censorship in, 5–6, 12, 15–18, 21–22, 53, 118–61, 170, 173, 176, 181–94, 198, 199; government of, 108, 110, 120, 171–72; *Hof- und Staatskanzlei* in, 15, 120; *Polizei- und Zensurhofstelle* in, 15, 120–21; *Theaterkommissäre* in, 120, 156

Baden, censorship in, 10, 12–13, 16
Bavaria, censorship in, 10, 12–13, 16
Bavarian Palatinate, censorship in, 12
Berlin: cultural life of, 69–70; political life of, 69–70; poverty in, 69, 73, 86–88
Biermann, Wolf, 9
Bourdieu, Pierre, 2
Brockhaus, Friedrich Arnold, 77
Brockhaus publishing firm, 70, 75, 77
Brühl, Karl Graf von, 78
Bundesakte of 1815, 6, 10
Burschenschaften, 11

Campe, Julius, 17–18, 95–96, 98
Carlsbad decrees, 11–13, 32, 70, 74, 95, 120
Catholicism, 4, 54–55, 65, 97, 104–6, 111–13, 183, 188, 192, 199
censors, 12–21, 31–32, 34–37, 43, 47, 56, 60, 65–66, 71–72, 112, 118–49, 151–57, 160–61, 170, 172–73, 175–76, 179–94, 198–201
censorship:
  effects of railway expansion on, 14
  effects on:
    anti-militaristic content, 152–56
    anti-Semitic content, 54
    atheist content, 33–35, 48, 55–57
    content relating to ethnic relations, 17, 119, 134, 136–42, 158, 160, 199
    content relating to the human body, 41–43, 47
    content relating to marriage, 176–79, 182–83, 189–90, 193, 200
    content relating to social relations, 16, 73–74, 82–83, 86–89, 104–5, 179, 181, 184–85, 197–99
    materialist content, 34–35, 48
    political content, 4–5, 17, 47, 73–87, 89–90, 98, 100–101, 103–4, 106–9, 111, 113, 119, 123, 143–56, 179–81, 184–85, 187, 189, 193, 197–99
    portrayal of nobility, 63–64
    portrayal of professional groups, 17
    pro-Enlightenment content, 148–52, 159
    sexual content, 35–39, 40–41, 44, 47–48, 58–61, 156–59, 173–76, 186–87, 188–89, 190–91, 193–94
    use of key words, 43–45, 144–45, 148, 179, 186–87

censorship: (*continued*)
  effects on: (*continued*)
    writing about family relationships, 39–41, 47, 61–62, 175–79, 182–83, 187, 189–90, 193, 200
    writing about religious matters, 4, 16–17, 32–35, 47–48, 53–57, 71, 76, 80, 89–90, 104, 106, 111–13, 120, 123, 127–36, 183–84, 188, 193–94, 197–99
  in geographic regions, states, countries, cities:
    Altenberg, 18
    Austria, 5–6, 12, 15–18, 21–22, 53, 118, 119–61, 170, 173, 176, 181–94, 198, 199
    Baden, 10, 12–13, 16
    Bavaria, 10, 12, 16
    Bavarian Palatinate, the, 12
    Federal Republic of Germany, 9
    Frankfurt am Main, 31–32
    German Democratic Republic, 8–9
    Hamburg, 13–14, 18, 99
    Hanover, 12, 18
    Hesse-Kassel, 17
    Holstein, 18–19
    Luxembourg, 12
    Prussia, 5, 12, 14–18, 21–22, 31, 33, 35, 47, 53–55, 57–60, 63, 65–66, 71–72, 74, 76, 81–82, 99, 102, 113, 198–99
    Prussian Rhineland territories, the, 71
    Saxony, 12
    Saxony-Altenburg, 12
    the Weimar Republic, 7
    Westphalia, 71–72
    Württemberg, 10, 12, 13
  instructions, 12, 82, 120, 127–28, 130–31, 136, 143, 145, 149, 152, 156, 157, 160–61, 176
  laws, 6–7, 9, 10–14, 16–17, 33, 35, 53–55, 57–60, 63, 65, 71, 74, 76, 128, 130, 173, 198, 199
  methods for resisting, 18, 19, 48, 56, 58, 60–66, 72–90, 97, 100–114, 151–52, 156, 158–60, 173–81, 183–84, 186–94, 199–201
  postpublication, 3, 6, 31
  pre-publication, 3, 19, 31, 72
  as protection of morality, 16, 17, 32, 35–39, 40–41, 44, 47–48, 55–57, 58–61, 61–62, 76, 123, 150–52, 154, 156–59, 160, 161, 173–79, 186–87, 188–89, 190–91, 194, 197–98
  as protection of personal honor, 57–58, 199
  structural, 2
  during time periods, historical eras, regimes:
    German Enlightenment, the, 5, 119–20
    Nachmärz, the, 6, 10
    Napoleonic period, the, 5–6
    National Socialism, 7–9
  of various forms of content, genres
    improvised content, 119
    expressionist plays, 7
    naturalist plays, 7
    theatrical performances, 6–7, 119–61, 170, 181–94, 198
Collin, Matthäus, 118
Cotta, Johann Friedrich von, 95–96

Daffinger, Moritz, 170–71
Danube flood of 1830, 17
Demagogenverfolgung, 79
Dietrichstein, Count Moritz von, 125–26

Enlightenment, 5, 10, 22, 119–20, 148–51, 159–60

Fallersleben, August Heinrich Hoffmann von, 18
Fallersleben, August Heinrich Hoffmann von, works by: *Unpolitische Lieder*, 18
Francis II of Austria, 120, 126, 151, 170, 176, 191–92
Frankfurt am Main, censorship in, 31–32
Frederick II of Prussia, 5
Frederick William II of Prussia, 5
Frederick William III of Prussia, 10, 74, 78
Frederick William IV of Prussia, 14
French Revolution, 5, 82, 97, 100–102, 113, 120, 143, 149
Freud, Sigmund, 2

German Confederation, 6, 10, 11–15, 18, 22, 74, 120–21
German nationalism, 11, 79, 82, 84–85
Gesellschaft zur Beförderung des Christentums unter den Juden, 80
Der Gesellschafter, 95
Glossy, Carl, 121
Goethe, Johann Wolfgang von, works by: *Italienische Reise*, 97
government: Austrian, 108, 110, 120, 171–72; German, 12–14, 95, 100, 103–4, 106–7, 114, 198; Prussian, 69, 71–72, 74–81, 84–86, 89–90, 98–99, 102, 104, 113–14, 201
Grabbe, Christian Dietrich, works by: *Dramatische Dichtungen von Grabbe. Nebst einer Abhandlung über die Schakspearo-Manie*, 31–32, 41, 45–47, 51, 53, 63, 65, 90, 201; *Herzog Theodor von Gothland*, 21, 29–48, 51, 56, 62, 65–66, 69, 89, 200; *Scherz, Satire, Ironie und tiefere Bedeutung*, 21, 51–66, 69, 89, 113, 199, 200

Grillparzer, Franz, works by: *Die Ahnfrau*, 119; "Campo Vaccino," 119; *Des Meeres und der Liebe Wellen*, 21, 170–94, 198, 200; *Ein treuer Diener seines Herrn*, 170, 191–92; *König Ottokars Glück und Ende*, 21, 118–61, 170, 185, 191, 199–200
Gubitz, Friedrich Wilhelm, 53
Gutzkow, Karl, 13, 18
gymnastics societies, 11

Habsburg Empire, 119–20, 136–39; ethnic relations within, 136–39
Hägelin, Franz Carl, 119, 121–22, 127, 131, 136, 143, 145, 149, 156–57, 160, 176
Hamburg, censorship in, 13–14, 18, 99
Hanover, censorship in, 12, 18
Hardenberg, Carl August von, 12, 81
Harrison, Nicholas, 20
Hauptmann, Gerhard, works by: *Die Weber*, 7
Hegel, Georg Wilhelm Friedrich, 70
Heine, Heinrich, works by: *Die Bäder von Lukka*, 96; *Briefe aus Berlin*, 21, 69–90, 101–2, 110, 113–14, 183, 197, 199–201; *Französische Zustände*, 18; *Die Harzreise*, 95; *Ideen. Das Buch Le Grand*, 101–2, 113; *Reise von München nach Genua*, 21, 95–114, 183. 198–200; *Reisebilder. Dritter Teil*, 96, 98–99, 107, 109–10, 113; *Reisebilder. Erster Teil*, 95; *Reisebilder. Vierter Teil*, 99; *Reisebilder. Zweiter Teil*, 95, 98, 102, 107; *Reisebilder* series, 77, 81, 83–84, 90, 95–97, 110
Henneberg, Berthold von, 4
Hesse-Kassel, censorship in, 17
Hofer, Andreas, 108

Hoffmann, E. T. A, works by: *Meister Floh*, 79
Hoffmann und Campe publishing firm, 95
Holstein, censorship in, 18
Houben, Heinrich Hubert, 19

Immermann, Karl, 98
Immermann, Karl, works by: *Das Trauerspiel in Tyrol*, 107

J. B. Wallishausser, 123–24
J. C. Hermannsche Buchhandlung, 31
Jacobin Terror, 102
Joseph II of Austria, 120
July Revolution of 1830, 13, 14, 98–99, 181

Karoline, Queen of Austria, 118
Kettembeil, Georg Ferdinand, 30–32, 34–36, 39–41, 43, 44, 47, 51, 53–57, 59, 63, 65–66
Köchy, Karl, 53
Kotzebue, August von, 11

Laube, Heinrich, 13, 18
Leipzig, battle of, 109
Leopold, Archduke of Baden, 13
liberalism, 6, 9–10, 12–14, 16–17, 31, 69–71, 77–80, 82–84, 103, 121, 181, 198
Literarisches Comptoir, 118
Ludlamshöhle, 171
Luxembourg, censorship in, 12

Mann, Klaus, works by: *Mephisto*, 9
March revolutions, 6, 14
Marengo, battlefield of, 100
Maria Theresia, Queen of Austria, 5
Metternich, Klemens von, 12, 120, 192
Migazzi, Archbishop of Vienna, 5
Montaigne, Michel de, 5

Montesquieu, Charles Louis de Secondat, 5
Morgan, Frau von, works by: *Italien*, 103
Morgenblatt für gebildete Stände, 96, 99, 107
Moser, Moses, 107
Müller, Beate, 2
Mundt, Theodor, 13

Napoleon, 84, 100, 102, 119
Nestroy, Johann, 123
Neue allgemeine politische Annalen, 95
New Censorship, 2–3
nobility, 63–64, 71, 97, 100, 102–3, 104–5, 106, 112–13, 122
northern Italy, Habsburg occupation of, 96, 109–11, 113

Ottokar, King of Bohemia, 119, 127–60

Palm, Philip, 6
Paul, Jean, works by: *Komet*, 79
Paumgartten, Charlotte von, 171
peasants, emancipation of, 102
Petri, Moritz Leopold, 53
Platen, Graf August von, 96
Platen, Graf August von, works by: *Der romantische Oedipus*, 96
Protestantism, 4, 54–55, 65, 95, 199
Prussia: censorship in, 5, 12, 14–18, 21–22, 31, 33, 35, 47, 53–55, 57, 60, 63, 65–66, 71–72, 74, 76, 81–82, 89, 99, 102, 113, 199; censorship authorities in, 82, 99–100; government of, 69, 71–81, 84–86, 89–90, 98–99, 102, 104, 113–14, 201; new liturgy of, 75, 80; *Oberzensurkollegium* of, 15, 71–72, 99, 113; promised constitution of, 81, 108–9
Prussian Rhineland provinces: censorship in, 71; trial by jury in, 84

Raimund, Ferdinand, 123
Raupach, Ernst, works by: *König Enzio,* 192
Restoration, 10, 19–22, 32–33, 43, 48, 71, 97, 100–104, 106–7, 108, 121–22, 171–72, 179, 182–83, 197–201
Rheinisch-westfälischer Anzeiger, 70–71, 72, 81
Romanticism, 21, 52, 58
Rudolf I of Austria, 119, 131, 132, 133, 134, 135, 136, 140, 143, 148–52, 154, 159–61
Russia, 106

Sand, Karl Ludwig, 11
Savigny, Friedrich Carl von, 73
Saxony, censorship in, 12
Saxony-Altenburg, censorship in, 12
Schauer, Friedrich, 2
Schläpfersche Verlagsbuchhandlung, 18
Schreyvogel, Josef, 118, 119, 122, 126, 138, 182, 188, 192, 193, 200
Schulz, Heinrich, 70, 72
Sedlnitzky, Count Joseph, 120, 126, 192
self-censorship, 6, 19–20, 172–81, 197, 201
Smolenitz, Marie von, 171
Sonnenfels, Joseph von, 119
Spontini, Gasparo Luigi Pacifico, 78–79, 85
Spontini, Gasparo Luigi Pacifico, works by: *Nurmahal, oder das Rosenfest in Kaschmir,* 85; *Olympia,* 78–79
Spontini-Weber affair, 78–79
Staël, Anne Louise Germaine de, works by: *Corinne ou L'Italie,* 103
Sterne, Laurence, works by: *A Sentimental Journey through France and Italy,* 97

Teutscher Beobachter, 13
Tieck, Ludwig, 29, 51
twenty-Bogen limit, 11, 18, 99
Tyrol, 104, 109; uprising in, 108

Vienna: Burgtheater in, 22, 118, 119, 122, 124–27, 129, 131, 133, 135, 137–38, 140, 142, 146, 148, 150–51, 156–57, 159, 160–61, 171, 173, 181–82, 187, 192; censorship in, 118, 119, 121–61, 170, 181–94; *Justizpalast* fire of 1927, 121; *Theater an der Wien* in, 122–23, 126–29, 131–35, 138–40, 142, 144, 146–48, 150–51, 153, 155, 157, 159–60; *Zentralrevisionsamt* in, 15
Voltaire, 5

Wars of Liberation, 79, 84, 107–8
Wartburg rally, 11
Weber, Carl Maria von, works by: *Der Freischütz,* 78
Wedekind, Frank, 7
Westphalia, 89; censorship in, 71–72
Wienbarg, Ludolf, 13, 18
Wiener Beschlüsse of 1834, 14
William I of the Netherlands, 12
Wirth, Georg, 18
Wolf, Christa, works by: *Der geteilte Himmel,* 8
Wöllner, Christian von, 5
Württemberg, censorship in, 10, 12

Young Germany, 13, 14, 18

Die zehn Artikel of 1832, 14
Zensurstil, 19, 20, 48, 56, 58, 60–66, 72–90, 97, 100, 114, 151–52, 156, 158–60, 173–81, 183–84, 186–87, 193–94, 199–201
Ziedler, Jakob, 123–24, 133, 136
Ziegler, Edda, 197, 201